Philosophy in Classical

Recent years have seen the beginning of a radical reassessment of the philosophical literature of ancient and classical India. The analytical techniques of contemporary philosophy are being deployed towards fresh and original interpretations of the texts. This rational, rather than mystical, approach towards Indian philosophical theory has resulted in a need for a work which explains afresh its central methods, concepts and devices. This book meets that need. Assuming no prior familiarity with the texts, Jonardon Ganeri offers new interpretations which bring out the richness of Indian theory and the sophistication of its methods. Original in both approach and content, *Philosophy in Classical India* contains many new results, analyses and explanations.

Discussing a diverse range of key Indian thinkers, Ganeri asks: What is the goal of their philosophical project and what are the methods of rational inquiry used in their pursuit? Recognising reason as the instrument of all philosophers, this book studies the active rational principles that drive classical Indian philosophy. The philosophers discussed here form a network of mutual reference and criticism, influence and response, and in their work one finds a broad vein of critical rationality in which reason is at once used constructively and to call itself into question. The inquiries of the classical Indian philosophers into the possibilities of human reason are considered afresh: new philosophical paradigms are unravelled, new applications for the concept of reason are discovered, and a common philosophical vocabulary is thereby enriched. *Philosophy in Classical India* rescues a story suppressed in Orientalist discourses of the East – the story of reason in a land too often defined as reason's Other.

Jonardon Ganeri read mathematics at Cambridge before pursuing graduate studies in philosophy at London and Oxford. He is the author of *Semantic Powers: Meaning and the Means of Knowing in Classical Indian Philosophy* (Clarendon Press, 1999). He is currently Spalding Fellow in Comparative Religions, Clare Hall, Cambridge.

Philosophy in Classical India

The proper work of reason

Jonardon Ganeri

To Robert

With best wishes

Jonardon

ROUTLEDGE
Taylor & Francis Group

London and New York

First published 2001 by Routledge
11 New Fetter Lane, London EC4P 4EE

Simultaneously published in the USA and Canada
by Routledge
29 West 35th Street, New York, NY 10001

Routledge is an imprint of the Taylor & Francis Group

Typeset by M Rules
Printed and bound in Great Britain by TJ International Ltd, Padstow, Cornwall

British Library Cataloguing in Publication Data
A catalogue record for this book is available from the British Library

Library of Congress Cataloging in Publication Data
A catalog record for this book has been requested

ISBN 0–415–24034–4 (hbk)
ISBN 0–415–24035–2 (pbk)

Contents

Introduction 1

1 The motive and method of rational inquiry 7

1.1 Early recognition of a 'practice of reason' 7
1.2 Rationality in the *Nyāyasūtra* 10
1.3 Rationality and the ends of life 15
1.4 Perception 17
1.5 Mind, attention and the soul 22
1.6 Rationality and extrapolation 25
1.7 Rationality and debate 28
1.8 Reason, scripture and testimony 35
1.9 Reason's checks and balances 37
Further reading 40

2 Rationality, emptiness and the objective view 42

2.1 Thought and reality 42
2.2 Emptiness and the objective view 43
2.3 Rationality in Madhyamaka 47
2.4 On causation 51
2.5 The impossibility of proof 58
2.6 A new paradox of motion 63
2.7 Self-refutation 66
Further reading 68

3 The rational basis of metaphysics 71

3.1 Order in nature 71
3.2 The categorial hierarchy 72
3.3 The structure of the world 77
3.4 The taxonomy of natural kinds 79
3.5 Absence as a type of entity 82
3.6 Higher-order absence 85

3.7 Navya-Nyāya logic 89
3.8 Number 91
Further reading 95

4 Reduction, exclusion and rational reconstruction 97

4.1 How to practise poverty in metaphysics 97
4.2 A skeletal ontology 98
4.3 Marking and similarity 100
4.4 The role of language in conceptual construction 104
4.5 The exclusion theory of meaning 106
4.6 Sentence meaning 111
4.7 Conditions on rational extrapolation 114
4.8 Reasoning from specifics 118
4.9 Are reason–target relations law-like? 121
4.10 The problem of grounding 123
Further reading 126

5 Rationality, harmony and perspective 128

5.1 A rationality of reconciliation 128
5.2 The many-sided nature of things 128
5.3 Disagreement defused 130
5.4 The epistemology of perspective 134
5.5 The logic of assertion 137
5.6 Assertion and the unassertible 141
5.7 The mark of a good reason 144
5.8 Integration and complete knowledge 147
Further reading 149

6 Reason in equilibrium 151

6.1 Reason and the management of doubt 151
6.2 The burden of proof 153
6.3 Criteria for rational rejection 155
6.4 Supposition and pretence 158
6.5 A new doxastic ascent 159
6.6 Epistemic equilibrium 162
Further reading 167

Notes 169
Texts 184
Bibliography 192
Index 203

Introduction

This is a book about philosophical theory in classical India. It is an attempt to understand the nature of the classical Indian philosophical endeavour, and in so doing to reveal a richness of projects and a diversity of methods. Reason is the instrument of all philosophers, but conceptions of the nature and function of reason vary along with varying ideas about the work for which reason is properly employed. Manu, the lawmaker, said that those whose only guide is reason should be banished from the company of the virtuous. That is the view too of the great narrators of the Indian epics. Reason unchecked was seen as a threat to the stability of Brahminical social order, as the tool of heretics and troublemakers. But the epic horror of pure reason was a disdain not for reason itself, but only for its capricious use, to undermine belief rather than to support it, to criticise and not to defend. Philosophy in India, or so I argue in Chapter 1, flourished in the space this distinction affords.

The mortal finger in Michelangelo's *Creation* stretches out, but cannot touch the divine hand. Is this an appropriate metaphor for reason itself? Does the subjectivity that goes along with being situated in the world preclude our attaining through reason an objective conception of it? Is the idea that human reason can find nature intelligible in some fundamental way misguided? This ancient problem is but one of the *leitmotivs* of philosophical inquiry in classical India, where radical critiques of reason are as plentiful as more moderate applications. Brahman, the still divinity, the Upaniṣadic symbol for objectivity itself, is that from which 'before they reach it, words turn back, together with the mind'.[1] But if there are limits to language and reason, can we by reason come to know what they are and where they lie? Or are the limits of reason themselves beyond reason's limit? Can it be rational to strive to transcend the boundaries of reason, to attempt what one knows to be impossible? If reason is by its very nature limited, then perhaps the subversion of reason itself becomes a rational end. That appears to be the conclusion of Nāgārjuna, the founder of Madhyamaka Buddhism, whose philosophical method I examine in Chapter 2. He reasons that the constructs of reason are as empty as the magician's hat, and he welcomes the predictable retort that his own reasoning is empty too.

Other paradigms abound in India of the nature of philosophical inquiry and the proper work of reason. Some are familiar, for instance the instrumentalist conception of reason as promoted by Kauṭilya, a royal minister, strategist and educator. Others, less so. In Chapter 3, I show how the Vaiśeṣika metaphysicians find in reason a tool for the construction of a formal ontology. A hierarchical theory of categories and natural taxonomies, alleged to be the metaphysics encoded in the Sanskrit language itself, is interpreted graphically, giving metaphysics a formal basis. The Yogācāra Buddhist, Diṅnāga is, by contrast, an ontological reductionist and a nominalist. He is uncompromising in his search for unity and simplicity in philosophical explanation, and he uses the method of rational reconstruction to rebuild our old conceptual superstructures on new, leaner, foundations. His system is my concern in Chapter 4. Chapter 5 concerns the Jaina philosophers, who look to reason as an instrument of harmonisation. The ancient philosophical controversies – so resistant to solution, so intractable to the up-front reasoning of debate, argument and evidence – call, it seems, for a new rationality, one whose function is to subvert the way ordinary language works, making explicit the hidden parameters in assertion, and so enabling the reasoner to harmonise apparently conflicting beliefs. The task of reason is again different in the new epistemology of the later classical writers. The problem now is whether the norms of reason can themselves be rationally justified, and the idea to be defended is that reason sustains a wide reflective equilibrium of beliefs, actions, principles and theories. It is in this way, I argue in Chapter 6, that an attempt is made to diffuse a critique of reason advanced by the formidable Advaita sceptic, Śrīharṣa – that reason seeks to justify itself only at the peril of a viciously infinite regress.

These are just some of the shifts and turns of the classical Indian concept of reason, some paradigms for a problematic notion. Many others do not get a mention here. In particular one may refer to the Mīmāṃsakas, who see in reason a hermeneutical instrument for the analysis of the Vedas, and to the Vedāntins, who wrestle with the relations between reason, authority and faith. My justification for omitting these approaches is only that a great deal has already been written about the place of reason in Indian philosophy of religion, and I want to focus on philosophical agendas overlapping, but not coextensive with the soteriological. Nor do I feel any need to follow the 'six systems' approach to the study of Indian philosophy, popularised by Max Müller and later by Sarvepalli Radhakrishnan,[2] but too simplistic to do justice to a complex web of interconnections, themes, personalities and transformations. The authors I do discuss form a moderately compact network of mutual reference and criticism, influence and response. In their work one finds a broad vein of critical rationality, in which reason is used both constructively and also to put itself in question.

What do we mean when we speak of a culture's notion of the rational? Not, of course, that the concept itself is culturally specific, but only that it is embedded, articulated and manifested in culturally specific ways. J. N.

Mohanty, a formidable interpreter of India's past, has observed that the role a concept of rationality has within a culture is a highly stratified one, its criteria and principles operating 'first of all in the life-world of the community concerned, then in the higher-order decisions of the scientists, law-givers and artists, finally in the theoretical discourse of the philosophers'.[3] There is much truth in this remark. New paradigms of what it is to act and believe rationally come into being as old concepts are criticised, revised and rejected. A particularly fine example of this approach to the analysis of Indian theory is Bimal Matilal's study of the concept of reason embedded in changing treatments of moral dilemmas in the epic literature and *dharmaśāstra*s.[4] His idea is that a diachronic study of conceptions about what constitutes an adequate resolution to a moral dilemma illuminates both shifts in the notion of reason itself, and also the mechanics of internal criticism, theory revision and paradigm rejection.

Forms of rationality are, I maintain, interculturally available even if they are not always interculturally instantiated. In an influential and thought-provoking essay, A. K. Ramanujan[5] has advanced a thesis contrary to mine. His claim is that there is a type-difference between Indian and western modes of reason. Drawing his conclusion from a range of linguistic and anthropological evidence, Ramanujan suggests that norms of reason are conceived as 'context-sensitive' in India, whereas in the West they are 'context-free.' The distinction is one he derives from linguistics, in which context-free rules, such as that every sentence has a verb, are contrasted with rules that are sensitive to grammatical context, such as the rule governing pluralisation of nouns in English. I have no objection as such to distinctions of this sort, but only to their application. It can at best be only a contingent truth, a historical fact about the exemplification of paradigms, that such a separation should exist, and if so it is of limited philosophical significance. In fact, my investigations here have convinced me that East–West type-difference hypotheses of such generality are definitely false.[6] Some paradigms for the rational can be found in both cultures, for example, instrumentalism and the epistemic conception of reason. Others, for instance the Jaina notion of a rationality of reconciliation, or the modelling of reason by game-theory, are found in one, but not the other. The point is to discover new forms of rationality and applications of the concept of reason, and so to enrich a common philosophical vocabulary. We become in this way aware of possibilities for reason we had forgotten or had not yet seen.

Might I not be accused of a reconfigured Orientalism in looking for expressions of rationality in Indian philosophy, on the grounds that the West is again setting the standard? As one critic has said, '[w]hy is a need felt to describe the "rationality" of the Indian philosophies, to assert that Indian philosophers were "as rational" as their western counterparts? Such a general project would not be conceived of with regard to western philosophy, because the West sets the paradigm. We look in our traditions for what is to be found in the West, like the sense-reference distinction. But why should we even look for such a distinction?'[7] I suggest that the criticism here depends on a failure to distinguish sufficiently carefully between philosophical *problems* and philosophical *explanations*. The point is not to comb the Indian literature for the sense-reference distinction, but for their solutions to the problem that distinction was invented to solve, a problem that is as real for Fregeans as for those who reject his distinction, as real for Indian philosophers of language as for their western colleagues.[8] If the objection is simply that 'rationality' is a western concept imperiously misapplied, my response would be that it is no more western than perception, thought, language or morality. The mistake here is in thinking of such philosophical concepts as internal to a theory, when in fact they are concepts about which there can be many theories (a distinction particularly well articulated in Canguilhem's philosophy of science[9]). Indeed, so far from being Orientalist, the project envisaged here is that of rescuing a story suppressed by Orientalism – the story of reason in a land too often defined as reason's Other.

In analysing the philosophical literature of classical India, then, I adopt an approach neither comparative nor historical. Philosophy is not history, even if both disciplines are relevant to the study of classical India. History studies ideas in their context – it situates an author in an intellectual milieu. Philosophy, on the other hand, tries to free an idea from its context – it separates the idea from what is parochial and contingent in its formulation. The historian of Indian philosophy must be sensitive to the character of a philosophical thesis, but ought not indulge in wanton borrowing from other philosophical literatures. David Seyfort Ruegg offered some timely methodological advice when he said that the historian of Indian thought should 'beware of anachronistically transposing and unsystematically imposing the concepts of modern semantics and philosophy, which have originated in the course of particular historical developments, on modes of thought that evolved in quite different historical circumstances, and which have therefore to be interpreted in the first place in the context of their own concerns and the ideas they themselves developed'.[10] The historian's worst crime is anachronism, displacing a concept and resituating it in some new and inappropriate context.

A philosopher has also to be guarded, but for different reasons. The philosopher must take care not to mistake contingent properties in the contextual formulation of an argument or idea for essential properties of the argument or idea itself. If the historian's worst crime is anachronism, that of the philosopher is parochialism, failing to separate the idea from its context. The philosopher's goal is to *decontextualise*. It is not to recontextualise, to situate old ideas within the context of current philosophical concerns, except in so far as those concerns are themselves context-neutral. The philosopher examining the Indian theories is for this reason justified in using the modern philosophical idiom as a generally shared and convenient vehicle in which to frame his discussion. The concerns of the classical Indians are clearly recognisable as philosophical, and in using a contemporary idiom, one's aim is to bring out the philosophical structure of those concerns, whether or not they coincide with anything in contemporary philosophical theory. My goal then is not the mere comparison of one idea with another, but the unravelling of new philosophical paradigms. It would be rather to miss the point to criticise that venture on the grounds of a difference in the preoccupations, religious beliefs and motivations of the classical philosophers. For discoveries made by the classical Indian investigators into the possibilities of human reason can be of interest and relevance even in different times and other cultures. There are indeed, as David Hume once said, more species of metaphor in this world than any one person can have dreamed.[11] My approach, distinct both from comparative philosophy and from the history of ideas, is instead a critical and analytical evaluation of conceptual paradigms in Indian theory.

To help those who are coming to the subject anew, I have added to each chapter a list of texts as a guide to further reading. I also give, in the list of philosophical texts discussed in this book, as comprehensive an indication as I can of what translations are available at the present time. Many of the important texts have been translated at one time or another, and even if some of the older translations are not to a modern standard, they do at least help open up the subject to non-Sanskritists. Unless otherwise specified, however, the translations in this book are my own.

I would like to express my gratitude to the British Academy, whose award under the Research Leave Scheme in 1999 freed me from departmental duties, and so gave me the time to prepare a typescript. Heartfelt thanks too to Gillian Evison, Simon Lawson, Helen Topsfield, Elizabeth Krishna and Kalpana Pant, librarians of the Indian Institute in Oxford, an invaluable research archive wherein I found all the materials I needed for this book. It is a pleasure to thank Roger Thorp and Hywel Evans at Routledge, who have been meticulous in overseeing the production of the book at every stage, and also to thank the referees for many helpful comments. Thanks too to Piotr Balcerowicz, Arindam Chakrabarti, Brendan Gillon, Stephen Phillips and Richard Sorabji for their sustained encouragement. The experience of trying for a number of years to teach courses on Indian Philosophy at King's College London and the University of Nottingham has been an important stimulus for the ideas developed in this book, and I have benefited from the keen critical faculties of my students in both institutions. Above all, however, it has been the teachings and writings of my late supervisor, Bimal Krishna Matilal, which have inspired and sustained me, as indeed they have many others, and it is with pleasure and gratitude that I dedicate this book to him.

Jonardon Ganeri

1 The motive and method of rational inquiry

1.1 EARLY RECOGNITION OF A 'PRACTICE OF REASON'

Reason can be used or abused. A cautionary episode in the *Mahābhārata* illustrates the point. Bhīṣma tells Yudhiṣṭhira that there is nothing more worth having than wisdom. Wisdom, he declares, is the greatest good, the refuge of all living things, the ultimate acquisition, and is considered by the virtuous to be heaven itself (12.173.2). But then, in case his point should be misunderstood, he recounts the story of Indra appearing in the form of a jackal (12.173.45–8):

> I used to be scholarly [says Indra], a reasoner, a scorner of the Veda. I was pointlessly fond of critical inquiry and the science of argument. I used to make declarations on the basis of logic; in assemblies, speaking with reasons, I harangued the brahmins and was rude during the Vedic recitations. I was an unbeliever, sceptical about everything, and though stupid, I thought myself wise. The status of a jackal that I have obtained is the result, Kāśyapa, of my misdeeds.

The terms in which Indra deprecates himself are important ones, for they gradually came to be associated with the practice of philosophy itself in India. Indra was a 'reasoner' (*haituka*), he was addicted to the study of critical inquiry (*ānvīkṣikī*) and to the science of argument (*tarka-vidyā*). That free thinking of this sort was seen as embodying a danger to the stability of orthodox brahminical learning is only too clear. In another epic narrative, the *Rāmāyaṇa*, Rāma advises his brother Bharata to steer well clear of such people (2.94.32–33):

> You must not associate with those 'worldly' (*lokāyata*) brahmins, dear brother. Their only skill is in bringing misfortune; they are fools who think themselves wise. In spite of the pre-eminent treatises on right conduct (*dharma*), these ignorant people derive their ideas from critical inquiry, and make declarations without any point.

These 'reasoners' represent a challenge and a threat to the existing tradition. They will assent to the deliverances of reason whether or not it agrees with the scriptures and the authorities on what is considered to be proper conduct. The lawmaker Manu therefore advises that a brahmin who has adopted the science of reasoning, treating with contempt the twin authorities on proper conduct (the scriptures and the texts on right conduct or *dharma*), should as an 'unbeliever' and a 'scorner of the Vedas' be driven from the company of the virtuous.[1]

It is not that in the great epics reason as such is condemned, but only its capricious use. The 'reasoners' are condemned for lacking any goal other than the use of reason itself; they believe in nothing and are sceptical of everything. They use reason to criticise the scriptures, but have no doctrines of their own. Reason, the message seems to be, is misapplied when it is used in a purely negative, destructive way. In other words, the proper use of reason should be to support, and not to undermine, one's beliefs, goals and values. The objection to the reasoners, as they are represented in the epics, is that for them the use of reason has become an end in itself. It is goalless, capricious, ungrounded.

The idea that the use of reason must be purposeful or goal-directed is taken up in the *Treatise on Gains* (*Arthaśāstra*), a famous book on government, politics and economics which dates from around 300 BC. Its author is Kauṭilya, supposed to have been the chief minister in the court of Candragupta, a Mauryan ruler who came to power at about the time of Alexander's death. The period following Alexander's campaign in India was in fact a time of intimate and extended contact between India and Greece. The ancient Greek chronicler Megasthenes frequently visited the court of Candragupta and in his *Indica* he presented to the Greeks a vivid account of the Indian society of those times. Fragments of this lost work quoted by later writers reveal Megasthenes to have been greatly impressed by similarities between Greek and Indian ideas, especially about space, time and the soul.[2] He is also said to have carried messages between Candragupta's son Bindusāra, the father of Aśoka, and Antiochus I. Bindusāra indeed asked Antiochus to send him Greek wine, raisins, and a Sophist to teach him how to argue. Antiochus replied by sending the wine and raisins, but regretted that it was not considered good form among the Greeks to trade in Sophists!

Kauṭilya's purpose in writing the *Treatise on Gains* was to educate future kings in the necessary skills required for a successful and prosperous rule. He states that there are four branches of learning in which a young prince should be trained: the religious canon composed of the three Vedas; the sciences of material gain, primarily trade and agro-economics; the science of political administration and government; and finally *ānvīkṣikī*, the discipline of critical inquiry, of which *sāṃkhya*, *yoga* and *lokāyata* are listed as the principal divisions. Significantly, he rejects explicitly the claim of Manu and others that the study of critical reasoning is tied exclusively to a religious study of the self and its liberation (*ātmavidyā*). Critical inquiry is an autonomous discipline (1.2.11):

> Investigating by means of reasons, good and evil in the Vedic religion, profit and loss in the field of trade and agriculture, and prudent and imprudent policy in political administration, as well as their relative strengths and weaknesses, the study of critical inquiry (*ānvīkṣikī)* confers benefit on people, keeps their minds steady in adversity and in prosperity, and produces adeptness of understanding, speech and action.

He reiterates an old couplet (1.2.12):

> The study of critical inquiry is always thought of as a *lamp* for all branches of knowledge, a *means* in all activities, and a *support* for all religious and social duty.

Shortly after the rediscovery and publication of the *Treatise on Gains* in 1909, Hermann Jacobi wrote an article arguing that Kauṭilya had to all extents distinguished and defined 'philosophy' in India.[3] Kauṭilya's separation of a study of 'critical inquiry' (*ānvīkṣikī*) from theological studies was enough, he conjectured, to justify the identification of 'critical inquiry' with philosophy. This rather important conjecture has been strongly disputed, on the grounds that critical inquiry as described by Kauṭilya consists simply in the art of investigating by reasons, and this is something that is practised in *all* branches of learning. Paul Hacker[4] makes the point that this 'critical inquiry' is not necessarily an independent system of thought, but is sometimes rather a *method*. In the same vein, it has very plausibly been conjectured[5] that the early references to *sāṃkhya*, *yoga* and *lokāyata* are not to well-defined schools of philosophical speculation, but reflect instead a methodological division. Thus *sāṃkhya* labels the methods of inquiry that rest on the intellectual enumeration of basic principles, *yoga* the methods of spiritual practice, and *lokāyata* the methods of worldly or empirical investigation.

We can agree with these conjectures without having to identify philosophy as a discipline with the having or inventing of a system of thought. Philosophy is circumscribed by adherence to a certain methodology and body of problems. Broadly, it is the *a priori* analysis of the interconnections and distinctions between groups of concepts to do with the nature of value, thought, existence and meaning. It is indeed possible to hear in Kauṭilya's remark about 'investigating . . . good and evil in the Vedic religion, profit and loss in the field of trade and agriculture, and prudent and imprudent policy in political administration' a suggestion that a reasoned investigation is an inquiry into the nature of the distinction between good and evil, the proper goals of political institutions, and so on. But the intended domain of application for critical inquiry seems to be much wider than that. It encompasses any situation in which one sets about achieving one's aims in a reasoned way.

There is a reasoned way to go about making a profit, a reasoned way to rule a country. The study of what such reasoning consists in is one thing, the *philosophical* investigation of the nature of profit or rule quite another. So *ānvīkṣikī* in Kauṭilya's sense is a study of the generic concept of rationality, as that concept features in questions about how rationally to think, how rationally to act, and how rationally to speak.

Kauṭilya's conception of rationality is goal-oriented and instrumental. The interest is in the reasoned way to achieve some goal, whatever that goal may be. The use of reason does not tell us for which goals one should strive, but only how rationally to strive for them. The *Arthaśāstra* is, after all, a manual of instruction for princes. The discipline Kauṭilya calls that of critical inquiry is the one which trains the prince in the way for him to fulfil his projects, having once decided what those projects are to be. The other sciences, of trade and agriculture, of policy-making and government, train him in the skills of choosing one objective rather than another. A person is rational when he uses rational methods to reach his aims. (Kauṭilya wanted kings to become philosophers, not as Plato that philosophers be made kings.) It is not enough to be rational that the aim be in some sense a 'worthy' one, for even worthy goals can be striven for by irrational means.

Bertrand Russell[6] said that 'reason' 'signifies the choice of the right means to an end that you wish to achieve. It has nothing to do with the choice of ends.' The epic horror of the reasoner concerned the *aimless* use of reason, using reason capriciously or solely to subvert the goals of others. Kauṭilya's defence makes rationality instrumental and therefore goal-directed. It follows, however, that a tyrant can be just as rational as a ruler who is beneficent, an atheist as rational as a believer. If rationality is instrumental, then to act rationally is not the same as to act well. Followers of reason alone still face the charge of immorality, hereticism and untruth.

1.2 RATIONALITY IN THE *NYĀYASŪTRA*

Gautama Akṣapāda's *Nyāyasūtra*, the redaction of which took place in the first or second century AD, deals with such themes as the procedures for properly conducting debates, the nature of good argument, and the analysis of perception, inference and testimony in so far as they are sources of knowledge. There is a detailed account of the causal structure of the mind and the nature of its operation. Certain metaphysical questions are addressed, notably the reality of wholes, atoms and universals. At the beginning of his commentary on this remarkable work, Vātsyāyana Pakṣilasvāmin (*c.* AD 400) wonders what it is that makes the Nyāya system distinctive. He answers as follows:

> Nyāya is the examination of things with the help of methods of knowing (*pramāṇa*). It is an inference supported by observation and authority.

> This is called a 'critical proof' (*anvīkṣā*). A 'critical proof' is the proof of things desired, supported by observation and authority. The discipline of critical inquiry is the one which pertains to it, and is also called the science of *nyāya* or the writings on *nyāya*. But an inference that contradicts observation and authority is only a bogus-*nyāya*.[7]

Vātsyāyana agrees with Kauṭilya that the study of critical inquiry is one of the four branches of study, but he insists that it has its own procedures or methodology. He claims that if critical inquiry did not have its own procedures then it would 'merely be a study of the soul's progress, like an Upaniṣad'. This is a rather important remark. Reasoned inquiry and scriptural studies are now claimed to have the same eventual goal or purpose; where they differ is in method. That marks a departure from Kauṭilya's purely instrumental conception of rationality, in which the use of reason could equally well serve any end. For Vātsyāyana wants to claim that there can be rational goals, as well as rational means, and so to distance the Nyāya system from the free-thinkers in the epics.

Let us first see that Vātsyāyana shares the epic horror of *aimless* reason. Reason, he says, can be used in one of three ways. One may employ it in a good and proper way (*vāda*), as one does when one's goal is to ascertain the truth of the matter. One may employ it in a bad or improper way (*jalpa*), as when one's goal is to defend one's position at all costs, using any intellectual tricks one can think of. Finally, one might employ reason in a negative and destructive way (*vitaṇḍā*). Here one has no goal other than to undermine one's opponent. People who use reason in this way are very like the sceptics and unbelievers of the epics, and Vātsyāyana disapproves. He claims indeed that to use reason in this way is virtually self-defeating:

> A *vaitāṇḍika* is one who employs destructive criticism. If when questioned about the purpose [of so doing], he says 'this is my thesis' or 'this is my conclusion,' he surrenders his status as a *vaitāṇḍika*. If he says that he has a purpose, to make known the defects of the opponent, this too is the same. For if he says that there is one who makes things known or one who knows, or that there is a thing by which things are made known or a thing made known, then he surrenders his status as a *vaitāṇḍika*.[8]

Vitaṇḍā is the sceptic's use of reason. Vātsyāyana's point is that someone who presents an argument against a thesis has at least that refutation as their goal, and so commits himself to the machinery of critical examination. But a *vaitāṇḍika* who accepts this gives up his claim to use reason aimlessly, without commitment. So the aimless use of reason is not just pernicious, it is self-defeating!

The salient point here is that reason must have a purpose, and the question is what that purpose should be. Vātsyāyana's answer is clever. He argues that a goal is a rational one if it is the rational means to some further goal. And he claims that whatever one's eventual goal is, the rational way to achieve it is through the acquisition of knowledge – knowledge about one's goal and how it might be achieved. So the acquisition of knowledge is always a rational goal. Indeed it is the rational goal par excellence, for knowledge is instrumental in the rational pursuit of any other goal:[9]

> Since there is success in one's activities when the awareness of one's object is produced by an accredited method of knowing (*pramāṇa*), the method of knowing is connected with the object. Without a method of knowing, there is no awareness of the object. Without an awareness of the object, there is no success in one's activities. But the knower, having grasped the object in thought by some suitable method, either desires it or wants to avoid it. His 'activity' is the effort prompted by his desire for or aversion of it. 'Success' is the coming together of that activity with its reward. Desiring the object, or wanting to avoid it, one either makes an effort to obtain it or else to avoid it. One's 'object' is the contentment [one feels] and the cause of that contentment, or the disdain and the cause of that disdain.

Let me take a simple example. Suppose my goal is to acquire a piece of silver. To succeed, I need to know where silver might be found, and how to recognise it; I need to be in a position to know, of some object, that it is made of silver. I need to know other things as well, such as that I have some way of acquiring the silver once identified. So the reasoned way for me to go about acquiring a piece of silver is to seek to acquire knowledge of the identifying traits, whereabouts and means of acquiring of silver objects. The acquisition of such knowledge becomes itself a goal, subsidiary to my principal aim of acquiring silver.

In the translation, I have tried to retain an ambiguity in the Sanskrit word *artha*, in rendering it as 'object'. It can mean both one's goal, such as acquiring silver, and also the thing which that goal concerns, the silver itself. It is the target of one's endeavour, both as the piece of silver, and equally well as the acquiring of that silver. Vātsyāyana suggests that it can also denote the satisfaction one feels on achieving one's goal, or the irritation of not doing so. Later on,[10] he stresses that, in virtue of the connection that exists between knowledge of the object and success or failure in one's goals concerning it, one should employ some suitable method of knowing if one wants to succeed. The theory of rationality in this way depends on a theory of the proper means of acquiring true beliefs.

Kauṭilya said that the study of critical inquiry is the study of the notion of 'investigating with reasons'. Vātsyāyana tells us what a 'reason' (*hetu*) is. It is a method of acquiring knowledge, a *pramāṇa*. For a 'reasoned' inquiry is one which is based on the acquisition of knowledge. The early Nyāya writers look closely at the characteristic method that constitutes a rational inquiry. The opening verse in the *Nyāyasūtra* is a list of sixteen items which, according to its author, comprise the subject matter of the Nyāya system. The first two items are the various methods of knowing and the domain of knowables. They constitute the Nyāya epistemology and metaphysics. The next seven are the theoretical components in the process of critical inquiry: doubt, purpose, observational data, doctrinal bases, extrapolative demonstration, suppositional reasoning, and a final decision. The final seven are terms of art in the theory of debate. *Nyāyasūtra* 1.1.1:

> The highest goal in life is reached through knowledge about the nature of:
>
> (a) knowables, methods of knowing,
> (b) doubt, purpose, observational data, doctrinal bases, the parts of a demonstration, suppositional reasoning, final decision,
> (c) truth-directed debate, victory-directed debate, destructive debate, sophistical rejoinders, tricks, false reasons, defeat situations.

A properly conducted inquiry, adds Vātsyāyana, is that process by which we move from an initial uncertainty about the nature of the thing or concept under investigation, to an ascertainment of its properties. The inquiry is permitted to draw upon such data as are incontrovertible or accepted by both parties in the dispute, and it proceeds by adducing evidence or reasons in support of one side or the other. The first element here is the existence of a doubt (*saṃśaya*) which initiates the investigation. A doubt is said to be a mental state whose content is of the form 'Does this object have a certain specified property or not?' Typical doubts discussed in the *Nyāyasūtra* (is the soul eternal or non-eternal?, is a whole object identical with the sum of its parts?) tend to be philosophical conjectures or hypotheses, but the method applies just as well to the resolution of empirical questions.

An inquiry must have a purpose. The assumption is that any form of rational behaviour must have some motivating purpose, the point for which one wishes to resolve the doubt. The inquiry can appeal to shared background doctrinal principles and empirical data. Here, by 'empirical data,' what is meant are the observational facts to which all parties can appeal. The background principles are called 'doctrinal bases' or 'proved doctrines', and might also include a category of *a priori* truths or principles. Gautama actually mentions several kinds of doctrinal base. In particular, there are those which everyone must accept, for example that objects of knowledge are established via means of knowing. Other doctrinal principles are in the form of conditionals, where both parties agree on the truth of the conditional, but dispute the truth of the antecedent. Also mentioned are assumptions which are made merely for the sake of argument. One or both sides might grant some principle, simply to facilitate the inquiry. In any case, having initiated an inquiry for some purpose, and taken into consideration both empirical evidence and such doctrinal or *a priori* considerations, the investigation concludes with the decision, which is a resolution of the initiating doubt.

Similar characterisations of the general structure of problem-solving are offered in the contemporary literature on formal heuristics.[11] There a problem is defined as one in which the following features are specified and delimited: *a goal* – a criterion of judging outcomes; *an initial state*, consisting of a situation and the resources available for the solution; a set of *admissible operations* for transforming states; *constraints* on states and operations; and *an outcome*. It would seem that the Nyāya account fits rather nicely this characterisation of the structure of a problem-solving set-up. The doubt is an initial state of uncertainty, the purpose is the goal, the admissible operations are the sanctioned methods of reasoning by extrapolative demonstration (Chapter 1.6) and supposition (*tarka*, for which see Chapter 6), the constraints are the observational data and doctrinal bases to which all parties agree, and the outcome is the final decision. A critical inquiry, then, is a formal heuristic for problem-solving.

Nyāyasūtra 1.1.1 makes a further demand on the type of proof procedure admissible in a critical inquiry. It insists that the inquirer be able explicitly to set out for others the piece of knowledge so acquired as the conclusion of a precisely formulated demonstration (*avayava*). In its general schematic form, a demonstration scheme has five steps:

(i) Preliminary statement of the thesis to be proved.
(ii) Citation of a reason.
(iii) Invoking an example.
(iv) Application to the present case.
(v) Assertion with confidence of the conclusion.

For example: (i) There is a fire on the mountain. (ii) Because there is smoke there. (iii) As in the kitchen. (iv) The mountain is the same. (v) Therefore, there is fire there. I will look in detail at the structure of such argument schemes in a later section (Chapter 1.7). I am interested here in what the demand for demonstration tells us about the nature of critical inquiry, an investigation 'with reasons'. The early Nyāya writers want to explicate the notion of a reason. Since the rational way to achieve one's goals is by acquiring knowledge about its constituents, it might seem that a reason is any method of acquiring knowledge (*pramāṇa*). However, the insistence now is that the rational inquirer be able to set out his reasoning in an explicit and canonical way. And a 'reason' is the premise or evidence (*hetu*) in such a suitably formulated argument. Vātsyāyana explains that the various means of acquiring knowledge have a subsidiary role here. They enter the account as the means by which each step in the explicitly formulated demonstration is proven:[12]

> The means of acquiring knowledge reside in those [demonstration steps]. The preliminary statement of the thesis is an item of testimony (*āgama*). The reason (*hetu*) is an item of inference. The example is an

> item of perception. The application is an item of 'analogical comparison'. The final conclusion exhibits the possibility of all these coming together in a single thesis. Such is a *nyāya* par excellence. With the help of this alone can truth-directed, victory-directed and destructive debate techniques be employed, never otherwise. Fixing the truth depends on this. The steps in the demonstration are sentences, and as such are included among the objects of knowledge; but they are mentioned separately for the above reasons.

Vātsyāyana's systematising idea is that the three strands out of which the Nyāya system is formed – theory of knowledge, study of critical inquiry and art of debate – can be brought together into a single discipline. In doing so, he introduces a new condition on a rational inquiry: that it be capable of being made public through verbal demonstration. A rational inquiry is, to be sure, a procedure for reaching one's goal which exploits knowledge about that goal and the most effective way to achieve it. But it must also be knowledge of the sort that can be displayed. It must be knowledge that is backed up by reasons of the sort that are potentially capable of convincing others, something that can stand up to the scrutiny of a debate.

There is a conflict here between two accounts of the source of rational norms. On the one hand, to proceed rationally is to proceed by acquiring knowledge of an appropriate sort. But on the other hand, to proceed rationally is publicly to adduce reasons and arguments for the knowledge one purports to have. The first is an epistemic conception of norms, while the second grounds norms in the public conventions of the debating hall. The early Naiyāyikas, drawing on their roots in the systematisation of debating theory, insist that rationality must be a public affair, an explicit demonstration in the five-step format, but they try to merge this idea with another, that the norms of reason are the norms of warranted belief. The tension between these two concepts of reason will manifest itself again as we examine in later sections other paradigms of rationality in the *Nyāyasūtra*.

1.3 RATIONALITY AND THE ENDS OF LIFE

The early Naiyāyikas have linked the pursuit of rational inquiry with the final ends of life. *Nyāyasūtra* 1.1.1 states that it is by understanding the nature of reasoned inquiry, epistemology and debating theory that one attains the 'highest goal' (*niḥśreyasa*). *Nyāyasūtra* 1.1.2 amplifies the point, adducing an exact sequence of causal relations between knowledge and liberation (*apavarga*).

The final aim of life is the permanent elimination of *duḥkha*. Duḥkha is a difficult term in Indian soteriology. Its meaning is: suffering, pain, discontent, frustration, displeasure. What then is the source of all this discontent? One source has already been mentioned by Vātsyāyana in the passage quoted before – the frustration of one's plans. Obtaining one's goals is an end in itself, but so too is the pleasure or contentment that success instils. It is not just that in obtaining the piece of silver, I gain as well the pleasures that go with possessing a valuable thing. It is also that fulfilling one's projects is a form of satisfaction in its own right. Vātsyāyana stresses, however, that the final aim of life must involve a separation from pleasures as well as pains. For pleasure is invariably attended by pain, as if it were honey mixed with poison! So the ultimate aim in life consists in the elimination of any attachment to the success or failure of one's projects, or the rewards or discomforts such projects bring.

Can a life of reason help one achieve this? Kauṭilya perhaps thought so, for he said that pursuing one's goals by means of rational inquiry helps to keep the mind steady in both adversity and prosperity. The Naiyāyika thinks so too (NS 1.1.2):

> Liberation results from the removal of the next member when the immediately preceding member is removed in the sequence of: wrong belief, bad qualities, actions, birth, suffering.

This is the pan-Indian *karma* theory, a causal theory of moral retribution. There is a direct causal link between the moral quality of one's present actions and one's future contentment or frustration in this birth or another (a commentator[13] points out that by 'actions' here what is meant is righteous and unrighteous conduct, since it is such conduct that is the cause of birth and rebirth). We observed earlier that with a purely instrumental conception of rationality, it is no more rational to do good than to do evil. To be rational is simply to set about one's aims in a reasoned way. In the context of a causal theory of moral retribution, however, it is rational to strive to do good. For given that one's final aim in life is to avoid frustration (presumably including the frustration of one's future plans), one has a reason to behave well now and do good. At least, one has a reason as long as one knows that there is a direct causal link of the sort described. After all, acquiring knowledge about the sources of frustration and suffering is the rational way to accomplish one's aim of eliminating them!

The rational life is a life best suited to eliminate at least one source of suffering, namely the frustration of having one's plans fail. So if one's ultimate end in life is to avoid suffering, and the main source of suffering is due to the frustration of one's plans, one has a reason to live a rational life. Moreover since, when one examines the general causes of suffering and frustration, what one finds is that future frustration is caused by past immoral deeds, one has a reason to have only moral deeds as one's goal. Someone who believes in the *karma* theory of moral retribution has a reason to strive to do good and not to do evil. One final link is needed to complete the picture. It is that bad or immoral deeds are the result of false beliefs. Once one knows this, one has a reason to strive for only true beliefs. For if one has only true beliefs, then one cannot do wrong, cannot incur the moral cost of future frustration, and so will succeed in life's ultimate goal of eliminating such frustrations. One has, therefore, a reason to strive to minimise false beliefs, and so to study the sources of true belief and knowledge. And, in so far as a study of the Nyāya system is the best method of achieving one's highest goals, one should study it through repeated reflection, discussion with others and by engaging in friendly debates (NS 4.2.47–9).

This then is the reason why the study of epistemology and critical inquiry, in short of the Nyāya philosophy, is instrumental in achieving one's final aims. There is an elegant explanatory closure here. One might not be inclined to agree with every step in the explanatory chain. While it is plausible that there is a dependency between the degree of success or failure of one's plans and the extent of falsity in one's beliefs, it is less easy to see that the dependency is mediated by the *moral* value of one's actions. Even if one were tempted to omit that link, or regard the tie between rationality and moral behaviour differently, the explanatory scheme affords a marvellous account of the relationship between the study of philosophy and the quest for life's final ends.

1.4 PERCEPTION

The Buddhist asserts that perception of objects is itself a rational activity. One does not, properly speaking, perceive the object at all, but only patterns of colour, sound, touch, smell and taste. From their sequence in time and arrangement in space, one infers the presence of an object of one kind or another. Reason here is a mental faculty of construction, synthesis and superimposition. It brings order to the array of sensory data. The early Naiyāyika, however, has tied reason to explicit demonstration and proof. He has no place for the idea of reason as an inner mental faculty of sensory integration. Since there is no logical connection between the capacity to see an object and the capacity to describe it, one is led instead to the idea that objects enter *directly* into the content of perceptual experience. The Naiyāyika rightly worries that if reason has a role in the construction or synthesis of the *objects* of perception, then realism about those objects is threatened. However, he allows reason to have a role in the *organisation* of the totality of one's perceptions. Kalidas Bhattacharya accurately, if enigmatically, assessed the idea when he said that 'thought as judgement, according to Nyāya, is either the perception of a passive unity of different data in substantive-adjective relation, or, going beyond perception, conscious management of data through actual use of language.'[14]

I begin with the *Nyāyasūtra* definition. Vātsyāyana would later classify the *sūtras* into three kinds: 'naming' *sūtras*, which introduce a topic or concept for analysis; 'defining' *sūtras*, which offer a definition of the concept in question; and 'critical' *sūtras*, which examine and evaluate the adequacy of the proposed definition. A definition is a property co-extensive with the concept to be defined. A definition is faulty if it is either too wide or too narrow – showing that it has neither of these faults is the purpose of the 'critical' *sūtras*. The Nyāya method here is not very different from the technique of finding necessary and sufficient conditions. Notice however that it does not tell us what the essence of the thing defined is, but rather gives us a syndrome, a criterion for distinguishing between it and all other kinds of thing.

Nyāyasūtra 1.1.4 is a 'defining' *sūtra*. It is the definition of perception:

> Perception is an awareness which, produced from the connection between sense-organ and object, is non-verbal, non-errant, and determinate in nature.

A perception is an awareness that stands in a certain special relation to its object. The attempt is to define that relation in purely non-cognitive terms. If the attempt is successful, then perception is a physical anchor between the subject and the external world. It is not itself cognitive, but rather supplies the raw material for cognition and so for reason.

What constraints are there on the physical relation that obtains between a perceiver's perceptions and the object perceived? A first constraint is just that the relation be physical, so that it is not explicated in terms of semantic relations such as that of denotation. This is what is meant by the assertion that perception is 'non-verbal'. Second, the relation has to have the right extension: it needs to hold between perceptions and the sorts of object one is normally regarded as capable of perceiving. Uddyotakara (*c*. AD 500) has a clear discussion of this point.[15] He notes that the relation must be capable of obtaining between the perceiver's perceptions and objects which are both nearby and far away; it must be a relation capable of obstruction by solid, opaque objects; it must connect the perceiver not only with the objects themselves, but also with their perceptible properties such as colour and shape, as well as with the perceptible properties of those properties; it must connect the perceiver not only with the front surface of a whole object, but with the object as a whole (for one sees the table and not just its surface); and finally, he asserts that it connects the perceiver with the *absences* of things, for apparently one can say that one *sees* the absence, and not merely that one fails to see.

It is hardly surprising that the Naiyāyikas find themselves unable to describe a single physical relation which obtains in all (and only) these circumstances, but perhaps they do not need to. For if it is part of the concept of perception only that it is grounded in a physical relation with a certain extension, then an adequate physicalist theory of perception needs only to specify what the extension of the underlying physical relation is. The discovery of the way that relation is realised in actual human perception might be a task assigned to the psychologist of perception, not to the philosopher.

The real interest in the *Nyāyasūtra* attempt to give a physical description of perception lies in the remaining two conditions. The point is that, no matter how well one succeeds in describing the underlying physical connection, there will be cases where that connection obtains, but the resulting awareness is not genuinely perceptual. Vātsyāyana points to cases of perceptual illusion and perceptual confusion:

> During the summer the flickering rays of the sun intermingled with the heat radiating from the surface of the earth come in contact with the eyes of a person at a distance. Due to this sense-object contact, there arises an awareness as of water. Such an awareness might be (mis-)taken as perceptual; hence the clause 'non-errant'. An errant one is of that wherein it is not. A non-errant one is of that wherein it is – this is a perception.
>
> Perceiving with the eyes an object at a distance, a person cannot decide whether it is smoke or dust. Such an indecisive awareness resulting from sense–object contact might be (mis-)taken as perceptual; hence the clause 'determinate in nature.'

These ambiguous passages led to a 'vortex of controversy' (Matilal 1995: 310) and eventually to a sophisticated theory of content. It is alleged that a person witnessing a mirage does not see the refracted sun's rays, even if in the right sort of physical connection with them. Neither does he see water, for there is none to be seen. Someone witnessing a mirage does not *see* anything, but only seems to see water. And a person who witnesses a ball of dust in the distance does not *see* the dust if he is uncertain whether it is dust or smoke. An object is not seen if it is not seen distinctly.

In both cases there is a natural temptation to say that the person does see something, but does not understand or know what it is that they see, or that they misconstrue what it is that they see, or that their perceptual appearance is non-veridical. One sees the refracted rays of light, but mistakes them to be water; one sees the ball of dust, but fails to determinate it as such. To say this would be to concede that the existence of an appropriate physical connection is sufficient for object perception. The difficulty with such a move is that, although it does indeed extrude rationality from the perceptual, it does it so completely that the perceptual cannot be a basis for rational thought. The 'objects' of perception are merely things in which one stands in a certain special physical relation, on a par with other objects one comes into physical contact with (e.g. by standing on or picking up). However, if perception is to be a foundation for rationality, there must be a way in which it is understood as making objects available in thought, as placing them within the ken of the observer.

Might we analyse the two additional clauses in terms of belief? If a person witnessing a mirage does not see the refracted rays of the sun, perhaps it is because he falsely believes them to be water. Similarly, one can perhaps say that the person looking at the ball of dust does not see it because he does not believe that it is dust (does not know whether it is dust or not). We might then think of taking the additional clauses as defining the perception of an object in terms of a physical connection, together with the absence of a belief that it is something it is not, and the absence of doubt or disbelief that it is something that it is. That is:

S's perception is of object x iff:

(1) S's perception stands in a relation R with x.
(2) R is physical (non-verbal).
(3) for all F, if S believes that Fx then Fx.
(4) for all F, if Fx then S does not disbelieve that Fx.

There are two objections to such a proposal. First, clauses (3) and (4) are much too strong. It is clearly possible to perceive an object and at the same time have false beliefs about it. I might, for example, perceive the table and yet believe that it is made of space-filling infinitely divisible stuff. Second, since belief implies rationality, the definition of perception in terms of belief is contrary to the attempt to extrude reason from perception.

The proper implication of the *Nyāyasūtra* definition is that the perception of objects is modulo a property. When I see an object (my desk, for instance) I do not simply see it, but I see it *as a table*. Here, the clause 'as a table' is to be read as an adverbial modifier of the seeing relation R. I stand in a 'table-seeing' relation to the object. The relativisation of the seeing relation by a property allows a reconstruction of Vātsyāyana's cases. The person who witnesses a mirage stands in a 'water-seeing' relation to the refracted rays. The errancy lies in the fact that they are seeing the refracted rays *as water*, when in fact the rays are not. And the person who witnesses a ball of dust, but fails to distinguish it as dust or smoke stands neither in a dust-seeing relation to the dust-ball, nor in a smoke-seeing relation, but equivocates. The correct way to read the definition then is:

S's perception is of object x iff:

(4) for some F, S sees x as an F, where

S sees x as an F iff:

(1) S's perception stands in a relation R with x.
(2) R is physical (non-verbal).
(3) Fx.

Clause (4) excludes the case of the ball of dust, for since there is no definite way by which the person sees the dust, the person does not see any object. It is necessary for object perception that the object is seen in some definite way. Clause (3) excludes the case of the mirage, for the person attempts to see the rays modulo *water* but the rays are not water. Notice here that 'non-errancy' signifies simply an absence of warping, a lack of discord between the perception and its object, and is not explicated in terms of a correspondence between the object and a perceptual content. We should think of this absence of warping as a property of the perceptual relation, much as transparency is a property of clear glass. Both are characterised in terms of the lack of a distortion or corruption of what is seen, and not in terms of representational correspondence. The passivity of perception is preserved; perception remains free from interpretation and construction.

It follows from the definition that if one perceives an object, and one does so by seeing it modulo its having a certain property, then it does indeed have that property. This is so even though one does not see *that* the object has the property. Perceiving x as F does not imply believing that x is F, but it does imply that one would be justified were one to believe that x is F. Perception is an evidential support for reason, without itself being reasoned (an idea echoed in Roderick Chisholm's critical cognitivism[16]). Later Nyāya writers draw a distinction between perception that is 'with imagination' and perception that is 'without imagination'. Bimal Matilal explains the philosophical use here of the term 'imagination' or *vikalpa* as standing 'for anything that, let us say, the mind adds to, or recognises in, the "given".'[17] In the Nyāya theory the object perceived (x) and also the mode under which it is perceived (F) constitute the perceptual given. It is the work of the 'imagination' to bring them together into a propositional judgment (x is F).

Buddhist objections to the Nyāya definition focus on instances where perception does seem to imply belief and inference. There is the case of Uddyotakara's rather remarkable claim that we perceive absences. I am looking for a pot. I look in the kitchen and see no pot. Uddyotakara says: I see the kitchen as qualified by absence-of-pot and thereby see the absence. The Buddhist Dharmakīrti objects that this is really a piece of reasoning, an inference from non-observation. The inference runs thus. None of the objects which I perceive in the kitchen is a pot. If there were a pot in the kitchen, I would see it, for my perceptual faculties are working normally and all other *ceteris paribus* conditions for perception are met. Therefore, there is no pot in the kitchen (see Chapter 4.9). Dharmakīrti's point is well taken, but it does not constitute a refutation of the theory. We may simply give up the strange claim that absences can be perceived.

Nyāyasūtra 2.1.31 rehearses an argument, apparently again due to Buddhists, which if sound *would* constitute a refutation. The argument is that our ordinary perceptual claims are disguised inferences. I cannot see the whole table from any one place. When I say that I see the table, what I mean is that I infer that there is a whole table on the basis that I have seen a part (its front surface). We never see wholes, but infer their existence from our more immediate perceptions. If the argument is that all perception is inferential, then Gautama's counter in *Nyāyasūtra* 2.1.32, that we see at least front surfaces, is conclusive. If the argument is that all perception of wholes is inferential, the Nyāya reply is that the whole is present in each of its parts. So we can perceive a whole just as we can perceive a property. One says that one sees the colour or shape of the flower in virtue of seeing the flower; so too one sees the whole in virtue of seeing a part.

What is at stake is the amount of work done in perception by reason. The Buddhist presses the Naiyāyika on the point that there is, in perception, an extrapolation and interpretation of what is immediately given. Allowing properties to enter the (non-conceptual) content of perceptual experience as adverbial modifiers offers a way of avoiding the unpalatable consequence that the perception of a whole is an inference. Attention is drawn to two kinds of properties of wholes: those that are properties of the whole without being a property of any its parts, and those that are properties of the whole only because they are properties of every part (see Chapter 3.6). The second sort 'saturate' the object, in rather the same way that sesame oil saturates the sesame seed. The property being-a-table or being-a-cow, on the other hand, applies to the whole, but not to any of its parts. It follows that seeing modulo such a property is seeing the whole and not its parts. This Nyāya rejoinder to the Buddhist criticism depends on one's being able to regard the property being-a-cow as an entirely objective feature of the perceived situation, not as itself a mere concept or mental construct. It is for this reason that, in the war for hegemony between the Buddhist and Nyāya philosophical views, some of the severest battles were those over the reality of universals and wholes.[18]

1.5 MIND, ATTENTION AND THE SOUL

Is the mind rational? Is it conscious? That depends on what we mean by 'mind'. The Naiyāyika, as generally for thinkers in classical India, sees in the mind (*manas*) something distinct from the soul (*ātman*). It is the soul alone which is the seat of reason, *qua* thinker, perceiver, enjoyer of pleasures and sufferer of pains. The mind is a mere instrument of the soul. It is that by which the soul controls the senses. The mind is given a second function: it is also that by which the soul perceives its own mental states. So the mind is both an inner sense and the controller of the outer senses, but all the while entirely directed by the soul. The mind is mechanical.

An enduring metaphor for the senses, due at least to Praśastapāda, is as windows onto the world. In a room with a window on every wall, each one represents a possibility of sensory contact with some aspect of the world. But only a possibility: in order to see out, one has to direct one's attention to one window rather than another. In the case of the senses, this role is assigned to the mind. It is a faculty of attention, that by which the soul directs its gaze through one sense rather than another. Another metaphor is helpful here. Think of the senses as converging railway tracks, meeting at a point and becoming a single track. The mind is the set of points at the junction. It is that by which the controller (the soul, the signalman) channels its attention in one direction rather than another.

A perception arises in the soul when there is a causal chain: from object to sense, from sense to mind and from mind to soul.[19] Uddyotakara observes that if this role of the mind in perception seems to have been forgotten in the *Nyāyasūtra* definition of perception, it is because a mind–soul link is not something *special* to perception, while a mind–sense link is *implied* by the mention of the sense–object connection.[20]

The existence of the mind as an inter-sensory switching device follows from an alleged deficiency in the powers of the conscious soul. This is that the soul can attend to at most one thing at a time. There is a strict sequence in the temporal order of thought. If the senses are functioning simultaneously, but one can entertain no more than one thought at a time, then one must have within oneself a capacity to choose between the deliverances of the senses (NS 1.1.16, NS 3.2.56). In reply to the obvious objection that we do seem to be able to attend to more than one thing at once, Vātsyāyana claims that this is an error produced by our inability to discriminate events which happen in very quick succession. He cites (NS 3.2.58) the illusion of a circling firebrand, appearing as if it were a continuous hoop, and more interestingly, the way one hears a sentence as a whole even though the letters and words are uttered in sequence.

This account of the mind is smooth. But a worry now presents itself. If the conscious soul fails to notice the distinctness in a sequence of perceptions, it seems to follow that the mind after all has a certain autonomy in operation. For if the soul is not quick enough to follow the mind's switchings from one perception to the next, how can it be controlling them?[21] And yet there is no question of assigning consciousness (*caitanya*) to the mind. *Nyāyasūtra* 3.2.38 is explicit:

> It [consciousness] is not a property of the mind, for reasons already given, and because of its being ruled by another, and because [there would then follow an] acquiring of the benefits of actions not performed.

The 'reason already given' is simply the definition itself of the soul, as the exclusive abode of thought, will, pleasure and pain (NS 1.1.10). The idea of 'benefits of actions not performed' is a reference to the *karma* theory of moral retribution. If the soul and the mind were distinct consciousnesses, then the future contentments or frustrations of the soul would depend on the present deeds of another, the mind. This contradicts the fundamental principle of the *karma* theory, that the benefits and costs of one's present actions accrue to oneself and not to someone else. Vātsyāyana uses the same line of reasoning against the Buddhist reduction of a person to a 'sum and series' of consciousness-moments (NS 3.2.39). If a person is a series of distinct consciousnesses, then the deeds of one reach their fruition in the contentments and frustrations of another, an injustice incompatible with the hypothesis of *karma*.

The more important assertion is that the mind is 'ruled by another'. It does not act independently, but only as directed by the conscious soul. It therefore cannot itself choose which sense to connect with. How then can the soul be unaware of its operation? A solution to the puzzle begins to emerge when we remember that the mind has another function, along with that of intersensory switch. It is also an inner sense, the means by which the soul perceives its own mental states. Vātsyāyana:[22]

> Memory, inference, testimony, doubt, intuition, dreams, suppositional argument, and perception of pleasure and pain are the proof of mind.

One conclusion we can draw from this is that the soul is not immediately aware of its own thoughts, for it requires an inner sense to perceive them. Thoughts, just like external events, can appear and disappear unperceived. So the mere fact that a thought occurs does not imply that it is taken notice of in consciousness. Once the point has been made that the mere occurrence of a thought is not sufficient for its being *noticed*, we see that the switching function of the mind need not determine which thoughts are noticed, but need only ensure that thoughts occur in succession. We can think of the mind as scanning the senses, constantly switching from one to the next. Its movement so conceived will be very swift, but entirely automatic and mechanical. Perceptions from all the senses occur rapidly, but sequentially in the soul.

To attend to something then, is not to direct the mind *qua* intersensory switch towards one rather than another sense faculty, but rather to direct it *qua* inner sense to some occurrent perception. The rapid movement of the mind need not be something of which the soul is aware. There is still a problem. If a perception comes before consciousness only if one chooses to direct the mind towards it, how can it be that one's attention is sometimes drawn by the perception itself? Standing on a thorn or a chip of stone will draw the attention even of a person whose mind is fastened on some other thing (NBh. under NS 3.2.32). The worry is that I will not notice the pain in my foot unless I direct my mind to attend to the deliverances of my tactile sense, but that there need be no motivation for me to do this in advance of noticing the pain. Unless it occurs to me to check whether my foot has been injured, I will not notice the pain! Even this, however, can be squared with a mechanistic conception of the mind. Let us say simply that some perceptions are so intense as to force the mind in their direction, not because it chooses to direct itself towards them, but simply because it is driven to do so by the intensity of the perception. A conception of the mind as entirely mechanical in operation has room to allow that this could happen. The 'movement' of the mind is an automated scanning of the senses, potentially diverted by the occurrence of intense perceptions and by the controlling influence of the soul. The mind is not itself a rational agent, and it is only in a relatively weak sense that the Indian soul–mind division is what one would now call a 'divided mind' hypothesis.[23]

What now is the place of reason in perception? The function of the soul is to integrate the content of distinct perceptions across times and between sensory modalities (NB 3.1.1). It has the power to identify the object of some past perception and an object currently being perceived. The identity 'this is the same as that' is not *given* in perception, but discovered or 'imagined' by the soul. The same is true across sensory modalities at a given time. Physical objects are perceived only by sight and touch, but the identification of an object held in one's hand with an object currently being seen with one's eyes is the work of reason and not of perception. Such identifications require one to be able to assume a point of view which spans times and crosses sensory modalities. Rationality then has a reconstitutive role in aligning our perceptions with each other, so that they come to represent a world of temporally extended and modality-independent objects.[24]

The possibility of trans-temporal and trans-modal identification of objects is said by the Nyāya to be the best argument for the existence of the soul as distinct from the mind or the senses, and as the final refutation of the Buddhist analysis of the person as a mere continuum of discrete consciousnesses. For how is a *re*-identification of an object possible by one who exists only for a moment? Only a single consciousness spanning time can 'simultaneously' witness the same object at two different times, and recognise it as the same. Only a single consciousness spanning sense modalities can 'simultaneously' witness a single object through two modalities, and recognise it as the same. The Buddhist asserts that a momentary consciousness can compare a *current* perception with a *current* memory (produced by the past perception of an earlier momentary consciousness), and so there is no need for there to be a single subject of the current and past perceptions. The Naiyāyika reply is that there is a *logical* difference between, on the one hand, judging that an object seen now is the same as an object seen some time ago, and, on the other, keeping track of an object over a period of time. It is perhaps like the difference between discovering that two different names refer to the same thing, and using a single name twice.[25]

The ability to turn fleeting modality-specific perceptions into thoughts about enduring physical objects is a concealed art of the soul. It is rational because it admits of a standard of correctness. Inter-perceptual identifications can be right or wrong – the degree to which one can make them accurately, and the extent which one can do so for perceptions more distant from one another in time or appearance, is the index of a rational capacity.

1.6 RATIONALITY AND EXTRAPOLATION

The discovery of identities among the contents of one's perceptions is a core function of reason. There is another. This is the capacity to extrapolate from what one has perceived to what one has not. That extrapolation is a key concept in the early history of Indian logic is clear from some of the examples

Vātsyāyana gives under NS 1.1.5.[26] Seeing a rising cloud, one infers that it will rain. An interesting variant is: seeing the ants carrying their eggs, one infers that it will rain. Seeing a full and swiftly flowing river, one infers that it has been raining. Seeing a cloud of smoke, one infers the existence of an unseen fire. Hearing a cry, one infers that a peacock is nearby. Seeing the moon at one place at one time and at another place at another time, one infers that it is moving (even though one cannot *see* it move). The medical theorist Caraka[27] has some other examples: inferring impregnation from pregnancy; inferring the future appearance of fruit from the presence of seeds. In the ancient Buddhist logical text, *The Essence of Method*,[28] we also find: inferring from a child's special mark that this person is that child, now grown up; inferring from the salty taste of one drop of sea water that the whole sea is salty. The *Ts'ing-mu*[29] (a commentary on Nāgārjuna's *Middle Stanzas*, for which see Chapter 2) has a similar example: inferring that all the rice is cooked on tasting one grain. And the *Vaiśeṣikasūtra* mentions another sort of extrapolation – the inference of an entire cow from the perception only of its horns.[30]

Extrapolation from the seen to the unseen can take place in any of the three dimensions of time – past, present and future. Our interest is in the Indian theory of rationality, and for this we want to look at answers given to the question: on what basis, if any, ought the extrapolation be made? For while dice-throwing, guesswork and divination are ways of extrapolating, they are not rational ones. Extrapolation, like critical investigation, must be done 'on the basis of reasons', and a theory of such 'reasons' is a theory of that in virtue of which an extrapolation is warranted. So we can discover Indian theories of rationality in their explanations of why the extrapolations in the examples mentioned above are warranted. Rationality now is the search for extrapolative licence.

While Vātsyāyana says only that there should be a *connection* between what is seen and what is inferred,[31] many of the early writers have a definite interest in prediction and scientific explanation, and assume that extrapolation is warranted when underwritten by a causal relation. On the other hand, it is clearly recognised too that not all warranted extrapolation is causal. The *Vaiśeṣikasūtra* lists, in addition, the relations of contact, inherence, coinherence in a third, and being contrary (VS 3.1.8, 9.18), while the early Sāṃkhya *ṣaṣṭitantra* has an overlapping list of seven.[32] Take the inference from a drop of salty sea water to the conclusion that the whole sea is salty. This is not an inference based on any causal relation between the drop of sea water and the sea as a whole; rather, the relation between them is mereological. One would say that it is an inference from sampling a 'typical' member of a group. This is a very common and useful form of reasoning (witness the example of checking that all the rice is cooked by tasting a single grain). It is not formally valid, but it is a pervasive and powerful species of informal reasoning. We will see in the next section that it acquires particular significance in the context of a debate.

There is also an intriguing example from Vātsyāyana I have not yet mentioned. This is the inference of the 'residual' by elimination.[33] Wondering whether sound is a substance, a quality, or an event, and finding reasons to deny that it is a substance or an event, one draws the conclusion that it is a quality. What is interesting is that the early writers are well aware that not all warranted inference can be reduced to the causal model. An adequate theory of inference has to find a description of the extrapolation-warranting relation at a level more general than that of the causal.

The difficulty in finding adequately general bases for extrapolative inference encouraged a scepticism about their existence. In one form, scepticism about the possibility of rational extrapolation is just the claim that there is no adequate extrapolative basis. It is the view allegedly of the Lokāyata 'materialist,' and most notably of the sceptic Jayarāśi (*c.* AD 600). An early version of the sceptic's argument is recorded in the *Nyāyasūtra* (NS 2.1.37):

> [Objection:] Inference is not a means of knowing, because there may be errancy arising from embankment, damage and similarity.

Gautama is referring to the examples of the swollen river, the ants and the peacock. His point is that the observed facts admit of different explanations: the swollen river might have been caused by a dam or embankment further downstream, the ants might be carrying their eggs because their nest has been damaged, and the peacock's cry might have been made by a human or animal impersonator. There are alternative causal explanations for each perceived event. This is a standard sceptical move. The sceptic introduces an alternative possible explanation (that our experiences are all dreams or produced by an evil genius, that the world was created five minutes ago with all its fossil records) and then claims that the existence of such an alternative explanation shows that one is not entitled to assume that the common-sense expanation is the correct one. Gautama's reply is interesting (NS 2.1.38):

> No. Because it is a different thing from a [mere] partial case, fear, and [mere] similarity.

The compact response is that there is an observable difference between a river which is swollen because of upstream rain and one which is swollen because of a downstream blockage, a difference between the orderly procession of ants when it is about to rain and their fearful scurrying when the nest is disturbed, and a difference between a genuine peacock's cry and that of an impersonator.

The implication of Gautama's reply for the rationality of extrapolation seems to be this. An extrapolation from the seen thing to the unseen thing is rational when there is a relation of some appropriate (as yet unspecified) sort between the two. The relation does not obtain between the unseen thing and something which merely resembles the seen thing. The rational extrapolator, therefore, must have the capacity to discriminate between the thing in question and other things which merely resemble it, but do not stand in the appropriate relation to the unseen thing. Only someone who can tell the difference between a flood river and a dammed river is entitled to infer from swelling to rain; only someone who can tell the difference between marching ants and frightened ants is entitled to infer from marching to rain; and only someone who can tell the difference between a peacock's cry and a human impersonator is entitled to draw the inference from cry to peacock.

The sceptic will reply, of course, that he can always find an alternative explanation for the occurrence of a perceived event, no matter how finely attuned the perceiver's discriminating powers. Even the best expert can be fooled by a good enough forgery. But the question is whether it is rational to concern oneself with such extreme sceptical possibilities. The Naiyāyika proposes a common-sense maxim for extrapolative reasoning: do not extrapolate beyond the level of your competence. The sceptic has a different maxim: do not extrapolate if there is any possibility of error. Since human beings have finite discriminatory capacities, there is always the possibility of error, and so the sceptic's maxim implies that it is never rational to extrapolate. (Jayarāśi[34] claims even that there is no rational extrapolation from the rising to the setting of the sun!) To reach the sceptical conclusion, however, the sceptic has further to prove that his maxim of extrapolation is the rational one to adopt, while the common-sense Nyāya maxim is not. And that is precisely what Gautama is here denying.

1.7 RATIONALITY AND DEBATE

H. N. Randle observed a long time ago that 'the Naiyāyika was from first to last a *tārkika*, a disputant.'[35] More recently, B. K. Matilal has called debate the 'preferred form of rationality' in classical India.[36] There is a good deal of truth in these observations. A sophisticated theory of rationality evolved in the arenas of debate. Kauṭilya observed that rationality is about the best means to an end, and the end of the debater is to win. But what counts as winning a debate? If the debate is the victory-at-any-cost sort, and a debater wins when his opponent is lost for words or confused or hesitant, then the best and so most rational way to proceed would be to employ such tricks as play on the opponent's weaknesses: speaking very quickly or using convoluted examples or referring to doctrines of which one suspects one's opponent is ignorant. In the other sort of debate, the truth-directed sort, 'winning' is a matter of persuading one's opponent, and also an impartial audience, that one's thesis is true, and the rational debater must find some other methods. Nothing is more persuasive than an argument backed up by well-chosen examples and illustrations. And so, when the Naiyāyikas came to codify the form of rational debating demonstration, the citation of examples was given at least as much prominence as the citation of reasons. When the Nyāya theory of inference was 'rediscovered' by Henry Colebrooke (he broke the news at a meeting of the Royal Asiatic Society in London in 1824), the Indologists of the day in their excitement failed to pay due attention to this fact, and were led to some rather extraordinary speculations about the origins of syllogistic theory. The Sanskritist Görres apparently arrived at the view that Alexander, having been in conversation with the logicians of India during his campaigns, sent some of their treatises back home to his tutor who worked them up into a system! Equally remarkable was Niebuhr's claim that the Indians must have derived their theory from the Indianised Greeks of Bactria (it is a view Vidhyabhusana was to repeat much later on). If there is a lesson here, it is that a little comparative philosophy is a dangerous thing.

The debating room is a theatre for the art of persuasion. It is a metaphor for any situation in which one wants to persuade others of the correctness of one's point of view. It will include by extension both the mundane situation of persuading one's companion that something is about to happen, and persuading a scientific or academic community of the truth of one's thesis. The model of rationality which comes out of the theory of debate is public, explicit, demonstrational. The norms of public reason are those of mutual agreement.

The proper way to formulate one's position is in accordance with a 'five-limbed' schema: tentative statement of the thesis to be proved; citation of a reason; mention of an example; application of reason and example to the case in hand; final assertion of the thesis (NS 1.1.32). Suppose I want to persuade my walking companion that it is about to rain. I might reason as follows: 'Look, it is going to rain. For see that large black cloud. Last time you saw a large black cloud like that one, what happened? Well, it's the same now. It is definitely going to rain.' In order to be able to generalise the structure of such patterns of reasoning, the Naiyāyikas make an important simplifying assumption. They assume that the underlying pattern is one of property-substitution. The claim is that all such patterns exemplify the same canonical form: *Ta* because *Ra*. An object (the *pakṣa* or 'site' of the inference) is inferred to have a property (the *sādhya* or 'target') on the grounds that it has some other property (the *hetu* or reason). The first simplification, then, is to think of reasoning as taking us from an object's having one property to that same object's having another.

The simplification scarcely seems justified. A cursory inspection of the cases mentioned at the beginning of the last section shows that only about half fit such a pattern. The cases of the swollen river, the ants, the peacock's cry, the fruit and the salty sea do not seem to fit at all. Neither can we fit reasoning to the remainder by elimination. The canonical schema seems to fit the case of the moon, the pregnancy and the child's special mark, but it is only at a stretch that one can force the case of smoke and fire into the pattern (an irony as this is a hackneyed example which all the logical texts quote). Bearing in mind the ways in which Indian logic was later to develop, one can be forgiven for feeling that this adoption of a property-substitution model at an early stage, while perhaps a helpful and necessary simplification for the sake of initial progress, also restricted the study of other patterns of inferential reasoning. Only the Jaina logicians explicitly tried to develop a theory of extrapolation free from this restriction (see Chapter 5.7).

What licenses the inference from *Ra* to *Ta*? The *Nyāyasūtra* answer is given in five brief and controversial aphorisms (NS 1.1.34–38):

> A reason is that which proves what is to be proved by being like an example.
>
> Again, by being unalike.
>
> An example is an observed instance which, being like what is to be proved, possesses its property.
>
> Or else, being opposite, is opposite.
>
> The application is an assimilation to what is to be proved 'this is thus' or 'this is not thus' depending on the example.

Likeness and unlikeness are relative to properties. Something is 'like' another thing if both possess a given property. They are unalike with respect to that property if they do not both share it. Now arguably the natural way to interpret these *sūtra*s is as follows. Either the locus of the inference is like the example (in that both possess the reason property, *R*) and, since the example has the to-be-proved property, so does the locus. Or else the locus of the inference is unlike the example (it possesses the reason property, but the example does not), and since the example *does not* have the to-be-proved property, the locus *does* have it. If we let '*b*' stand for the example, then we seem to have:

a is like$_R$ b	a is unlike$_R$ b
Tb	$\sim Tb$
$\therefore Ta$	$\therefore Ta$

This formulation actually makes the inference a generalisation of the inference from sampling. The example is a typical member of the class of things having the reason property. And it has this other property, the to-be-inferred target property. But the site of the inference is also a member of the class of things having the reason property. So it too has the target property (the negative formulation is similar). This is a powerful form of reasoning, one which we engage in all the time. It is not formally valid, but it is a pervasive type of informal reasoning. We employ it whenever we infer that an object has a property on the grounds that it belongs to a type, the typical members of which have that property. Compare: this grain of rice is typical of the whole pan of rice, and it is cooked. So any other grain will be cooked as well. This drop of water is typical of the entire sea, and it is salty. So this other drop must be salty as well.

We said that in the debating model, rationality is subject to public norms of correctness. In arguments of the kind being considered, public norms do indeed have a role to play, for they determine whether the object adduced by the debater as an 'example' is adequate. For something to be capable of playing the role of example, it must be generally and uncontroversially accepted as a member of *R* and as a *T*. The debater must, when he chooses an example, be careful to select one that will fit public criteria of acceptability. Warranted extrapolation, clearly, is context dependent and occurs, in particular, only when there is a background of shared knowledge. For one grain of rice is an adequate exemplar of all only if it is commonly known that all the rice has been cooked in the same pan, at the same temperature, and with the same amount of water. It is for this reason that the pattern of reasoning here is neither formally valid nor reducible to an Aristotelian syllogism.[37]

There is a strong pressure, nevertheless, to fit such arguments into a deductive-nomological model. These arguments, the thought goes, rest on an underlying lawlike universal generalisation – that all the members of kind *R* are *T*s. The argument is then enthymematic for a deductively valid one: *Ra*, all *R* are *T* ∴ *Ta*. The role of the example, it is alleged, would be to provide empirical support for the universal rule, either by being something which is both *R* and *T*, or by being something which is neither *R* nor *T*. The pioneer indologist, Stanisław Schayer, had a different idea.[38] He read the step labelled 'example' in the five-step proof as an application of a logical rule, the one we would now call 'universal instantiation'. This is the rule that permits one to infer from '$(\forall x)(Rx \rightarrow Tx)$' to '$(Ra \rightarrow Ta)$'. And he read the step called 'application' as the application of another logical rule, *modus ponens*. But he still sees the overall inference as a formally valid one whose validity is a consequence of the fact that there is a hidden premise '$(\forall x)(Rx \rightarrow Tx)$'.

More light can be thrown on this point if we examine the early Nyāya account of a pair of debating moves called the 'likeness-based' rejoinder and 'unlikeness-based' rejoinder. A sophistical rejoinder (*jāti)* is a debating tactic in which the opponent tries unsuccessfully to produce a counter-argument, an argument designed to prove the opposite thesis. It is sophistical because the counter-argument is based on a false or superficial resemblance. *Nyāyasūtra* 5.1.2–3 state:

> When there is assimilation through likeness or unlikeness, the likeness-based and unlikeness-based rejoinders lead to the opposite property.
>
> [The reply is:] the proof [of the thesis] is just like the proof of a cow from cowhood.

One debater, debating properly, tries to prove that a certain object has a certain property by pointing out that it is like another object which does have that property. (The black cloud overhead now is like the cloud we saw yesterday – both are black. But that cloud caused it to rain, so this one will too.) The opponent now tries to counter by pointing out that the object is also like an object which does not have the property. (The black cloud overhead is like the white cloud we saw the day before yesterday – both are clouds. But that cloud did not cause rain, so this one won't either.)

a is like$_{R1}$ b	a is like$_{R2}$ c
Tb	$\sim Tc$
$\therefore Ta$	$\therefore \sim Ta$

As an argument, the rejoinder seems to follow the very same pattern as the original one, so why is it false? The existence of such rejoinders shows that mere likeness is not sufficient for good argument. The likeness has to be of the right type. When is the likeness of the right type? The *Nyāyasūtra*'s very cryptic comment is that the 'right type' is the type displayed by the relationship between a cow and its genus cowhood. Vātsyāyana, the commentator, is unclear and confused on this point. He does, however, make one important observation:[39]

> If one proceeds to establish the required inferable property on the basis simply of likeness or unlikeness then there will be lack of regularity (*vyavasthā*). Irregularity does not arise with respect to some special property. For something is a cow because of its likeness with another cow, which likeness is actually cowhood, not the cow's having dewlap, etc. It is because of cowhood that a cow is unlike a horse, etc., not because of a difference of particular qualities. This has been explained in the section on the limbs of a demonstration. In a demonstration, each limb serves a single purpose because they are connected with the means of knowing. The irregularity rests only on a bogus reason.

If the likeness must be of the right type, then the reason property, as determiner of the likeness relation, must also be of the right type. The object under investigation must be like objects which belong to a group, the typical members of which have the target property. Vātsyāyana implies that if the property in question is a property shared by typical members of the class of cows, then the reason property must be the class-essence cowhood.

In the last section, we saw that rational inference is linked with warranted extrapolation, and we wondered what it was that made an extrapolation warranted. The problem we have here is similar. We are now asking for the conditions under which it is admissible to extrapolate a property from one object to another. It appears to be admissible to extrapolate the property 'rainmaker' from one black cloud to another black cloud, but not from a black cloud to a white cloud. It appears to be admissible to extrapolate the property 'has a dewlap' from one cow to another cow, but not from one four-legged animal (a cow) to another (a horse). There seems to be an order in the world of objects, a structure which licenses the extrapolation of properties in some directions, but not others. Objects are grouped together on the basis of their likenesses and unlikenesses to one another. The possibility of likeness-based and unlikeness-based rejoinders shows, however, there are many different ways of making these groupings, many different metrics of likeness. So the problem is this – given some arbitrary property we wish to extrapolate from one object to another, how do we decide which such metric determines a standard for proper and warranted extrapolation? For an extrapolation may be warranted under one likeness relation, but not another. So not every inference of the standard pattern is permissible:

a is like$_R$ b
Tb
$\therefore Ta$

The response given in the tradition to this problem is to impose further constraints on the relation of likeness. Relevant or extrapolation-warranting likeness consists in the sharing of a property at least as narrow in extension as the property to be extrapolated. The idea is clearly expressed and ably defended by Diṅnāga (Chapter 4.7), and for that reason he is rightly thought of as one of India's finest logicians. I also think that the pre-Diṅnāga Naiyāyikas would not have developed the theory of inference in the way they did unless they had some such idea in their minds. But I do not believe we should be led by this to try to reinterpret what they said as an unequivocal expression of the idea. Matilal puts the matter well when he says that 'the conception of a universal connection is being hinted at on the analogy of a universal property.'[40] The *hint* was there, but it was for Diṅnāga to lend that hint articulation (and perhaps it is only at moments when a theory is being revised that a precise definition is needed). The important point is this need not be read as the introduction of a new *premise* into the inference pattern, but rather as a condition on when an inference is admissible. The constraint is of the form: it is valid to infer Ta from Tb if a is like$_R$ b when b, the example, is relevantly like a (i.e. when the property it shares with a is narrower in extension than the property being extrapolated). An inference rule is not another premise in the inference, but rather that in virtue of which the inference is valid or invalid. And the treatment of the early Nyāya theory as a theory of inference from sampling shows how the rule that there be a 'universal connection' (*vyāpti*) of this kind between the properties is not an enthymematic premise, but a genuine inference rule of an informal logic.

Five sorts of bogus reason (*hetvābhāsa*) are mentioned in *Nyāyasūtra* 1.2.4: the *wandering*, the *contradictory*, the *unproven*, the *counter-balanced* and the *untimely*.[41] Of special importance here is the one called the 'wandering' (for the 'unproven' and the 'counter-balanced', see Chapter 1.9). This was interpreted by later Naiyāyikas as meaning that the reason property deviates from the target, and so as a case in which the criterion enunciated in the above paragraph is violated. If a faulty reason is one which is present somewhere the target property is not, then by contraposition, a proper reason is one which is not present somewhere the target property is not, and so is at least as narrow in extension. The *Nyāyasūtra* definition is, however, less than explicit, and Vātsyāyana's explication of this most important *sūtra* is all over the place:

> The wandering is that which does not remain at only one end. (NS 1.2.5)
>
> An example is: sound is eternal because it is intangible. A pot is tangible and is seen to be non-eternal. Sound is not tangible in the same way. What then? It is intangible. One might say, therefore, that because it is intangible, sound is eternal. However, in this example, tangibility and non-eternality are not grasped as standing in a prover–proven relationship. For example, an atom is tangible and it is eternal. And when something like the soul is the example, then the reason, which is taken to be 'because of being intangible' in accordance with the *sūtra* 'a reason is that which proves what is to be proved by being like an example (1.1.34),' deviates from eternality. For a thought is intangible as well as non-eternal. So, as there is deviation in both sorts of case, there is no prover–proven relationship as the mark of a (proper) reason is absent. One end is eternality, one end non-eternality. So we understand 'being at one end'. Opposite to that which is at one end is that which does not remain at only one end, because it is a pervader (*vyāpaka*) of both ends.

Four inferences are compared. (1) A pot is non-eternal. Sound is unlike a pot – one is tangible, the other intangible. So sound is eternal. However, we also have this. (2) An atom is eternal. Sound is unlike an atom – one is tangible, the other intangible. So sound is non-eternal. Again, we have: (3) The soul is eternal. Sound is like the soul – both are intangible. So sound is eternal. But also: (4) A thought is non-eternal. Sound is like a thought – both are intangible. So sound is non-eternal. The implication is that what undermines the inference is the existence of examples which do not fit, i.e. counter-examples. Another maxim of extrapolation is in play: do not extrapolate if you know of any counter-examples (there is no implication that the extrapolator is obliged to look for counter-examples, however). A prover–proven relationship is one for which no counter-examples exist. What Vātsyāyana lacks, however, is a clear grasp of what makes something a counter-example. He does not see that only a thing which is intangible and non-eternal ought to be thought of as a counter-example to the inference from intangibility to eternality. Something which is tangible and eternal (an atom) is *not* a counter-example. For the existence of tangible eternal things is not inconsistent with the rule underpinning the inference, that whatever is intangible is eternal. It is the gaining of a clearer grasp of the notion of a counter-example that leads one to an understanding of the proper form of the prover–proven relationship. Again, Diṅnāga is extremely precise on the nature of counter-examples

(Chapter 4.7), and can take a lot of the credit, even if the essential point had been appreciated before him.

My point has been that there are many ways to arrive rationally at belief, other than that of formal deduction. Informal argument schemes, such as the inference from sampling, are just as much ways of reaching beliefs that it is rational for someone to hold, and it is with this wider concept of rational belief that we make better sense of the early Nyāya philosophical enterprise.

1.8 REASON, SCRIPTURE AND TESTIMONY

Is it rational to believe the testimony of others or the statements of the scriptures? Does the assumption that it is rational to believe what we hear or read require us to think of rationality in a new way? We have so far encountered two epistemic models of rationality: the perceptual model, according to which rationality provides norms for the temporal and cross-modal integration of perceptual experiences; and the extrapolative model, according to which rationality provides norms for the extrapolation from the perceived to the unperceived. The Naiyāyika thinks that belief in the testimony of others is indeed rational, but that neither the perceptual nor the extrapolative model of rationality can account for why this is so. Testimony is a *sui generis* source of rational belief (i.e. a *pramāṇa*).

The Nyāya theory of testimony is simple. Nyāyasūtra 1.1.7 states that testimony is the utterance of a 'credible person' (*āpta*). On this *sūtra*, Vātsyāyana adds the following important comment:

> A credible person is a speaker who has knowledge of the object and is motivated by the desire to tell of the object as known. This definition of a credible person is equally applicable to the seer (*ṛṣi*), the noble (*ārya*), and the outsider (*mleccha*).[42]

The comment is important because it implies that the scriptures do not have any special claim to our assent, but are to be believed for precisely the same reasons as any other piece of testimony, namely because the transmitter is credible. A credible person is one who is knowledgeable about the subject matter, and who has a sincere desire to communicate that knowledge, and can come from any walk of life or branch of society.[43] Vātsyāyana elaborates the point while discussing the *Nyāyasūtra* argument (NS 2.1.68) that the authority of the Veda is just like that of a medical treatise, in that it rests on the credibility of the communicator. He comments:

> To what is this authoritativeness due? It is due to the direct knowledge of what is prescribed, compassion for fellow beings, and the desire to communicate rightly. Credible communicators, having direct knowledge of what they prescribe, show compassion for fellow beings, (advising) 'this

> is to be avoided,' 'this is a cause of pain,' or 'this is to be attained' and 'this is the means to its attainment.' For creatures who cannot themselves understand, there is no other way of knowing all this . . . Thus a credible communicator is a source of knowledge.[44]

When a person speaks who is knowledgeable, well motivated and caring, it is rational to believe what they say. The scriptures, as it happens, are transmitted to us by such persons, and so we are entitled to believe them and regard what they say as a valuable source of knowledge, especially about moral and soteriological matters we would not otherwise be informed of. It is rational to believe the scriptures in just the same way and to just the same extent as it is rational to believe a medical text about medical matters, or any other experts about their respective field of competence.

A dilemma threatens this account of testimonial rationality. Must we *know* that the speaker has the qualities of competence, sincerity and compassion in order to be entitled to believe her, or not? It can hardly be right to say that we are entitled to believe any utterance we hear, and just hope that its author is competent and sincere. That would be an epistemic charter for the gullible.[45] But if we have first to establish that the speaker is competent and sincere, then it seems that our grounds for believing are inferential, and the rationality implicated in testimony is nothing but a variety of extrapolative rationality. We reason, in effect, that the present utterance is relevantly similar to past utterances of the same speaker, which have been seen to be true. Someone who accepts this (David Hume is a notable case) is led to conclude that it is indeed rational to believe the utterances of a sincere and competent speaker, but that no new model of rationality is involved.

What saves the Nyāya theory is the idea that one can 'monitor' the competence and sincerity of the speaker without forming any *beliefs* about her competence or sincerity. One might simply have an internal 'lie-detector' subconsciously monitoring for signs of blushing, fidgeting, and so on. The existence of such a mechanism makes the following counterfactual conditional true: if the speaker were lying, one would come to believe it. In the presence of a sub-doxastic faculty of this sort, one need not attempt to acquire knowledge about the speaker's credentials. For one's readiness to assent to what is being said will be overridden if she were to lie. Assent is made rational in a negative way, by the absence of evidence that the speaker is deceitful, rather than by positive evidence that she is sincere. It is rational in the same way that it is rational for one to believe that one has not just trodden on a nail. One need have no positive reason for so believing (a visual inspection of the foot, for example) for one knows that, if one had just trodden on a nail, one would have come to know about it. The 'reasoning' is *ab ignorantiam* and not inductive.[46]

While the worry about the reduction of testimony to inference is raised in the *Nyāyasūtra* (NS 2.1.49–51), this defence is not to be found there. It emerges in the later idea that a precondition for testimony is the 'absence of knowledge of unfitness' and not the 'knowledge of fitness', Vātsyāyana says only that testimony depends on the speaker's credibility and that 'inference is not like this'.[47]

1.9 REASON'S CHECKS AND BALANCES

I began this examination of rationality in the early Nyāya with a description of the disreputable 'reasoners' mentioned and criticised in the epics. The ill-repute was on the grounds that their use of reason was unmotivated, groundless, unconstrained. The Naiyāyika is very careful to avoid this charge. The very term *nyāya*, which Vātsyāyana identified with reasoned inquiry itself, is contrasted with another, *nyāyābhāsa* – a pseudo-inquiry. A pseudo-inquiry is one which, although otherwise in accord with the rules governing proper reasoning (setting out the demonstration in a five-limbed format and with a proper reason property), *contradicts observation and authority* (see Chapter 1.2). The same point is made time and again. A properly conducted debate, one which is friendly and truth-directed, is one which proceeds with the help of the methods of knowledge-acquisition, employs the five-limbed format, and is not in contradiction with any doctrinal base (NS 1.2.1). A reason property which proves a thesis contradictory to a doctrinal base is a mere bogus reason (NS 1.2.6). Reason in Nyāya has had its wings clipped. It can override neither observation nor authoritative doctrine!

Descartes observed that our perceptions can sometimes contradict one another, and that when they do it is the role of reason to adjudicate. A tower might look round from a distance, but square closer up. A star and a distant lamp both look like specks of light, but one is vastly larger than the other. It is reason (belief and inference) that tells us that the star is larger than the lamp, even though they both look the same size. It is reason that allows us to decide whether the tower is really square or round. How, then, can one deny that reason sometimes overrides perception? However, there *are* cases where perception overrides reason. Vātsyāyana tries to find a case where a reasoned argument meets all the criteria as laid down in the theory of inference, but whose conclusion has to be rejected because it goes against perception. His example is: fire is not hot, because it is a creation, like a pot. Fires and pots are alike in that they are both products of human effort (let us restrict the extension of 'fire' to those produced by humans). A pot, however, is a thing made of clay and so is not hot (material things are composed out of the four material elements, earth, water, fire and air, and only those containing elemental fire are hot). So fire too is not hot! The inference goes through even if we insist on a universal connection between reason and target. For it is indeed true that, among everything seen, created things are not hot. The point is that the inference extrapolates from the seen to the unseen, and fire's heat therefore belongs here with the unseen. The thermal properties of fire, as the matter under investigation, are, as it were, *sub judice*. Every created thing ever encountered (excluding fire) has been found to be cold. So, extrapolating, fire too as a created thing must be cold. Uddyotakara says that the inference is *baffled* by a perception of fire.

The conflict here is between a prediction based on an inductive generalisation and an actual observation. In general, one faces a choice whenever one has both an inference to the truth of some conclusion and strong evidence that the conclusion is false. One can either reject the evidence for the falsity of the conclusion, or else reject one of the premises in the inference. The examples of Descartes are cases where the first option is the correct one to choose. The evidence of the senses is defeated in one case by its own internal inconsistency and in the other by a generalisation with enormous empirical support (that things look smaller when they are further away). But the example of Vātsyāyana is a case where the second option is the correct one. In the face of incontrovertible observation, one must reject the similarity metric on the basis of which the extrapolation was made.

When is it rational to reject the premise, when the conclusion? Is this not a question for reason itself to decide, and when it decides in favour of the conclusion (i.e. of perception) does it not therefore decide to override itself? It is to avoid the apparent absurdity of such a result that the Nyāya insist on there being two different models or faculties of reason: reason as the rational extrapolator, and reason as the rational integrator of mental contents (perceptual and inferential). Integrative reason strikes a balance between perception and extrapolation, preferring one or the other according to its own standards. What is true of the relation between perception and inference is true too of the relation between testimony and inference, and true also of the relation between perception and testimony. What is the norm on integration? What principle does it follow in deciding who to override? Maximising consistency is the obvious answer, but there is scope for weighting. The Nyāya, it would seem, wants to weight testimony (and especially scriptural testimony) more heavily than anything else, and to weight observation more heavily than extrapolation. The pure reasoner of the epics would maximise the weight given to inference – no doctrine is unrevisable, no scripture sacred – or else, like the materialist, to observation. Such an anti-dogmatism may have led him to be banished from the company of the virtuous, but for us a question still remains. If there is a choice of weightings, which one is the rational choice? On what principle does one choose? The search for reasons goes on. Only at the end of this book will we see how the later Naiyāyikas brought this search for reasons to a close (Chapter 6).

Can reason really override itself? As we have seen (Chapter 1.7), five sorts of bogus reason are mentioned in *Nyāyasūtra* 1.2.4. In two of them, the *unproven* and the *counter-balanced*, reason acts as its own regulator. These are important, for they are favourite weapons of the sceptic. The situation called 'counter-balanced' is one in which, in order to resolve the point at issue, the debater adduces a reason which might equally well prove the point either way. The reason meets all the criteria for warranted extrapolation, and would have been entirely adequate in settling the matter, were it not for the possibility of an equally acceptable and adequate extrapolation to the opposite conclusion. Vātsyāyana's example is: sound is non-eternal because we do not apprehend in sound the properties of eternal things, just like the pot, etc. The objection to this otherwise admissible extrapolation is that it is reversible. For we can equally well argue as follows: sound is eternal because we do not apprehend in sound the properties of non-eternal things, just like the sky, etc. This too, on its own, would have been an admissible extrapolation. (A simpler, if not entirely suitable, example would be: sound is eternal because it is eternal; and: sound is non-eternal because it is non-eternal.) In the absence of any ground for preferring one of these over the other, the most reasonable thing to do is to accept neither. Behind this bogus reason is another maxim of extrapolation: when faced with equal, but opposite bases for extrapolation between which you cannot choose, *do not extrapolate*. When reasons are balanced against each other, one is driven instead towards the sceptic's *ataraxia* (see Chapter 2.5).

The other bogus reason of interest to us here is the one called 'unproven', or, more literally, 'same as the thesis' (*sādhyasama*). The reason is one which has not itself been established, and in that sense is in the same state as the thesis to be proved. Vātsyāyana's intriguing example is: a shadow is a substance because it moves. We have again an otherwise admissible extrapolation, but one that would be a false move in a debate. The problem is that the movement of shadows is not itself an established fact: it is neither a shared doctrine nor an indisputable observation. For one needs to know whether shadows are seen to move like men, or whether what takes place is a succession of perceptions of dimly lit things produced by the obstruction of the light by a moving cover. Extrapolation proceeds from the seen to the unseen, or more generally, from the proven to the unproven. The underlying maxim on extrapolation is therefore: only extrapolate from what you have already established. The fault of being 'the same as the thesis' is a violation of this maxim.

The Mādhyamika sceptic Nāgārjuna uses this fault to devastating effect. He argues that any reason adduced to refute the sceptical thesis will suffer the fault of being the same as the thesis. For if the sceptical thesis is that nothing can be known, then to refute it is to prove that something can be known. But if it is not yet established that anything can be known, one can adduce no known or established fact to prove it. So any putative reason one adduces to prove that something can be known will be the 'same as the thesis' in being as yet unproven. The two propositions, 'A proves B only if A is proven in advance of B' and 'B = something is proven' in combination entail that A has to be something which is proven in advance of anything being proven, and this entails that there is no such A. The sceptic's thesis is indefeasible!

Such is the account of reason as it was conceived in early India. The concept is a shifting, not to say shifty, one, an interplay of different themes. The collection of ideas presented here was supposed to describe the way people actually do reason and explain why they are justified in doing so. It is a common-sense theory of common sense. In the subsequent chapters, I will look at attacks on this account from several directions. The Mādhyamika sceptic's claim that reason is *self-defeating* has already been mentioned. It is self-defeating because, if true, it is provable that nothing is provable (Chapter 2). The Jainas are diametrically opposed: reason, they say, is *over-complete*: everything is provable (Chapter 5). And Diṅnāga, a founder-member of Yogācāra-Vijñānavāda Buddhism, is neither a sceptic nor a syncretist, but a *unificationist* about reason. What he rejects is the idea that there is a plurality in the concept of rationality (rationality *qua* integrator, *qua* extrapolator, and *qua* recipient of testimony). Such a unification of reason, it turns out, necessitates a radical departure from naiveté (Chapter 4). At the end of the book, we will return to Nyāya, and see how in the later period, responding to the many and varied assaults on the concept of rationality embedded in common sense, it revitalised its defence of the common-sense account.

FURTHER READING

Texts

Gautama *c.* AD 150, *Nyayasūtra* (NS).
Vātsyāyana *c.* AD 450, *Nyāyabhāṣya* (NBh).

Rationality, philosophical method (1.1–3)

1 Arindam Chakrabarti, 'Rationality in Indian Philosophy,' in Eliot Deutsch and Ron Bontekoe eds., *A Companion to World Philosophies* (Oxford: Blackwell Publishers, 1997), pp. 259–278.

2 Wilhelm Halbfass, 'Darśana, Ānvīkṣikī, Philosophy,' in his *India and Europe: an Essay in Understanding* (Albany: State University of New York Press, 1988), pp. 263–286.

3 Bimal Krishna Matilal, 'On the Concept of Philosophy in India,' in *Philosophy, Culture and Religion: Collected Essays* (Delhi: Oxford University Press, 2001).

4 Bimal Krishna Matilal, *Perception: An Essay on Classical Indian Theories of Knowledge* (Oxford: Clarendon Press, 1986), Chapter 3.

5 C. Ram–Prasad, *Knowledge and the Highest Good: Liberation and Philosophical Inquiry in Classical Indian Thought* (Basingstoke: Macmillan, 2000).

Perception, mind (1.4–5)

1 Bimal Krishna Matilal, *Perception: An Essay on Classical Indian Theories of Knowledge* (Clarendon Press, Oxford, 1986), Chapters 6, 8.
2 Bimal Krishna Matilal, 'A Realist View of Perception,' in P. K. Sen and R. R. Verma eds., *The Philosophy of P. F. Strawson* (New Delhi: Indian Council of Philosophical Research, 1995), pp. 305–326; reprinted in his *Philosophy, Religion, Culture: Collected Essays* (Delhi: Oxford University Press, 2001).
3 Arindam Chakrabarti, 'I Touch What I Saw,' *Philosophy and Phenomenological Research* 52 (1992), pp. 103–117.
4 Kishor Chakrabarti, *Indian Philosophy of Mind: The Nyāya Dualist Tradition* (Albany: State University of New York Press, 1999).

Extrapolation, informal logic, debate (1.6–7)

1 Esther Solomon, *Indian Dialectics* (Ahmedabad: B. J. Institute of Learning and Research, 1976), 2 volumes.
2 Mrinalkanti Gangopadhyay, *Indian Logic In Its Sources* (Delhi: Munshiram Manoharlal, 1984).
3 Claudius Nenninger, 'Analogical Reasoning in Early Nyāya-Vaiśeṣika,' *Asiatische Studien* 48 (1994), pp. 819–832.
4 Claus Oetke, 'Ancient Indian Logic as a Theory of Non-Monotonic Reasoning,' *Journal of Indian Philosophy* 24 (1996), pp. 447–539.
5 Bimal Krishna Matilal, *The Character of Logic in India* (Albany: State University of New York Press, 1998).

Testimony, tradition (1.8–9)

1 Bimal Krishna Matilal and Arindam Chakrabarti eds., *Knowing from Words* (Dordrecht: Kluwer, 1994).
2 J. N. Mohanty, *Reason and Tradition in Indian Thought* (Oxford: Clarendon Press, 1992), Chapters 8, 9.
3 Jonardon Ganeri, 'Testimony,' in *Semantic Powers: Meaning and the Means of Knowing in Classical Indian Philosophy* (Oxford: Clarendon Press, 1999), pp. 72–81.

2 Rationality, emptiness and the objective view

2.1 THOUGHT AND REALITY

Is reality accessible to thought? Could it not be that there are limits on our cognitive capacities, and the way the world is, whatever that might be, is something beyond our powers of understanding? What there is in the world might extend beyond what we, in virtue of our natural cognitive endowment, have the capacity to form a conception of.

The thesis is a radical form of scepticism. It is a scepticism about what we can conceive rather than about what we can know. Nāgārjuna (*c.* AD 150), founder of the Madhyamaka school of Indian Buddhism, is a radical sceptic of this sort. Indeed, he is still more radical. His thesis is not merely that there may be aspects of reality beyond the reach of conception, but that thought entirely fails to reach reality. If there is a world, it is a world about which we can form no adequate conception. Moreover, since language expresses thought, it is a world about which we cannot speak.

> Where the reach of thought turns back, language turns back. The nature of things (*dharmatā*) is, like *nirvāṇa*, without origin and without decay. (MK 18.7)

> Not dependent on another, calm, not conceptualised by conception, not mentally constructed, not diverse – this is the mark of reality (*tattva*). (MK 18.9)

This indeed is for Nāgārjuna the true meaning of the Buddha's teachings, a meaning so disruptive to common reason that the Buddha was reluctant to spell it out.

> For that reason – that the truth (*dharma*) is deep and difficult to understand – the Buddha's mind despaired of being able to teach it. (MK 24.12)

A century of scholarship on the Madhyamaka system has seen a plethora of interpretations. David Seyfort Ruegg has remarked on a situation in which 'the doctrine of the Madhyamaka school, and in particular that of Nāgārjuna, has been variously described as nihilism, monism, irrationalism, misology, agnosticism, scepticism, criticism, dialectic, mysticism, acosmism, absolutism, relativism, nominalism, and linguistic analysis with therapeutic value.'[1] More recently, thematic relationships with antirealism[2] and the Derridean technique of deconstruction[3] have received attention. Nāgārjuna is certainly a complex and at times ambiguous thinker. He writes in an aphoristic style, he may have shifted his position in the course of his career, and no-one is entirely sure whether many of the works usually attributed to him are his own compositions. The exegetical problems remain fully to be resolved. What we can be sure of is that Nāgārjuna did indeed compose two fascinating philosophical documents, the *Middle Stanzas* (*Mūlamadhyamakakārikā*: MK) and his *Reply to Critics* (*Vigrahavyāvartanī*: V), whose great value lies in the undisputedly radical nature of their ideas. What seems clear is that Nāgārjuna thinks that the conceptual scheme implicit in common sense presupposes the existence of a world of stable, self-sustaining objects, and that his philosophical method consists in demonstrating that existential presuppositions of this sort are never true. To reach the sceptical thesis one needs a more general result, that the common-sense scheme is the only possible conceptual scheme. For if nothing of the sort that thought presupposes exists, then anything – if there is anything – which does exist is inaccessible to thought.

2.2 EMPTINESS AND THE OBJECTIVE VIEW

The theory of emptiness (*śūnyatā*) is Nāgārjuna's most celebrated doctrine. It is a theory about the nature of our understanding of our own experience, and its relation to the world. It is a theory about our capacity for objective thought. Experience represents itself as being about external objects, yet all but the most unreflective know that their experience is sometimes misleading. Among Nāgārjuna's favourite examples are witnessing the illusory objects conjured up in a magical trick, apprehending an object in a dream, and thinking that the objects of stories and fables, such as the city of celestial musicians, are real (MK 7.34, 17.33, 23.8). We may add holograms, hallucinations, objects seen in film projections. If one is to be able to understand such experiences for what they are, the unreflective view must be replaced with a more objective one, a view achieved by reflecting on the origin of such experiences. One must attain a perspective on one's own experience which enables one to think of illusions, dreams and holograms along with their etiology, and so to explain their occurrence without recourse to the assumption that they have genuine content. The process of stepping back from the contingencies of appearance produces a sequence of progressively more objective conceptions. If the process can be completed, it is completed in the attainment of an 'objective view'[4] or 'absolute conception'.[5]

Nāgārjuna presses us towards an objective view. He observes that there are types of experience for which, when we place them within our conception of the world, we can find an adequate explanation without having to suppose that there actually exist things of the sort represented in the experience. We are not deceived by the magician's illusion because we can explain the appearance in terms of the magical trick. The new understanding we have come to is a conception of such experiences as ones whose objects are, in Nāgārjuna's term, 'empty'. They are empty because they depend for their apparent existence on other factors, such as the magician, the dream, the holographic projector, or the fictional narrative.

> Emptiness is proved on the grounds that things do not have self-standing natures (*svabhāva*). The dependent nature of things is what is called 'emptiness,' for a dependent nature is one which is not self-standing. (V 21–22)

> We claim that dependent origination is emptiness. It is a derivative designation, and it alone is the middle way. (MK 24.18)

One is in a position to think of an experience as empty if one can explain its occurrence in terms of a set of causes none of which is an object of the type the experience presents. The ability to think of one's experiences in this way depends on one's having taken the first step towards an objective stance.

Someone who has taken this first step towards objectivity will contrast two kinds of experience. Part of one's experience is now understood as arising in dependence of a deviant etiology. The remainder of one's experience, however, has to be understood in another way, as being about what causes it. The conceptual scheme encoded in common sense offers just such an explanation. What are the key elements in the common-sense scheme, the most deeply ingrained categories in our thinking about the constituents of our surroundings and our interactions with them? In the chapters of the *Middle Stanzas*, Nāgārjuna identifies the following concepts: origin, motion, sensory perception, physical objects and their properties, desire, causation, past and future, suffering (*duḥkha*), combination, the idea that things have a self-standing nature or essence, bondage and release, agency, the self, the flow of time, creation and decay, and the possibility of error. Our common-sense understanding of the world is as one containing stable, self-sustaining objects which move about and causally influence one another, which we can see in virtue of their causal influence upon us, which are caused to come into being and eventually to decay, and which stand in spatio-temporal relations to one another and to us. The *karma* hypothesis appears here too as a deeply entrenched ingredient in the classical Indian common-sense understanding of moral consequence (Chapter 1.3).

The common-sense understanding of ordinary (non-deviant) experience is of experience as caused by the object it purports to represent. Such experience is said to have a 'support' (*ālambana*) in the world of objects (see Chapter 4.10). When one thinks in this way of one's experience as caused by the object it represents, one has a certain conception of objects. They are conceived of as things which can be perceived and can also continue to exist unperceived. Nāgārjuna claims that they are conceived of as things which have a 'self-standing nature' or *svabhāva.* This complex and ambiguous term conveys notions of permanence, stability, endurance, independence, essence, identity. It stands for the idea of an object which can exist independently of any perception or experience, and which, by existing for a duration of time, can be perceived more than once at different times. It is a conception of things 'out there' which make intelligible our having the experiences we do when no other explanation of their origin can be found.

The common-sense understanding of our experiences and conceptions is a step in the direction of objectivity, a step away from an uncritical acceptance of the existential presuppositions of experience and conception. The crucial move is the next one. Nāgārjuna describes it as a move from 'conventional' truth (*saṃvṛtti-sat*) to 'ultimate' truth (*paramārtha-sat*). We may regard it as the step from the common-sense scheme to an absolute conception. What happens when we take another step away from appearance, when the conception of these two kinds of experience itself becomes part of what we want to understand? The possibility explored by Nāgārjuna is that our conception of experience, as produced by self-sustaining and independent objects, is itself a fiction of the common-sense scheme. To put it another way, when we step back from the common-sense scheme, what we come to understand is that we have no independent conception of an independent reality, but conceive it only as containing things which are not empty. The common-sense scheme applies to such things because we have a category of experience for which we can find no 'deviant' causal explanation. What we now discover is that it is a mistake to take this inability to comprehend all of our experience in the way we comprehend dreams and illusions as grounds for thinking that such experience must be thought of as caused by an explanatorily independent world of objects. Nāgārjuna recommends calmness in place of striving for such explanations:

> Those with little understanding who see only the existence and non-existence of things fail to see the calmness of what is experienceable. (MK 5.8)

When one steps out of the common-sense conception and towards an objective view, the view to which one is led is that *all* conception is empty. The idea of experience explained by thinking of it as caused by explanatorily independent objects is seen now for what it is – a fiction of the common-sense scheme. Such experience ought to be conceived of simply as experience for which the experiencer cannot find the explanation. It is the proper function of rationality to lead one to a critical assessment of one's own conceptual scheme, to an understanding of the operations and deceptions of common sense, and so eventually to an objective view. Nāgārjuna's claim is that when reason is so used, the objective understanding one attains is that the 'naive' view, the view that there is a role for objects in the causal explanation of experience, is nothing but an appearance of explanation, created by the naive view itself. An objective understanding is an understanding that all conception and all experience is empty.

> Just like a master, by his magical powers, fashions a magical figure, and this magical figure in turn fashions another magical figure – in that way, an agent is like the magical figure and his action like the other figure fashioned by the first. Afflictions, actions, bodies, agents and effects are like a city of celestial musicians or a mirage or a dream. (MK 17.31–33)

The form of understanding encoded in common sense is more objective than blind trust in one's experience because with it one understands that some experience is 'genuine' and other experience is mere 'appearance'. The new view, the view Nāgārjuna thinks can be reached by a critical exercise of reason, is that the explanation of 'genuine' experience offered by common sense is itself a mere appearance of an explanation. Common sense deceives us, just as common experience does. Common experience deceives us into thinking that magical projections and other mere appearances exist. Common sense deceives us into thinking that genuine experience is explained with reference to a world of objects. When we achieve an objective understanding, we realise that common sense is itself the projection of a magician, a magical figure which fashions another magical figure in the form of the distinction between genuine experience and mere appearance. Nāgārjuna's point, and it is a theme running right through his work, is that common sense deceives us when it appeals to the idea of an 'independent' object, which explains why we have the experiences we do, but is not itself within the explanatory web. But it is better to accept that some experiences are unexplained, than to appeal to an idea which gives only an impression of being an explanation, but in fact offers no real explanation. The same point is what leads him to his attack on the ideas of an uncaused causer, an unproved prover, an unmoving mover and an unperceived perceiver. The circle of explanation (or causation, or proof, or motion, or perception) must be (but cannot be) closed.

The Nyāya model of rational inquiry is itself a model embedded within common sense. It is the intuitive, natural, naive account of the rational processes of belief-formation, revision and rejection. For the common-sense appeal to the idea that beliefs are true when they are caused by what they represent is itself a certification of certain methods of belief-formation as rational. Nāgārjuna has a quite different conception of the means and ends of rationality.

2.3 RATIONALITY IN MADHYAMAKA

Rationality is the means by which one 'steps back' to a more objective view. Rationality is a mode of critical evaluation of one's conceptual scheme. A more objective understanding is one in which one understands that things are not necessarily as they appear. It is a view from which one can see how and where one's earlier conceptions are misleading. One learns not to trust one's perceptions when a large object far away looks small, or a stick half submerged in water looks bent, and in learning this one exercises a mode of self-critical reason. So too rational people learn not to trust their conceptions when they presuppose the existence of independent, self-standing objects. From the vantage point of an objective view, it is easy to see that one's old conceptions had false presuppositions. The real trick, however, is to be able to expose those presuppositions while still 'within' the old conception, and so to lever oneself up to a more objective view. This levering-up-from-within requires a new way of reasoning: Nāgārjuna's celebrated *prasaṅga*-type rationality. It is a self-critical rationality which exposes as false the existential presuppositions on which one's present conceptions are based.

One feature of those presuppositions is especially important. A conceptual scheme does not presuppose a world of *objects* so much as a *structure of division*. A conceptual scheme is a grid of divisions and relations imposed upon an undifferentiated, amorphous reality. A system of concepts is a way of cutting, grouping and relating. It represents a choice about where the boundaries of objects should fall. Modern studies of the notion of an object encoded in common sense suggest that common sense encodes principles of cohesion ('surfaces lie on one object if and only if they are connected'), principles of contact ('surfaces move together if and only if they are in contact') and principles of continuity ('an object traces exactly one connected path over space and time').[6] Other notions of an object, other carvings of reality, are possible, for example, the notion of an object in Vaiśeṣika ontology (for which, see Chapter 3), or those encoded in modern physical theory. What a conceptual scheme presupposes, then, is that the ways of cutting, grouping and relating which it encodes correspond to natural structures of division and organisation in the world. It is on *this* presupposition that the Mādhyamika process of rational self-criticism bears.

A simple example will illustrate the kind of reasoning Nāgārjuna thinks is needed if one is to expose the presuppositions of one's conceptual scheme from within. A non-compound monadic concept '*F*' has the following application-condition: it applies only to things which are *F*. It is therefore a concept whose application presupposes that there is a condition which divides the domain into two. For our purposes, the condition can be thought of either as 'belonging to the class of *F*s' or 'possessing the property being-*F*'. Now take an arbitrary object, *a*, from some antecedently specified domain. There are apparently two possibilities for *a*: either it falls under the concept, or else it does not. That is, the two options are:

(I) *F* applies to *a*.
(II) *F* does not apply to *a*.

Suppose that one can disprove *both* of these options. How one would try to do this will vary from case to case, depending on the individual concept under scrutiny. But if one is able to disprove (I) and to disprove (II), then the concept in question can have no application-condition. The presupposition for the application of the concept, that there is a condition (class, property) effecting a division within the domain, fails. A later Mādhyamika master[7] expresses the idea exactly:

> When neither existence nor non-existence presents itself before the mind, then, being without objective support (*nirālambana*) because there is no other way, [the mind] is still.

Sentences are used to make statements, but if the statement so made is neither true nor false, then, because there is no third truth-value, the statement must be judged to lack content.[8]

Nāgārjuna's developed strategy involves a generalisation. A generalisation is needed because many if not most of the concepts under scrutiny are *relational* rather than *monadic*; centrally: causes, sees, moves, desires. When a concept is relational, there are four rather than two ways for its application-condition to be satisfied (Figure 2.1):

(I) R relates *a* only to itself.
(II) R relates *a* only to things other than itself.
(III) R relates *a* both to itself and to things other than itself.
(IV) R relates *a* to nothing.

As an illustration of the four options, take R to be the square-root relation √, and the domain of objects to be the set of real numbers. Then the four possibilities are exemplified by the numbers 0, 4, 1 and –1 respectively. For $\sqrt{0} = 0$, $\sqrt{4} = 2$ and also -2, $\sqrt{1} = 1$ and also -1, while finally -1 does not have a defined square root among the real numbers. The list of four options is what is called in Madhyamaka a *catuṣkoṭi*.

> Everything is thus, not thus, both thus and not thus, or neither thus nor not thus. That is the Buddha's [provisional] instruction. (MK 18.8)

> Some say that suffering (*duḥkha*) is self-produced, or produced from another, or produced from both, or produced without a cause. (MK 12.1)

> Since every factor in existence (*dharma*) is empty, what is finite and what is infinite? What is both finite and infinite? What is neither finite nor infinite? (MK 25.22)

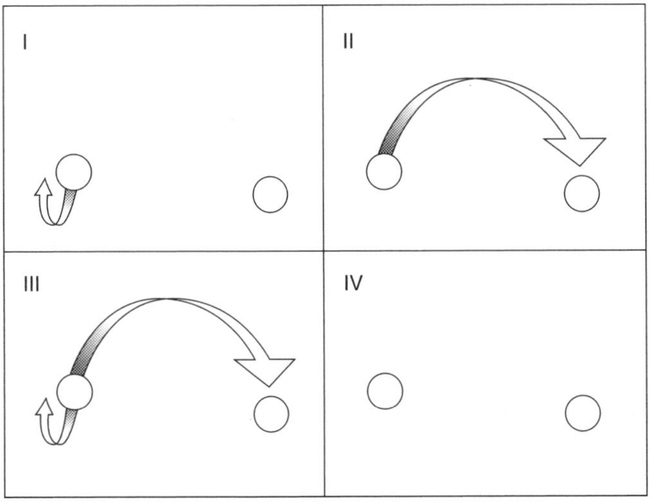

Figure 2.1 The four options.

It is easy to see that the four options are mutually exclusive and jointly exhaustive. For the class of objects to which R relates *a* is either (IV) the empty set ∅ or, if not, then either (I) it is identical to {a}, or (II) it excludes {a}, or (III) it includes {a}. Not every relation exhibits all four options. (I) is not exhibited if R is anti-reflexive. (II) is not exhibited if R is reflexive and bijective. (IV) is not exhibited if R is defined on every point in the domain. Note in particular that if R is the identity relation, then neither (III) nor (IV) is exhibited, not (III) because identity is transitive, and not (IV) because identity is reflexive. Indeed, options (III) and (IV) are not exhibited whenever R is an equivalence (transitive, symmetric and reflexive) relation.

The next step in the strategy is to construct subsidiary 'disproofs', one for each of the four options. Although there is no pre-determined procedure for constructing such disproofs, by far the most commonly used method is to show that the option in question has some unacceptable consequence (*prasaṅga*). A major dispute for later Mādhyamikas was over what sort of reasoning is permissible in the four subsidiary disproofs, the proofs that lead to the rejection of each of the four options. It is a difficult question to answer, so difficult indeed that it led, at around 500 AD, to a fission within the school of Madhyamaka. The principal group (Prāsaṅgika, headed by Buddhapālita) insisted that only *prasaṅga*-type, 'presupposition-negating' reasoning is admissible. This faction is the more conservative and mainstream, in the sense that their teaching seems to be in keeping with Nāgārjuna's own method of reasoning. The important later Mādhyamika masters Candrakīrti and Śāntideva defended this view. A splinter faction, however (Svātantrika, headed by Bhāvaviveka), allowed 'independent' inference or inductive demonstration into the disproofs. Perhaps this was done so that the inductive methods developed by Diṅnāga (Chapter 4.7) could be deployed in establishing the Mādhyamika's doctrinal position. Clearly, the fewer restrictions one places on the type of reasoning one permits oneself to use, the greater are the prospects of successfully finding arguments to negate each of the four options. On the other hand, we have seen that the citation of paradigmatic examples is essential to this type of reasoning (Chapter 1.6–7), and it is hard to see how one could be entitled to cite examples in support of one's argument, when the very conception of those examples is in question.

The effect of the four subsidiary disproofs is to establish that none of the four options obtains:[9]

> Neither from itself nor from another, nor from both, nor without a cause, does anything whatever anywhere arise. (MK 1.1)
>
> One may not say that there is emptiness, nor that there is non-emptiness. Nor that both, nor that neither exists; the purpose for so saying is only one of provisional understanding. (MK 22.11)

The emptiness of the concept in question is now deduced as the final step in the process. For it is a presupposition of one of the four options obtaining that the concept does have an application-condition (a class of classes or relational property). If all four are disproved, then the presupposition itself cannot be true. When successful, the procedure proves that the concept in question is empty, null, *śūnya*. This is Nāgārjuna's celebrated and controversial '*prasaṅga*-type' rational inquiry, a sophisticated use of rationality to annul a conceptual scheme.

A statement is truth-apt if it is capable of being evaluated as either true or false. When Nāgārjuna rejects each of the four options, he is rejecting the claim that a statement of the form '*a*R*b*' is truth-apt, since the four options exhaust the possible ways in which it might be evaluated as true. But if the statements belonging to a certain discourse are not truth-apt, then the discourse cannot be part of an objective description of the world (a joke is either funny or unfunny, but it cannot be evaluated as true or false). The *prasaṅga* negates a presupposition for truth-aptness and so for objective reference.

Nāgārjuna applies the procedure in an attempt to annul each of the concepts I listed above as the basic ingredients of the common-sense scheme. In each case, his method is to identify a relation and prove that none of the four options can obtain. On closer inspection, it turns out that his argumentation falls into two basic patterns.[10] One pattern is applied to any concept involving the idea of an ordering or sequence, especially the concept of a causal relation, of a temporal relation and of a proof relation. The paradigm for this argument is Nāgārjuna's presentation of a paradox of origin (MK Chapter 1), which serves as model for his analysis of causation (MK Chapter 8), the finitude of the past and future (MK Chapter 11), and suffering (MK Chapter 12). The argument seeks to establish that a cause can be neither identical to, nor different from, the effect. If nothing within the domain is uncaused, then the four options for the realisation of a causal relation are foreclosed.

The other pattern of argumentation in Nāgārjuna is essentially grammatical. When a relational concept is expressed by a transitive verb, the sentence has an Agent and a Patient (the relata of the relation): for example, 'He sees the tree,' 'He goes to the market,' 'He builds a house.' The idea of the grammatical argument is that one can exploit features of the deep case structure of such sentences in order to prove that the Patient can be neither identical to the Agent, nor include it, nor exclude it, and that there must be a Patient. Nāgārjuna uses this pattern of argumentation in constructing a paradox of motion (MK Chapter 2), and this chapter serves as a model for his analysis of perception (MK Chapter 3), composition (MK Chapter 7), fire (MK Chapter 10), and of bondage and release (MK Chapter 16). Indeed, the same pattern of argument seems to be applicable whenever one has a concept which involves a notion of a single process extended in time. In the next three sections, I will reconstruct respectively Nāgārjuna's arguments against causation, proof and motion. What we say about these prototypical cases will apply *inter alia* to all other concepts to which the two basic strategies apply.

2.4 ON CAUSATION

How does the causal argument go? In a passage on the origins of suffering, a theme so central to Buddhist soteriology and the Buddha's teaching, Nāgārjuna rehearses the general pattern of argumentation:

> Some say that suffering is self-produced, or produced from another, or produced from both, or produced without a cause. (MK 12.1)
>
> If suffering came from itself, then it would not arise dependently; surely *those* sensory and bodily aggregates arise in dependence on *these* sensory and bodily aggregates. (MK 12.2)
>
> When being self-produced is not established, how could suffering be caused by another? Whatever caused the suffering of another must have caused its own suffering. (MK 12.7)
>
> If suffering were caused by each, it could be caused by both. Not produced by another nor self-produced. How could suffering be uncaused? (MK 12.9)
>
> Not only are the four options impossible in respect to suffering, none of the four options is possible even in respect to external things (*bhāva*). (MK 12.10)

The relational concept under scrutiny is 'originator of'. The object in question here is suffering, but Nāgārjuna extends the argument to include any object within the causal order. Let us then take some arbitrary object, *a*. The four options are (I) that *a* originates in itself, (II) that it originates in some other, (III) that it originates in itself and originates in some other, and (IV) that it has no origin. And, if we read these passages along with others in the *Middle Stanzas*, the four disproofs have something like the following structure.

Disproof of (I). If *a* is self-originating then it exists and perpetuates itself independently of anything else. For *a* is self-originating just in case a necessary and sufficient cause of its existence at time *t* is its existence at time $t - \delta$, and so on backwards in time. It follows that there is no point in time at which *a* comes into existence, for its existence at one instant is necessary for its existence at the next. It also follows that there is no point in time at which it goes out of existence, for its existence at one time is sufficient for its existence at the next. So calling something 'self-causing' is just a rather misleading way of saying that it is eternal. This is misleading because it is wrong to think of eternal entities as 'causal' at all. They are outside the causal realm. This is the *prasaṅga*, the unacceptable consequence of the initial hypothesis.

Disproof of (II). The claim is that only things other than *a* can be causes of *a*. If *a* originates from some other thing, then one must ask wherefrom this other thing originates. It cannot originate from itself. This is because, in the previous argument, *a* was an object chosen arbitrarily. So that argument will apply with equal force to the originator of *a*. But if the originator of *a* itself originates from some other, we have the beginning of an infinite chain of distinct causes (MK 7.19: 'If another originates this, then origination is infinitely regressive'). It cannot, however, be a matter of logical necessity that the world of objects is infinite.

Disproof of (III). The remaining possibility is that at some point a causal ancestry loops back on itself. An object in such a loop would be caused by all the members of the loop, and so have both itself and other things among its sufficient causes. However, the argument against (I) proved that *a* is not a sufficient cause of itself, and the argument against (II) proved that no other thing is a sufficient cause of *a*. So (III) is disproved by either of the previous arguments.

Disproof of (IV). Can something exist and have no originating cause? One may be inclined to think of numbers, universals and other abstract objects, but Nāgārjuna has specified that the argument is applicable only to *bhāvas*, and we may take a *bhāva* in this context to be an object *within* the causal order. Elsewhere, he insists that 'there is nowhere an existing thing without a cause' (MK 4.2).

An interesting dialectical strategy underpins this sequence of arguments. (I) in general asserts that R relates *a* to itself *and* that R does not relate *a* to any other thing. The disproof consists in showing that R does not *even* relate *a* to itself. Similarly (II) in general asserts that R relates *a* to other things *and* that R does not relate *a* to itself. It is disproved by showing that R does not *even* relate *a* to other things. The arguments against (I) and (II) are then individually sufficient to disprove (III), that R relates *a* to itself and to other things.

Suppose we let 'A' stand for 'R relates *a* to itself,' and that we let 'B' stand for 'R relates *a* to other things.' The dialectical structure is now:

Option	*Thesis*	*Disproof strategy*
I	A & ¬B	disprove A
II	B & ¬A	disprove B
III	A & B	disprove A or disprove B
IV	¬A & ¬B	eliminated by fiat

So (III) is disproved both by the disproof of (I) and by that of (II). Nāgārjuna might have chosen a different dialectical strategy here. He might have chosen to disprove (I) by disproving 'A', and to disprove (II) by disproving '¬A'. The disproof of (III) would then follow from the disproof of (I), but not from that of (II). He might also have chosen to disprove (I) by disproving '¬B', and to disprove (II) by disproving 'B.' The disproof of (III) would then follow from the disproof of (II), but not from that of (I). To use either of these alternative strategies, however, one would have to be happy with the idea that a proposition and its negation can simultaneously be disproved. The important point is that, whichever strategy one uses, the disproof of (III) is trivial once one has a disproof of both (I) and (II).

The way that (IV) has been disproved is instructive too. In fact, it is not so much disproved as ruled out by fiat. For we restrict the domain to objects within the causal order, leaving no room for an object within the domain and yet uncaused. This is a characteristic function of the fourth option. It is used to delimit the domain is such a way that everything within the domain has the property under scrutiny (in this case, the property having-an-origin).

Nāgārjuna has sometimes been understood differently.[11] It has been claimed that Nāgārjuna derives his argument against origin from a paradox about change. Nāgārjuna does indeed formulate the paradox of change in one place:

> If a thing were by nature to exist, then it could not fail to exist, for a change of nature is certainly not possible. (MK 15.8)
>
> In the absence of a nature, what can undergo the process of change? On the other hand, if a nature is present, what can undergo the process of change? (MK 15.9)

The argument against (I) might then be that a thing that comes into being out of itself cannot change from one moment to the next, and if it does not change then nothing *new* has come into being. And an argument against (II) might be that if one thing can change into something completely different from itself, then there is nothing to regulate what produces what. If an oak tree can originate from an acorn, then why not from a mustard seed? The general strategy here is to argue that once we allow that R can relate *a* to things other than itself, there can be no regulation as to which other things *a* is so related. This is the *prasaṅga*, the unacceptable consequence, of assuming (II).

If this is Nāgārjuna's argument, it is a difficult one to defend. The idea that the effect must resemble or pre-exist in its cause has always been enticing, but it has little to recommend it. I think Nāgārjuna has a much stronger argument in mind. The idea that things have causes, if applied universally, forces us into the unacceptable position of having to accept infinite causal chains or else causal loops. The alternative, to allow there to be exceptions to the proposition that things have causes and admit there to be uncaused causers, is to make an *unprincipled* distinction. For there is no rational criterion with which to divide things into the caused and the uncaused.

Let me try to clarify the structure of this argument. Graham Priest[12] has shown that there is a general structure common to many of the most familiar paradoxes. A paradox arises whenever one has a function or operation which is bound to a domain and yet which goes beyond that domain. A paradox is thus the result of a pair of arguments. One proves *closure* – that the result of performing the operation in question falls within a given domain. The other proves *transcendence* – that the result of performing the operation in question falls outside the domain. The pattern of arguing from the four options itself conforms to this schema. For I observed that the effect of rejecting option (IV) is to delimit the domain of entities to which the argument applies. So the rejection of (IV) is an assertion of closure. And the rejection of the first three options jointly constitutes the proof of transcendence, that the operation must nevertheless go beyond the domain.

For the paradox of origin, take the domain to be the class C of things which have causal originators, and the operation to be a function δ from objects to their originators. The idea behind the proof of transcendence is that the repeated application of the 'originator of' function to an arbitrary object *a* eventually takes us out of the domain C. The originator of the originator of . . . of the originator of *a* is not in C:

$$\exists n\ \delta^n a \notin C \qquad \text{Transcendence}$$

Closure, on the other hand, is the thesis that no matter how often the 'originator of' function is iterated, it never maps out of C:

$$\forall n\ \delta^n a \in C \qquad \text{Closure}$$

The proof of closure is, as I noted earlier, the role of the refutation of the fourth option in the *catuṣkoṭi*. For this option states that objects arise uncaused, while closure states that no object lacks a causal originator. I regard this as having the force of a stipulation on what 'object' means in this context.

The function of the first three options in the *catuṣkoṭi* is to prove transcendence. Iteration on the 'originator of' function eventually maps out of the domain C. The proof is by reductio. Let us assume that for any value of x, the originator of x is in C. Then either (i) $\delta x = x$ or (ii) $\delta x \neq x$. Now (i) states that x is its own originator – it is option (I) in the *catuṣkoṭi*. The argument against this is that if an object is its own originator, then it must be eternal, and if it is eternal then it is not within the causal domain, the domain of things which have causes. That is, if $\delta x = x$ then $\delta x \notin$ C. Calling something 'self-originating' is misleading. It gives the impression that such things do have causal origins, but is really nothing more than a confused neologism for saying that they are eternal and so *acausal*.

Let us suppose then that the originator of x is something different from x. Consider the originator of the originator of x, i.e. $\delta^2 x$. Again, either (i) $\delta^2 x = x$ or (ii) $\delta^2 x \neq x$. The first possibility is that there are loops of causation, in which x is caused by y, and y is caused by x. So the originators of x are x itself and y (I am assuming that causal origination is a transitive relation). This is option (III) in the *catuṣkoṭi*, the option that things originate both from themselves and from others. The argument against this is that we again have self-origination, and so again the object is eternal and so acausal. Another objection would be that it contradicts the idea that a cause must precede its effect, but this is not a principle on which Nāgārjuna places any great weight.

The only remaining possibility is that $\delta^2 x \neq x$, the originator of the originator of x is not identical to x. Since we have already shown that the originator of the originator of x is not identical to the originator of x (because no object is identical to its originator – the rejection of option (I) of the *catuṣkoṭi*), it follows that x, δx and $\delta^2 x$ are distinct entities. Likewise, $\delta^3 x$ cannot be identical to $\delta^2 x$ or δx, and if it were identical to x there would again be a causal loop, this time with three rather than two members. One can clearly go on and prove that the nth order originator of x is distinct from any lesser order originator of x unless two lower order originators of x are identical or there is a causal loop with n members. As long as there are no causal loops, it follows by induction that the nth order originator of x is distinct from all lower order originators of x. So there is an infinite sequence of distinct higher order originators of x. This is the possibility excluded by the rejection of option (II) in the *catuṣkoṭi*. One argument would be that the domain C is finite. Another is that causal explanation would be vitiated – one never reaches the explanans.

This then is how Nāgārjuna seeks to prove the transcendence part of the paradox. It is interesting to see in Sextus Empiricus a parallel argumentative strategy.[13] The strategy of the Pyrrhonic sceptic is one of seeking to demonstrate that the reasons for and against a thesis are equally strong. The Pyrrhonic sceptic then recommends that the rational course is to suspend all judgment and in doing so to reach a state of equipoise. From an Indian point of view, this would be a route to scepticism via the fallacy of the 'counter-balanced' reason (Chapter 1.9). Sextus[14] argues that it is very plausible that there are causes, for

> [I]f there were no causes, everything would come from everything else, and by chance. For example, perhaps horses would come from mice, and elephants from ants; and in Egyptian Thebes there would have been rainstorms and snow and the south would have had no rain, if there had not been a cause on account of which the south is stormy in winter and the east is dry. Further, anyone who says there are no causes is refuted; for if he claims to make this statement simply and without any cause he will not be worthy of belief; while if he says that he makes it because of some cause, he is positing a cause while wishing to deny it, in granting a cause why causes do not exist.

On the other hand, Sextus argues that it is also very plausible that there are no causes. One of his arguments is that it is impossible to conceive of a cause before apprehending its effect as its effect, and this leads to a circularity. Another argument is that

> [A]s we are questioning the very existence of causes, it will be necessary for him to supply a cause of the cause of there being a cause, and a cause of that, and so on ad infinitum. But it is impossible to supply an infinite number of causes; therefore, it is impossible to assert with firm assurance that anything is the cause of anything.

Another of Sextus' arguments against there being causes is this:

> Whence some people say also the following: The cause must either exist at the same time as its effect, or before it, or come into being after it. But to say that the cause is brought into existence after the genesis of its effect would be ridiculous. But neither can it exist before it, as it is said to be conceived relatively to it, and the Dogmatists hold that relatives, *qua* relative, coexist and are conceived together with one another. Nor can it exist at the same time as the effect; for if it is productive of the effect, and if what comes into being must come into being through the agency of what exists, it is necessary that the cause first become a cause, and then, this being done, produce the effect. Consequently, if the cause comes into being neither before nor at the same time as the effect, and the effect does not come into being before it, it does not, I suppose, have any existence at all. It is also clear, I think, that by these considerations, too, the concept of cause is once again destroyed.

The dialectical aims of Sextus and Nāgārjuna are rather different, as I have already observed. In brief the difference is that Nāgārjuna thinks that there can be *no* reasons for thinking either that there are causes or that there are no causes, while Sextus thinks that there are plausible reasons for thinking *both* that there are causes and that there are no causes. Yet there are certainly echoes of Nāgārjuna in the above passages. Nāgārjuna, to be sure, is not as unclear as Sextus seems to be about the distinction between reasons and causes (although that confusion undoubtedly arose in connection with the Sanskrit term *hetu*, which can mean both 'reason' and 'cause'). On the other hand Nāgārjuna's argument against there being reasons, to which we shall turn next, does indeed exploit the idea of an infinite regress, and the pattern of arguing from 'the three times' (past, present and future), which Sextus applies to the question of the existence of causes, is applied by Nāgārjuna to the putative existence of movement and other temporal processes.

Nāgārjuna's paradox of causation is this: the concept of a cause is incoherent because, *given certain plausible assumptions*, it is self-contradictory. The concept is an empty one, failing to correspond to anything in the structure of the real world: an apparently unacceptable conclusion derived from apparently acceptable premises via an apparently acceptable argument. Something must give! Some authors[15] have claimed to find fallacies in Nāgārjuna's argumentation. I accept that Nāgārjuna is not above using sophistical tricks, such as equivocation and the like, but I hope that the reconstruction of his argument I have given above is free from the sorts of fallacy of which he has been accused. Another response would be to deny that Nāgārjuna is employing the common-sense concept of a cause. His argument depends for its plausibility on the falsity of the following contentions: that to be self-caused is to be causal; that there are causal loops; and that there are infinite causal chains. Might one not argue that one or more of these contentions is consistent with the common-sense notion of a cause? There is, perhaps, nothing so very counter-intuitive about the idea of causal chains stretching back into the infinite past, or of causation going round in loops.

I believe that no such defence of common sense is necessary. The idea that the common-sense scheme is best-suited or even well-suited to provide an adequate explanation of the world has lost its grip with the rise of scientific theory. We are happy to be told that the 'solid' table is really mostly empty space, that there is a finite maximum speed faster than which nothing can travel, and so on. Nāgārjuna's error, I suggest, is to be located in the extrapolation of his argument against the coherence of common sense to the coherence of any system of concepts, or rather, in his implicit assumption that the common-sense scheme is the only possible conceptual scheme. I believe that we can accept that he has shown that the common-sense concept of a cause is incoherent, but reject the further claim that the structure of reality lies beyond the powers of human conception. The reason is this. Nāgārjuna's method is to expose the existential presuppositions of a conceptual scheme, and demonstrate that they cannot obtain. The truth of any assertion of the form '*x* is caused by *y*' presupposes that there are causal relations, and having shown that there is no value of '*y*' for which that assertion is true, the conclusion is drawn that the presupposition fails. The problem for Nāgārjuna is that scientific theories do not *presuppose* the existence of entities, but *posit* them. Theoretical terms are introduced by explicit stipulations. A scientific conception of the world does not rest on a set of existential presuppositions, whose falsity would render the conception empty. It rests on a set of explicit stipulations. So the existence of entities denoted by the terms of such stipulations is not a presupposition of the theory's having content, but that in virtue of which the theory is true or false.

Nāgārjuna does not draw the crucial distinction. It is the distinction between the ordinary terms in a language and the terms which are introduced by explicit stipulation. Other Indian philosophers did appreciate the importance of this distinction. The grammarian Bhartṛhari, called terms of the first sort *ājānika* 'immanent', and terms of the second sort *ādhunika* 'novel'. Great weight was placed on this distinction by the scientific rationalists in India, the Vaiśeṣikas, and especially by Praśastapāda (a contemporary of Bhartṛhari). The point is that the existence of a reference is *presupposed* only by the use of immanent terms in the language, and not by the use of stipulatively introduced ones, for which the existence of a reference is part of what is explicitly stipulated.[16] This vital distinction shielded the construction of scientific theory from Nāgārjuna's destructive arguments, and allowed for a new conception of rationality (see Chapter 3). The great advantage of Diṅnāga's formulation of the Buddhist position over Nāgārjuna's is precisely that it bears upon the realism of scientific accounts of conceptual structure (Chapter 4). Such structures, he claims, approach reality asymptotically, but never reach it.

I have run ahead of myself. Let us go back to Nāgārjuna, and examine his demonstrations of the impossibility of proof and the paradox of motion.

2.5 THE IMPOSSIBILITY OF PROOF

Beliefs are justified with reference to the means by which they are acquired – this is the central claim of the theory of knowledge known as the *pramāṇa* theory (see Chapter 1). Nāgārjuna considers the theory to have a flaw so fundamental as to render it paradoxical. His argument depends on what would now be called a 'doxastic ascent'. Ernest Sosa[17] says:

> It is sometimes held, for example, that perceptual or observational beliefs are often justified through their origin in the exercise of one or more of our five senses in standard conditions of perception. The advocate of doxastic ascent would raise a vigorous protest, however, for in his view the mere fact of such sensory prompting is impotent to justify the belief prompted. Such prompting must be coupled with the further belief that one's senses work well in the circumstances, or the like. For we are dealing here with *knowledge*, which requires not blind faith but reasoned trust. But now surely the further belief about the reliability of one's senses cannot rest on blind faith but requires its own backing of reasons, and we are off on the regress.

Nāgārjuna's formulation of the criticism is similar:

> If just such objects are established for you through the means of knowing, tell me how you establish those means of knowing. If the means of knowing are established through other means of knowing, then there is an infinite regress (*anavasthā*). Neither the beginning nor the middle nor the end can then be established. (V 31–33)

Nāgārjuna compares the means of knowing with measuring instruments. Just as one cannot use a pair of scales to measure weight unless one knows that the scales have been properly calibrated, so too one cannot use some method as a means of knowing to 'measure' an object of knowledge unless one knows that the method *is* an adequate means of knowing.

The literal meaning of *anavasthā* is 'lack of grounding'. If A is proved through B, and B proves A only if it is itself proved, then a proof of A necessitates a proof of B (the doxastic ascent). The argument iterates, and unless the iteration can be made to come to rest somewhere, A will lack a proof. The doxastic ascent switches the burden of proof from the thing to be proved to the means by which it is to be proved. The idea that such a switching of the burden of proof is legitimate is at one with the idea that it is a fallacy of reason to establish one's conclusion on the basis of unproved reasons. This was the fallacy called the 'unproven' or *sādhyasama*, the reason's being in the 'same predicament' as what is to be proved. Admitting the legitimacy of doxastic ascent is equivalent to accepting that this is indeed a fallacy. Nāgārjuna does regard this as a fallacy; indeed, the principal fallacy from which his critics' arguments suffer (MK 4.8–9).

The relations 'is proved by' and 'originates in' both generate infinite chains by being indefinitely iterable. We can ask for the proof of the proof of A, just as we can ask for the originator of the originator of *x*. As in the paradox of origin, there are just two ways to block the infinite regress. One is by appeal to the existence of termini of proof, propositions that are either self-proving or else require no proof. The other is by appeal to the existence of loops of proof, allowing proof relations to go round in a circle. These are options Nāgārjuna examines systematically in V 33–51. His objection to the idea that there are two classes of proposition, those that must be proved through some means of knowing and those that need not, is that this distinction lacks any basis in reason:

> If the means of knowing are established without any means of knowing, then your position is abandoned. There is a discordance, and you should state the distinguishing reason (*viśeṣa-hetu*). (V 33)

This is an important methodological point. Distinctions should not be postulated on an *ad hoc* basis. A good philosophical theory tries to give a unified explanation of a diversity of facts. Dividing the facts into different types for which there are different explanations leaves explanatory gaps in the account. One should introduce a distinction only if it corresponds to some natural division in the phenomena under examination, and not simply to solve a problem in one's theory. To block the threatened infinite regress by saying that there are unproved provers is to postulate a category simply for theoretical expediency, and not because there is any independent ground for doing so.

Even if there is no independently motivated distinction between the unproved and the proved, perhaps there is a well-founded distinction between what is self-proved and what is proved by another. Everything must be proved, but might not the means of knowing be self-proving? This seems to have been the view of Gautama, the author of the *Nyāyasūtra* (*cf.* NS 2.1.19). The proposal is, it seems, analogical. The sources of proof are like sources of light. A source of light illuminates other things and at the same time illuminates itself. Likewise, a source of proof proves other things and at the same time proves itself (V 33). Nāgārjuna is apparently responding to the *Nyāyasūtra* view here. His response is to dismiss as defective the assertion that a source of light illuminates itself! To say that something is illuminated is to say that it ceases to be in the dark. But a source of light is not illuminated, for it is never in the dark, and if it is not illuminated, then it certainly is not self-illuminated. Nāgārjuna's point perhaps is that an object is visible just in case light is coming from it, and since this description is true of both illuminators and things illuminated, there is no need to say that an illuminator must be illuminated in order to be visible. There is a hint in this reply of a 'grammatical' basis to Nāgārjuna's argument (the influence of grammar on Nāgārjuna's way of arguing is much more apparent, however, in the argument we will consider in the next section). The implication is the Agent and the Patient cannot be identical when the verb is 'illuminates'. The statement 'A illuminates A' is not well formed. It is not well formed because 'A illuminates B' means something like 'the addition of A in the circumstances results in B's ceasing to be in the dark,' and that implies that A is something that can be added to a circumstance in which B is already present.

Nāgārjuna, I think, employs a sophistical debating trick in this curious argument. The light analogy uses a causative form *pra-√kāś*, whose meanings include both 'to make bright, illuminate, irradiate', and by extension 'to make clear, evident, manifest'. The point of the analogy is most plausibly that a source of light makes itself evident *in the very act* of making some other object evident, for the object could not be made evident unless by a source of light. It is only in 'quibbling' on the meaning of a word that Nāgārjuna is led in this context to discuss the capacity of light to illuminate itself. What Nāgārjuna ought to discuss, but does not, is whether a means of knowing can prove itself *in the very act* of proving something else.[18]

Nāgārjuna, fortunately, has another argument against the idea that the means of knowing prove themselves. It is that if they prove themselves independently of any reference to what it is that they prove, then they cannot be proof of anything (V 40–41). His point is easiest to see if we remember the analogy between means of knowing and measuring instruments. How might one go about 'measuring' a pair of scales, that is to say, checking that it is correctly calibrated? The only way, it seems, is to test its performance against things of known weight. The same is true of a means of knowing such as observation. In order to check that my visual sense is working properly, I test it by reading an optician's chart. If I want to check that I know a method for solving quadratic equations, I solve a few textbook problems and then check in the back of the book that I have the right answers.

Nāgārjuna is swift to point out that the method of proof by testing against known cases cannot block the threatened regress (V 42–43). The reason is simple: the test cases must have been established first. An attempt to block the regress along these lines would result in the technical fault of 'proving the proved' (*siddhasādhana*). The methods of proof under investigation are being proved by comparing them to known cases, but those cases are known only because proven by those methods of proof. So one is attempting to prove something which must already have been proved, that the methods of proof in question are adequate and reliable. Couldn't one counter by pointing out that the method of proof used to establish the test case is not the same as the method of proof under scrutiny? I solve the test problems, but someone else prepared the answers in the back of the book. For otherwise one would have the situation which Nāgārjuna ridicules when he asks whether a son can be produced by a father and the father by that very son (V 49–50). But it is clear that the alternative is not much better. For if objects have to proved by a means of knowing, and the means by objects, one ends up proving nothing (V 45–48).

Nāgārjuna sums up the entire argument in a triumphant final verse:

> The means of knowing are not established by themselves or by one another or by other means of knowing. Nor are they established by the objects known, nor accidentally. Perception is not established by that very perception, inference is not established by that very inference, comparison is not established by that very comparison, and testimony is not established by that very testimony. Nor are they established by one another, i.e. perception by inference, comparison and testimony, inference by perception, comparison and testimony, comparison by perception, inference and testimony, and testimony by perception, inference and comparison. Nor are perception, inference, comparison and testimony established, respectively, by another perception, another inference, another comparison and another testimony. Nor are the means of knowing established by the objects known, taken collectively or severally, included in their own field or in those of the other means of knowing as well. Nor are they established accidentally. Nor are they established by a combination of the causes mentioned before, whatever their number: twenty, thirty, forty or twenty-six. In these circumstances, your statement

> 'Because the objects known are to be apprehended through the means of knowing, those things are known to exist as well as those means of knowing' is not valid. (V 51)

This is a fine example of Nāgārjuna's general dialectical strategy. The strategy is to find a rule such as 'A proves B only if A is itself proven' or '*x* can cause *y* only if *x* is itself caused', and to make every possible application of the rule onto the domain. What happens when one takes the set of objects (including provers and things proven), and tries to apply the rule at every point, is that one discovers one cannot do it. Nāgārjuna then concludes that the rule cannot be applied, and so that the concept it governs is empty.

Formally, the argument follows very similar contours to the argument against causation. The domain is the class of propositions with proofs, and the operation is the function 'proof of *x*'. Here closure is the thesis that every proposition has a proof – there are no unproved provers. Transcendence then follows from the plausible contentions that there are no proof loops, for this would lead to a vicious circle, and that there are no infinitely long proof chains, for this would lead to a lack of grounding. However, while I was willing to accept that Nāgārjuna had uncovered an incoherence in the ordinary concept of a cause, I do not think that he has succeeded in anything comparable here. For the rule on which his argument plays, that A proves B only if A is itself proven, is not actually a rule governing the notion of a proof. Some reasons, reasons based on observation, are defeasible – observation in itself provides one with reasons to believe, unless one comes to have reasons to suspect it. So the correct rule on proof by observation is: A proves B unless A is disproven. In other words, proof by observation is non-monotonic.[19] Perception as of a table proves the existence of the table; perception as of a table, together with evidence that one is hallucinating, does not. The Naiyāyikas beginning with Uddyotakara were very clear about this.[20]

What happens now to the fallacy of the unproven, on which Nāgārjuna said that his refutation depended? One needs to be able to draw a distinction between purely extrapolative reasoning, inference from the observed to the unobserved, and demonstration-based reasoning, a public setting out of one's thesis with supporting reasons and examples. Extrapolation rests on observation, and observation can prove without being proved. The second rule is the right one here, and there is no fallacy of the unproven. Demonstration, however, rests on convincing one's audience by citing reasons, and reasons are convincing only if they are themselves proven. So the proper domain of the fallacy of the unproven is only that of reasoning by demonstration. The crucial distinction one needs is the one Diṅnāga was later to codify and make explicit with his terms 'inference for oneself' and 'inference for others'.[21] Once again we see that Nāgārjuna's arguments are ones which would have been highly persuasive at the time, and which are refuted only by distinctions clearly recognised much later.

2.6 A NEW PARADOX OF MOTION

Nāgārjuna's celebrated argument against motion is interesting in its own right, but it also functions as a paradigm for a pattern of argumentation he thinks is widely applicable. Kamaleswar Bhattacharya[22] has described the argument as having a grammatical basis, because it exploits the Sanskrit grammatical theory of 'deep case' or 'thematic role' (*kāraka*). This is a theory of the underlying semantic structure of sentences rather than their surface grammar, and Nāgārjuna's argument might therefore be better described as 'semantic'. In any case, the fact is that the argument is a general one, applicable whenever one has statements with certain semantic properties. It does not depend on particular properties of the concept of motion.

The Sanskrit theory of deep case is an approach to the analysis of sentences which takes the verb to be the core of a sentence, around which nouns stand in a variety of relationships. A verb denotes an activity or event, and each noun in the sentence denotes a thematic causal factor connected with that event. In the sentence 'Sītā cooks rice,' for example, the activity of cooking has for its Agent Sītā and for its Patient rice. Agency is a thematic deep case relation, a relation explicated in terms of Sītā having a certain causal role with respect to the activity. One suggestion is to think of the Agent as an affector, and the Patient as the thing affected. The Sanskrit grammarians do not quite say this, however, but prefer to say that the Agent is 'what is independent', and the Patient is 'what is most desired' by the Agent. Other thematic roles capable of being occupied include Instrument ('that by means of which the Agent performs the activity'), Target, Donor and Place (the 'location' of the activity).[23]

When there is a moving, there is also an Agent of moving, the 'mover', defined as that which is moving, as well as a Patient of moving, the 'being moved over', here identified with the Place of the moving. The paradox Nāgārjuna exposes is one to do with the nature of such definitions. A thing has the properties by which it is defined, and the mover is defined to be that which is *now* moving. Nothing in the past or in the future can satisfy this definition, for nothing in the past or the future has the property of being *now*. But a movement cannot be entirely in the present moment, for movement requires duration. Similarly, the being moved over is defined to be the place *now* being moved over, and that cannot be a position already moved over, nor a position yet to be moved over. But a movement cannot be located in the point between the already moved over and the yet to be moved over, for movement requires displacement.

> How indeed can it be said that a mover moves, when without a movement there is no mover. (MK 2.9)

> From the perspective of one who thinks that a mover moves, there would be the consequence of a mover without movement. But of a mover there is movement. (MK 2.10)

> If a mover were said to move, there must be two movements, one by which he is called a mover, and one by which the mover moves. (MK 2.11)
>
> If without motion one cannot posit a mover, how can one posit a mover standing still? (MK 2.16)
>
> One does not stand still where one is moving, nor where one has moved nor where one has yet to move. Moving, starting to move and ceasing to move are the same. (MK 2.17)
>
> The motion by means of which the mover is so-called is not the motion by means of which he moves. He does not exist before that motion, so what and where is the thing that moves? (MK 2.22)
>
> The motion by means of which the mover is so-called is not different from the motion by means of which he moves. There cannot be two motions in a single mover. (MK 2.23)
>
> So there is no motion, no mover and no place to be moved over. (MK 2.25)

Nāgārjuna draws a distinction between the event of movement (*gamana*), or movement at an instant, and the process of movement (*gati*), or movement over a duration. A process of movement cannot be identified with any one event of movement, nor with a succession of such events. For if there are two movements, then there are two movers, and then there is here no single mover in a process of motion. The same argument applies to any process. The seer sees the seen. The 'seer' is, by definition, one who now sees. This is a definition nothing past or future can satisfy, and yet seeing necessarily requires duration, for it is a causal process extending between the seer and the thing seen (MK Chapter 3).

An obvious solution is simply to allow that a single enduring substance can be the 'mover' in a succession of movements. One who wishes to say this has to be able to maintain that an object can be identically present at different times. For only an object present *now* can be that which *now* moves, and only an object present in the immediately succeeding instant can be that which moves at that instant. If these two movers are one and the same, it follows that the mover is identically present at different times. That invites the objection that the mover will be the substratum of contradictory properties. The present movement ceases, and is replaced by the next movement in the sequence; so the mover will both have the present movement and also not have it. But this is impossible.

> If it cannot be said that there is a movement without a mover, then how will there be a mover without that movement? (MK 2.7)
>
> Just as a mover does not move, so too a non-mover does not move. Apart from the mover and the non-mover what third thing can move? (MK 2.7)

Later Nyāya writers found a general solution to the problem of contrary temporal properties. Their solution is to introduce adverbial modifiers (delimitors) on the property possession relation. An object as delimited by one time can possess a property, even if the object as delimited by another time does not.[24] This solution was not apparent in Nāgārjuna's time. Indeed, the problem of temporary intrinsic properties is a live one even today, where one finds both promoters and detractors of the adverbial solution.[25]

Nāgārjuna's argument has naturally been studied in comparison with those of Zeno.[26] Here are Zeno's arguments as reported by Aristotle:[27]

> [The Dichotomy] The first asserts the non-existence of motion on the ground that that which is in locomotion must arrive at the half-way stage before it arrives at the goal.
>
> [Achilles] The second . . . amounts to this, that in a race the quickest runner can never overtake the slowest, since the pursuer must first reach the point whence the pursued started, so the slower must always hold a lead.
>
> [Arrow] Zeno argues fallaciously; for if, he says, everything always rests when it is against what is equal, and what is in locomotion is always in the now, the arrow in locomotion is motionless. But this is false, for time is not composed of indivisible 'nows', no more than is any other magnitude.
>
> [Stadium] The fourth is the one about equal bodies which move in opposite directions past equal bodies in a stadium at equal speed, the one row from the end of the stadium and the other from the middle – in which he thinks it follows that half the time is equal to double.

The only one of Zeno's arguments bearing any resemblance to that of Nāgārjuna is the flying arrow, although there is no general agreement in the interpretation of either paradox. Jonathan Lear[28] has proposed an interpretation of the arrow under which there is a substantial agreement with my interpretation of Nāgārjuna. The force of the argument, according to Lear, is that the present tense 'is moving' cannot be applied to a period of time, as a period cannot be present, and yet nothing at an instant is moving.

Nāgārjuna's paradox of motion is a paradox of definition. The phrase 'the mover' is defined as 'that which now moves'. It is, therefore, defined only for the present time, and not for any past or future time. One cannot truly say that the mover will move or that the mover has moved. One can indeed assert again, a moment later, 'the mover is moving', but this new utterance of 'the mover' is again defined only for its time of utterance. There is nothing in virtue of which one can say that the denotation of the previous utterance is the same as the denotation of this one: whence Nāgārjuna's claim that if there are two movements, there must be two movers. Movement, however, requires a duration, and so one can never say that a single thing, the mover, is moving.

Consider again the statement 'the mover will move.' Nāgārjuna's argument depends on the claim that, because the phrase 'the mover' is not defined at future times, this statement, uttered in the present, cannot be true. However, 'the mover' *is* defined in the present, and what is to stop us from asserting of some present thing that it will be moving in the future? What stops us is the existence of truth-value links between statements in different tenses uttered at different times. The statement '*a* will be *F*' is now true just in case the statement '*a* is *F*' will be true. So the statement 'the mover will move' is now true just in case the statement 'the mover is moving' will be true. But that future statement can never be true, because the description 'the mover' is not defined at any future time (and a future utterance of 'the mover' is an utterance of a different description, defined only in the future).

The puzzle arises because we are dealing with descriptions of an unusual type, ones whose matrix is an indexical property – the property of being the Agent of a movement occurring *now*. Many definite descriptions are indeed like this, for instance 'the Prime Minister', which is really an abbreviation for 'the *current* Prime Minister'. Clearly, in truth-value links of the sort I have just described, we have to take into account this indexicality in the description. The statement 'The *current* Prime Minister will resign' is true just in case the future statement 'The *past* Prime Minister has resigned' will be true. When we make explicit the shifting value of the temporal index, the paradox disappears. For the truth-value link we are after is this one: the statement 'The present mover will move' is true just in case the statement 'The past mover is moving' will be true. Such truth-value links show how the sentence 'the mover will move' can after all be true.

2.7 SELF-REFUTATION

'With relief, with humiliation, with terror, he understood that he too was a mere appearance, dreamt by another.' Thus ends a story by Jorge Luis Borges entitled 'The Circular Ruins'.[29] It is a story about a magician who sets out to dream into reality another man, and who completes his task only to discover that he himself is nothing but a dream. According to Nāgārjuna when one achieves an objective view of one's conceptions, what one finds is that all conception is empty. Does that mean that the objective view is empty too, that the concept of emptiness is as empty of content as the concepts it describes? Does Nāgārjuna's thesis defeat itself? The charge was one vigorously pressed by Nāgārjuna's opponents, and in order to respond to it, he wrote a new book, his *Reply to Critics*. This book begins with a formulation of the self-refutation charge:

> If a self-standing nature of things, whatever they may be, exists nowhere, your statement must lack a self-standing nature. It is not, therefore, in a position to deny the self-standing nature of things. (V 1)

Let us recall what the emptiness thesis claims. It claims that no thesis or theory formulated in terms of the categories and concepts of the common-sense scheme has objective content, because a presupposition of that conceptual scheme, that there are self-standing objects, is false. The emptiness thesis itself, however, is not a thesis *within* the common-sense scheme, but a thesis *about* it. It does not itself presuppose that there are self-standing objects. There appears to be a straightforward *non sequitur* in the self-refutation charge, as Nāgārjuna himself points out:

> This statement of mine, though lacking a self-standing nature because dependently originated, is engaged in the task of establishing the nature of things as lacking a self-standing nature. In these circumstances, your statement is not proper. (V 22)

Similarly, when Nāgārjuna famously claims to have no 'doctrine' (*pratijñā*) of his own (V 29), he might simply be using the term 'doctrine' to mean a thesis resting on the same presuppositions as the common-sense scheme, and it is quite evident that the emptiness thesis is not a 'doctrine' in that sense.[30] Indeed, Nāgārjuna sometimes speaks as if he has a viable alternative ontology on offer, an ontology consistent with the teachings of the Buddha, in which entities exist only in relations of dependent origination with one another and lack any self-standing nature. The world, in this alternative ontology, is rather like a net, where entities are merely the knots in interlocking ropes of dependent origination, acquiring whatever capacities they have in virtue of their relative position in the whole network and not in virtue of having intrinsic properties (V 22).

This sits ill, however, with the concept scepticism Nāgārjuna also avows.[31] If common sense is the only possibility for an objectively well-grounded conceptual scheme, and if even common sense fails, then no conception can be well grounded. The emptiness thesis belongs to an ungrounded, dream-like discourse, and within that dream-discourse other, embedded dreams are described, the dreams that are common-sense theories. Nāgārjuna exploits a comparable literary device, the idea of a magic trick *within* a magic trick:

> Suppose a magic man created by a magician should obstruct another magic man created by his own magic and occupied by something . . . [then] the magic man who is obstructed is void, and he who obstructs is also void. In like manner, a negation of the intrinsic nature of all things by my statement is possible, even though this statement is void. (V 23)

Another sort of conceptual ascent has occurred here. It is like a novel the narrator of which is a literary theorist who declares that all novels are merely empty fictions. Within the novel, the narrator's declaration has the desired effect of making the other characters understand better the nature of fictional discourse. This is so even though the narrator's statement itself is merely an empty fiction. Nāgārjuna would like to explain the therapeutic efficacy of his own teaching the same way. His denial that things have self-standing nature can make one see that one's experiences are dream-like, empty, even though that denial is only dream-like too (V 23–28).

It might be argued that Nāgārjuna's position is self-refuting because it is self-referential. For the statement 'This statement is empty' is, if true, then empty and so not true, and, if empty, then true and so not empty. The only remaining possibility is that the statement is false. If it is false, then it is not empty, and Nāgārjuna is wrong to say that the emptiness thesis is itself empty. Nāgārjuna's point, however, is that one can agree that the emptiness thesis is empty without agreeing that it is self-referential. Conception is like a hierarchy of dreams within dreams within dreams, carried on indefinitely. Whenever we take a step back to a more objective view, we ascend a level in this hierarchy, and realise that our conceptions at the previous level were themselves all empty. And this thought, that all those conceptions are empty, is itself recognised as another empty thought when we take the next step through the hierarchy of empty conceptions. So the emptiness thesis is formulated at each level in the hierarchy, but recognised as itself empty in the next level up. It never applies to itself.

Nāgārjuna gives up on the idea that conception is 'supported' by the world. Conception is always a dream within a dream. The real problem with the Madhyamaka method is that it is piecemeal. All it can show is that specific concepts, particularly the concepts of the common-sense scheme, are dream-like, ungrounded, empty. What it does not prove is the emptiness of *all* concepts, and especially those concepts, such as emptiness itself, which do not presuppose that there are self-standing objects. Nāgārjuna may have shown that the concepts of common sense have false presuppositions; what he has not shown is that the same is true of any possible system of concepts. Perhaps then there is still another use of reason, a use neither to codify common sense (Chapter 1) nor to leap-frog out of it (Chapter 2), but to construct 'sophisticated' or 'scientific' (non-common-sensical) theories of the world. After examining one such theory, Vaiśeṣika metaphysics (Chapter 3), we will be in a position to see how the Buddhist challenge is reconfigured in the work of Diṅnāga (Chapter 4).

FURTHER READING

Texts

Nāgārjuna *c.* AD 150, *Mūlamadhyamakakārikā* (MK, *The Middle Stanzas*).
Nāgārjuna, *Vigrahavyāvartanī* (V, *Reply to Critics*).
Candrakīrti *c.* AD 600, *Prasannapadā* (P).

Emptiness (2.1–2)

1 David Seyfort Ruegg, *The Literature of the Madhyamaka School of Philosophy in India* (Wiesbaden: Otto Harrassowitz, 1981).

2 C. W. Huntington, *The Emptiness of Emptiness: An Introduction to Early Indian Madhyamaka* (Honolulu: University of Hawaii Press, 1989).

3 David Burton, *Emptiness Appraised: A Critical Study of Nāgārjuna's Philosophy* (London: Curzon Press, 1999).

The four options, the dialectical method (2.3)

1 Richard H. Robinson, 'Some Logical Aspects of Nāgārjuna's System,' *Philosophy East and West* 6 (1957), pp. 291–308.

2 David Seyfort Ruegg, 'The Uses of the Four Positions of the Catuṣkoṭi and the Problem of the Description of Reality in Mahāyāna Buddhism,' *Journal of Indian Philosophy* 5 (1977), pp. 1–71.

3 Brian Galloway, 'Some Logical Issues in Madhyamaka Thought,' *Journal of Indian Philosophy* 17 (1989), pp. 1–35.

4 Frank Hoffman, 'Rationality in Early Buddhist Four-Fold Logic,' *Journal of Indian Philosophy* 10 (1982), pp. 309–337.

5 Vijay Bharadwaja, 'Rationality, Argumentation and Philosophical Embarrassment: A Study of Four Logical Alternatives (*catuṣkoṭi*) in Buddhist Logic,' *Philosophy East and West* 34 (1984), pp. 303–319; reprinted in his *Form and Validity in Indian Logic* (Shimla: Indian Institute for Advanced Study, 1990), Chapter 4.

Causation, proof, motion (2.4–6)

1 Richard Hayes, 'Nāgārjuna's Appeal,' *Journal of Indian Philosophy* 22 (1994), pp. 299–378.

2 Bimal Krishna Matilal, *Perception* (Oxford: Clarendon Press, 1986), Chapter 2.

3 Mark Siderits, 'Nāgārjuna as Anti-Realist,' *Journal of Indian Philosophy* 16 (1988), pp. 311–325.

4 Kamaleswar Bhattacharya, 'Nāgārjuna's Arguments against Motion: Their Grammatical Basis,' in G. Bhattacharya et al. eds., *A Corpus of Indian Studies: Essays in Honour of Professor Gaurinath Sastri* (Calcutta: Sanskrit Pustak Bhandar, 1980), pp. 85–95.

5 Kamaleswar Bhattacharya, 'The Grammatical Basis of Nāgārjuna's Arguments: Some Further Considerations,' *Indologica Taurinensia*, 8–9 (1980–1), pp. 35–43.

6 George Cardona, 'A Path Still Taken: Some Early Indian Arguments Concerning Time,' *Journal of the American Oriental Society* 111.3 (1991), pp. 445–464.

Self-refutation (2.7)

1 Richard Robinson, 'Did Nāgārjuna Really Refute All Philosophical Views?' *Philosophy East and West* 22 (1972), pp. 325–331.

2 David Seyfort Ruegg, 'Does the Mādhyamika Have a Thesis and Philosophical Position?' in B. K. Matilal and R. D. G. Evans eds., *Buddhist Logic and Epistemology: Studies in the Buddhist Analysis of Inference and Language* (Dordrecht: Reidel Publishing Company, 1982), pp. 229–238.

3 Paul Sagal, 'Nāgārjuna's Paradox,' *American Philosophical Quarterly* 29.1 (1992), pp. 79–85.

3 The rational basis of metaphysics

3.1 ORDER IN NATURE

Indian philosophical literature abounds with lists, enumerations, catalogues and classifications. There are lists of the different means of knowing, of the categories of knowable things, of the variety of psychological and physical constituents of a person, and, generally, of the modes, realms and states of existence. Our interest is in the rationale behind these classifications. What function do the classifications serve? What are the criteria underpinning them? Wilhelm Halbfass[1] says that these lists answer 'the question of being' in India, so that a list of the different kinds of being tells us what it is to 'be'. Taxonomies are cheap – there are many ways of dividing objects into groups – and the choice of one particular way of dividing from the others is the selection of an ontology. One approach to the Indian categories, indeed the traditional approach, has therefore been to explore the reasons for choosing one way of classifying rather than another. I think a fresh approach is needed. Remembering that the classifications are *given* rather than *chosen* for all but the original compilers of the sūtra-texts (and perhaps not even for them), the real interest is in the methods of *rationalisation* – how a predetermined list is made sense of, and in the methods of *revision* – how the list is modified in accordance with the principles by which it is rationalised.

My focus in this chapter is on the ontology of the Vaiśeṣika school, a school and a set of thinkers predisposed towards the study of the metaphysical structure of the natural world. I will examine too the logical theory that is integral to this ontology, as it was formulated and developed by the logicians of Navya-Nyāya. I want to present a stark and beautiful theory, a theory whose importance has not been fully appreciated by scholars who have charted the contours of Indian philosophical thought. The theory I have in mind emerges as a rationalisation of the early Vaiśeṣika theory of the categories. My contention is that three revisionary Vaiśeṣika thinkers – Bhāsarvajña (*c.* AD 950), Udayana (*c.* AD 1050) and Raghunātha (*c.* AD 1500) – saw that there is a graph-theoretic basis to the Vaiśeṣika notion of a category. If I am right, then an old idea about Indian philosophy must be given up as a dogma – the idea that mathematical concepts play no part in Indian philosophical thought about order in the natural world.

3.2 THE CATEGORIAL HIERARCHY

A theory of 'category' is a theory about the notion of a type of thing. When Gilbert Ryle[2] accused Descartes of making a 'category mistake' in treating the mind as if it were a thing of the same type as the body, he appealed to a principle about categories – that organisations, structures and arrangements are different in kind from the objects organised, structured or arranged. A social organisation is not simply another thing of the same type of thing as the people who belong to it; and, by the same token, neither is a class a thing of the same kind as its members, or a property the same kind of thing as its instantiations. Modern ontologies usually take the kinds of thing to be objects, events and classes; some add states, properties and tropes.

Let us review the contours of the traditional Vaiśeṣika account. Classical Vaiśeṣika lists six *kinds* of thing: substance, quality, motion, universal, individuator, inherence. Later Vaiśeṣika adds a seventh: absence. The basic stuff of the cosmos in the Vaiśeṣika world-view is atomic. Atoms are uncreatable, indestructible, non-compound substances. Atoms can coalesce into composite substances and can move. Indeed, the only changes in this cosmos are changes in the arrangement, properties and positions of the atoms. Creation is a matter of coalescing, destruction of breaking (and even God does not *create* the cosmos *ab nihilo*, but only 'shapes' it, as a potter shapes clay into a pot). A compound substance is a whole, composed out of, and inhering simultaneously in each of, its parts. These substances are individuated by the type and organisation of their parts. A 'quality' in classical Vaiśeṣika is a property-particular – for example, a particular shade of blue colour or a distinct flavour (what one would now call a 'thin' property). Qualities inhere in substances and in nothing other than substances. A 'motion' is another sort of particular; it too inheres in a substance and in nothing but a substance. Universals inhere in substances, qualities and motions. A universal inheres simultaneously in more than one, but has nothing inhering in it. Lastly, the 'individuator' (*viśeṣa*) is a distinctive and eponymous component in classical Vaiśeṣika ontology. An individuator inheres in and is unique to a particular atom: it is that by which the atomic, partless substances are individuated.[3]

Two principles lie at the heart of the Vaiśeṣika system: a principle of identity and a principle of change. The Vaiśeṣika principle of change is this: *a* becomes *b* iff the parts of *a* rearrange (perhaps with loss or gain) into the parts of *b*. 'Motion' is that in virtue of which the parts rearrange or stay together. There are basic or partless parts, the atoms, which, precisely because they have no parts, are incapable of becoming anything else. They move about, but are eternal and indestructible. The Vaiśeṣika principle of identity is this: $a = b$ iff the parts of *a* are numerically identical to and in the same arrangement as the parts of *b*. 'Quality' is that in virtue of which the parts are numerically identical or different. Atoms, precisely because they are partless, require a different principle of identity: atoms are distinct iff they have distinct individuators. Universals are limits on the degree of possible difference and change. One thing cannot change into another thing of an entirely different *sort* (a mouse into a mustard seed). One thing *a* can become another thing *b* iff the same universal resides in both *a* and *b*, that is, if *a* and *b* are of the same sort (as Udayana[4] puts it, universals *regulate* causality).

This is the motivation for there being six 'types' of thing (substances, qualities, motions, universals, individuators, inherence). The problem is to find a proper philosophical basis for the notion of a 'type' of thing thus appealed to. In his *Lakṣaṇāvalī,* Udayana reconstructs the categories in a new way, a way which I shall claim explicates the notion of a type *graph-theoretically*. What is a graph? It is a simple sort of relational structure, consisting of a set of nodes or vertices, and a set of edges (an edge being defined as a pair of nodes). A graph is 'directed' if the edges have a direction. Graphs, like many other mathematical structures, are realised in natural phenomena. A striking example is molecular structure: it is because the structure of a molecule is a graph that one can use a graph to depict one:

H – O – H

The implicit structure of the Vaiśeṣika ontology is that of a directed graph. The inherence relation connects things in the ontology in inheror–inheree pairings. So the substances, qualities, motions, universals and individuators are represented as the nodes of a graph whose set of edges represent the inherence relation. A fragment of the graph might look like this:

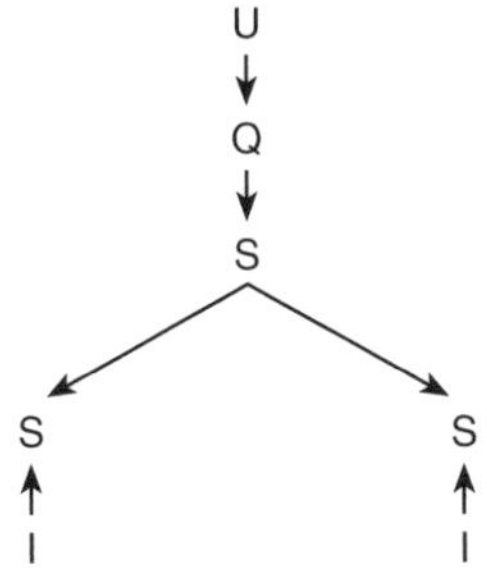

This graph represents the following state of affairs: a universal U inheres in a quality Q which inheres in a substance S. That substance is a dyad composed of two atoms in which it inheres, and each of which has inhering in it an individuator I. The structure of the world is a directed graph.

The nodes in a graph can be classified according to the number of edges terminating in them, and the number of edges starting from them: so the *valency* of a node in a directed graph is an ordered pair of integers (n, m). What Udayana saw in the *Lakṣaṇāvalī* is that things of different types in the Vaiśeṣika ontology correspond to nodes of different valencies. His brilliant idea is to use the idea of valency to *define* the categories of substance, quality, motion, universal and individuator. He begins with a classification of the categories into the four valency-groups (+, +), (+, 0), (0, +) and (0, 0):[5]

5 Non-eternal [= compound] substance, quality, motion, universal, and individuator inhere.

6 Eternal [i.e. atomic] substance, inherence, and absence lack the property of inhering.

7 Substance, quality, and motion are inhered in.

8 Universal, individuator, inherence, and absence have nothing inhering in them.

In particular then, atoms have valency (+, 0), universals and individuators have valency (0, +), while compound substances, qualities and motions have valency (+, +).

Notice that Udayana says that the inherence relation itself has a valency, (0, 0). We should not take this to mean that the inherence relation is to be represented by a node disconnected from the rest of the graph, but rather that it does not correspond to any *node* in the graph at all. The first and most fundamental graph-theoretic type distinction is the distinction between a node and an edge, and the inherence relation is represented in a graph by the set of edges, not by any node. The set of edges represents the extension of the inherence relation.

If the categories are to be distinguished from one another according to the valency of the nodes in that graph which is isomorphic to the world of things, then further specification is needed. The distinction between universals and individuators is simple: an individuator has valency (0, 1) while a universal has valency $(0, m)$, with $m > 1$:

202 A universal has nothing inhering in it, inheres, and is co-located with every difference.

203 Individuators lack the property of being inhered in, inhere, and lack the property of inhering by being co-located with every difference.

Udayana's phrase 'co-located with every difference' is a technical device for expressing the idea that a universal inheres in more than one. For if an inheror inheres in exactly one thing x, then all other things are loci of difference-from-x, and the inheror is not co-located with difference-from-x. However, if the inheror inheres in two things x and y, then difference-from-x is located in y and difference-from-y is located in x, and the inheror is co-located with both differences. So something co-located with every difference-from each of the things in which it inheres is necessarily located in more than one thing. Notice that in classical Vaiśeṣika, individuators are said to have no universals inhering in them precisely because they are fundamental units of individuation, having nothing in common with one another.

Any node with valency $(0, m)$ with $m > 1$ is now to be called a 'universal', and any node with valency (0, 1) is to be called an 'individuator':

UNIVERSAL

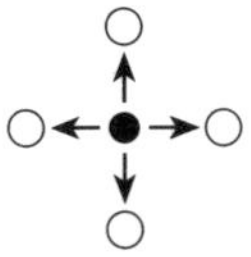

INDIVIDUATOR

The valency of atoms is different from that of qualities or motions, but we still need a general definition of *substance*, covering both atomic and compound substances. For compound substances, like universals, but unlike atoms, inhere in other things (their parts). Udayana in fact offers four definitions, of which the first three repeat older definitions. The fourth definition, however, is completely original:

9 A substance is not a substratum of absence of quality.

10 Or, it belongs to such a kind as inheres in what is incorporeal, inheres in what is not incorporeal and does not inhere in what inheres in what is not corporeal.

11 Or, it belongs to such a kind as inheres in space and in a locus, but not in smell.

12 Or, it is that in which inheres that in which inheres that which inheres.

The first of these definitions is the classical one in Vaiśeṣika[6] – a substance is that which possesses qualities. Udayana returns to this definition in his famous, but conservative commentary, the *Kiraṇāvalī*. He thinks of replacing it in the more experimental *Lakṣaṇāvalī* with a definition that makes no reference to any other category and indeed is phrased entirely in terms of the notion of inherence: a substance is 'that in which inheres that in which inheres that which inheres'. In other words, a substance is to be represented by a node such as this:

SUBSTANCE

The point of the definition is that a substance possesses qualities, and qualities possess universals, and nothing else in the ontology possesses something which possesses something. For universals and individuators possess nothing, while qualities and motions possess universals and nothing else.

Let us define a 'path' between one node and another in the obvious way: there is a path from node **x** to node **w** if there is a sequence of nodes <**x**, **y**, . . ., **w**> such that there is an edge from **x** to **y**, an edge from **y** to **z**, . . ., an edge from **v** to **w**.[7] Define the 'length' of a path as the number of edges between the first and the last node. Udayana's definition of a substance is now: a node is a substance iff there is a path at least of length 2 leading to it. Substances inhere in their parts; so the definition entails that every part of a substance is a substance.

The classical conception of qualities and motions makes them almost identical: they both inhere only in substances, and they both are inhered in only by universals.[8] Praśastapāda's remark[9] that the qualities other than contact, breaking, number and separateness 'inhere in one thing at a time' should not be construed as implying that they inhere in only one thing, but only that this group of qualities are *monadic* (non-relational) properties. These features are enough to distinguish qualities and motions from all else: from universals and individuators (which do not have anything inhering in them), and from substances (which are inhered in by things that are themselves inhered in). It explains too why qualities cannot inhere in qualities – if they did then they would be equivalent graph-theoretically to substances.

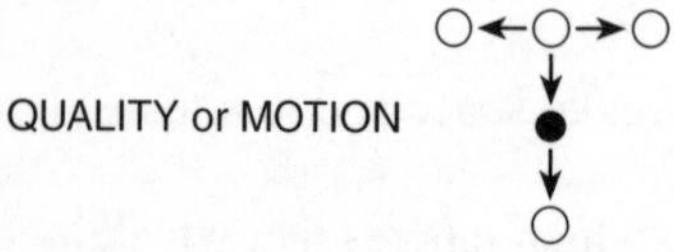

What is difficult is to find any principled way to distinguish between qualities and motions. There was indeed a persistent revisionary pressure to assimilate these two categories. Bhāsarvajña[10] heads the revisionary move, stating unequivocally that motions should be treated as qualities because, like qualities, they reside in substances and possess universals. From a graph-theoretic perspective, this revision is well motivated: qualities and motions are represented by nodes of the same valency, and so are things of the same *type*. Udayana chooses the harder way, and tries to formulate definitions that will accommodate the distinction. The classical Vaiśeṣika idea[11] that motions are what cause substances to come into contact with one another is reflected in his definitions:

126 A quality belongs to such a kind as inheres in both contact and non-contact, and does not inhere in the non-inherent cause of that sort of contact which does not result from contact.

190 A motion belongs to such a kind as inheres in the non-inherent cause of contact and does not inhere in contact.

These definitions introduce two new relations, contact and causation, neither of which is explicable in terms of inherence nor belongs to the graph-theoretic interpretation of the categories. The very success of that interpretation gives a rationale to the revisionary pressure. Finding a pattern into which all but a few items of some phenomenon fit grounds a presumption that those items are in some way discrepant. This is a general principle of scientific and rational inquiry (we will encounter it again in Chapter 6.6), and we can see it has been used by Bhāsarvajña to motivate revisions in the classical Vaiśeṣika theory. Rationality appears here in the form of *principled* revision.[12]

3.3 THE STRUCTURE OF THE WORLD

The definitions of the categories generate constraints on permissible graphs. What is the simplest solution to those constraints (the simplest possible world)? Any path must have a beginning and an end. Only atoms can end paths, and only universals and individuators can begin them. A graph consisting of a single path, beginning with an individuator and ending in an atom (I→S) is not well formed, however, because a substance must be the end of a path of length at least 2. So the atom, besides its individuator, must have inhering in it a quality, and in that quality a universal. However, a universal must inhere in at least two things, so there must be a second quality, a second atom and a second individuator. The simplest well-formed graph is therefore:

○ → ○ ← ○ ← ○ → ○ → ○ ← ○

In accordance with the definitions, we can identify this as a metaphysical structure of the form:

I → S ← Q ← U → Q → S ← I

Let us consider in this context the merits of another proposed revision to the classical system. The two great revisionaries are Bhāsarvajña and Raghunātha. I have already mentioned one revision: the assimilation of motions and qualities to a single category. Another candidate for revision must surely be the category of individuator. Raghunātha[13] indeed argues that individuators should be eliminated, on the ground that since the old school has to allow the self-individuation of the individuators, one might just as well permit the self-individuation of atoms. In other words, the charge is one of redundancy, the introduction of individuators only postponing the necessity for self-individuation. And graph-theoretically it is clear that the individuators can be deleted from a graph without altering its connectedness, for they are merely inert nodes adorning each atom.

There is still more structure in the Vaiśeṣika graph. Intuitively the ontology 'descends' from a top level of universals, down through the qualities-cum-motions and compound substances, on through the simpler substances, and ending at a bottom level of atoms. This intuition can be made more precise. Notice first that there are no closed cycles in the Vaiśeṣika graph. A cycle is a directed self-terminating path <**x**, **y**, **z**, . . ., **x**>. The members of a cycle must have valency (+, +). So no universal or individuator can be a member of a cycle, because neither has anything inhering in it. No quality or motion can be a member of a cycle, because only universals inhere in qualities and motions, and there are no universals in a cycle. No atomic substance can be a member of a cycle, because atoms inhere in nothing. That leaves only cycles of compound substances. But there can be cycles of substances only if a substance can have as a part something of which it is a part and so (if the part-of relation is transitive) be a part of itself.

If there are no cycles then paths have determinate lengths. So let us now define the 'level' of a node as the length of the longest path leading to it. Universals and individuators all belong in level 0 – they are not inherees. Nothing other than universals and individuators are in level 0 – substances, qualities and motions *are* inherees. Level 1 is the level of all and only qualities and motions – all are inhered in by universals and universals alone. Further, it follows from the definition of Udayana that substances are in level 2 or below. Indeed, the levels from 2 down are populated by substances and substances alone. Every path comes to an end with some atomic substance.

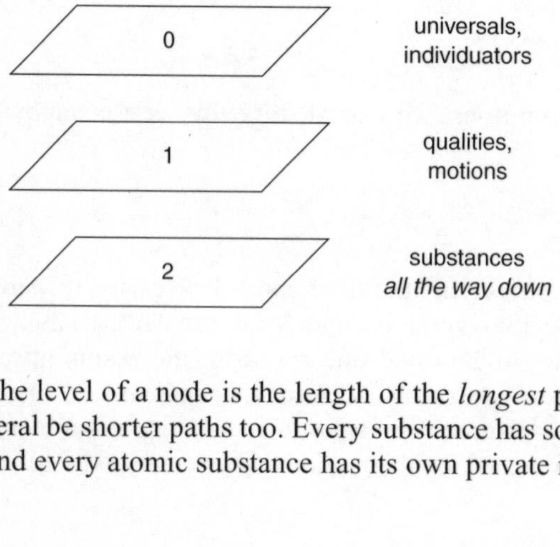

The level of a node is the length of the *longest* path to it, but there will in general be shorter paths too. Every substance has some universals inhering in it, and every atomic substance has its own private individuator.

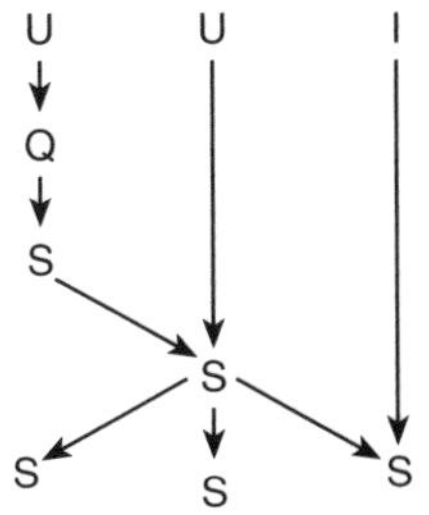

Musashi Tachikawa[14] has aptly compared the structure of the world in Vaiśeṣika metaphysics with a mobile hanging from the ceiling. We must remember, however, that the whole branching graph of substances is 'suspended' by threads running down from the top level of universals and individuators to each and every substance in the lower levels. So another comparison would be with a group of marionettes: the bodies of the puppets are the branching structures of substances, and the strings will be the threads running up to the level of universals and individuators.

3.4 THE TAXONOMY OF NATURAL KINDS

Udayana in the *Kiraṇāvalī*[15] lists six specific constraints on the category of universals. They are (1) that a universal not reside in fewer than two things; (2) that no two universals reside in exactly the same things; (3) that no two universals are 'crosscutting,' *partially* overlapping one another; (4) that no universal lead to an infinite regress; (5) that no universal undermine the very nature of the entity in which it resides; and (6) that no universal be incapable of being related to the things in which it purports to reside. These conditions can be interpreted graph-theoretically. The function of constraints (4), (5) and (6) is to stop properties *of* the graph becoming nodes *in* the graph. There can be no universal *inherencehood (i.e. that which all the edges have in common), because the edges of a graph are not nodes. So *inherencehood is ruled out by (6). There can be no universal *individuatorhood (i.e. that which all the individuators have in common), because an individuator by its very nature has nothing in common with anything else. So *individuatorhood is ruled out by (5). No universal can inhere in other universals, for, were this to occur, then that universal could have further universals inhering in it, and so on *ad infinitum*. So *universalhood and any other such merely ostensible property (*upādhi*) of universals are ruled out by (4). Neither is one permitted to generate a regress by introducing a node $\mathbf{n}_1$ connected to every other node, then a second node $\mathbf{n}_2$ connected to every other node including $\mathbf{n}_1$, and so on *ad infinitum*.

The first three constraints are conditions on the connectedness of the graph. We have encountered the first already, that nodes representing universals must have an 'out-valency' greater than one – that is the feature of their valency which distinguishes them from individuators. Constraints (2) and (3), however, are substantive and new. Constraint (2) is a unique-ness condition: for any given set of nodes, there is at most one universal node connected to each and every member. So graphs like this are ruled out:

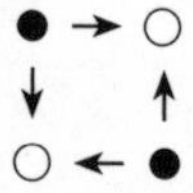

This graph represents a situation in which two universals (the upper left and lower right corners) reside in exactly the same pair of things (the upper right and lower left corners). The general effect of (2) is to rule out reduplication within the graph (and so within nature). It is an Occam's razor on nodes rep-resenting universals, a block on there being two nodes having exactly the same edges with other nodes. We will see that the same principle of non-reduplication is extended to other types of node as well.

The third constraint rules out crosscutting among universals, that is, the sit-uation in which two universals reside jointly in some things and individually in others. There is a considerable modern discussion of the thesis that cross-cutting systems of categories cannot explain genuine natural kinds.[16] This is the typical sort of graph the condition rules out:

u_1 u_2

$$\bigcirc \leftarrow \bullet \rightarrow \bigcirc \leftarrow \bullet \rightarrow \bigcirc$$

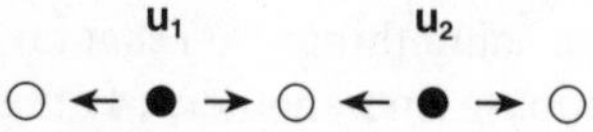

It is clear that the 'no crosscutting' condition induces a hierarchy in the domain of universals. The nodes in level 0 are ordered within the level into hierarchical groupings (each individuator being a hierarchy unto itself). Vaiśeṣika writers talk of the universals as being arranged in a 'higher–lower' relationship (VS 1.2.3). They posit the existence of a unique 'highest' uni-versal – called 'being' *bhāva* or 'existentness' *sattā* (VS 1.2.18) – a universal that stands as higher in the higher–lower relationship with every universal other than itself,[17] and they add that other universals stand in the relationship as higher to some universals and as lower to others (VS 1.2.5). The only exceptions are the 'ultimate species' (*antya viśeṣa*), said never to stand as higher, in the higher–lower relationship, to any other universal (VS 1.2.6).

Ian Hacking[18] defines a scientific taxonomy as a class of entities *C* and a transitive asymmetric relation *K*, such that: (i) *C* has a head, a member of the class that does not stand in relation *K* to any other member, but such that every other member stands in this relation to it; and (ii) every member except the head stands in the relation *K* to some other member. He adds that such taxonomies sometimes terminate in a bedrock of categories that cannot be further subdivided. It is clear that the Vaiśeṣika theory satisfies this definition of a scientific taxonomy. The class of universals is the domain, the higher–lower relationship is a transitive and asymmetric relation, the universal existentness is a head member, and the ultimate species constitute a bedrock. This lends a degree of support to Bimal Matilal's conjecture that the Vaiśeṣika universals are comparable to natural kinds.[19]

The thesis that natural taxonomies cannot be crosscutting, while certainly the majority view, is not universally accepted. One author[20] dissents on the grounds that the different colours *red* and *blue* are to be found in the same object, a vase painted both red and blue. The traditional Vaiśeṣika reply, that *red* and *blue* merge in the vase to form a single, new colour, is rather less convincing than the Buddhist analysis of the vase into parts, some red and some blue. Another[21] argues that the ban on crosscutting would lead to a catastrophic diminution in the number of universals, for the univeral relations *far* and *near* crosscut all other universals. A different argument rests on the standard, but curious, unwillingness to distinguish between artifact kinds and natural kinds, from which it follows that *vase* and *gold* crosscut in a golden vase. Rather more convincing is an example from the modern literature, the kinds *parasite* and *insect*, and with it the suggestion that scientific taxonomies are interest relative.[22]

There is one further rule on the connectivity of the graph (in fact, it is a consequence of Udayana's first condition). This is the rule that no universal can be 'unexampled' (*aprasiddha*), inherent in nothing. The underlying principle is that every node must be connected to at least one other node – there can be no isolated nodes. And this, I think, is only an instance of a still more general rule, that the graph forms one connected whole, and does not factorise into separate and unconnected parts. The graph represents the world, and the world is a single, connected unity.

Are there conjunctive and disjunctive universals? Suppose that the set of nodes to which the nodes **x** and **y** have edges is equal to the set of nodes to which another node **z** has edges. Then $\mathbf{z} = \mathbf{x} \vee \mathbf{y}$ (**z** is the disjunction of **x** and **y**; the identity follows from Udayana's second condition). Conversely, if **z** is a node with edges to just those nodes to which **x** and **y** both have edges, then $\mathbf{z} = \mathbf{x} \wedge \mathbf{y}$ (**z** is the conjunction of **x** and **y**). Daniel Ingalls[23] says that Navya-Nyāya do not have general terms for logical sum and logical product, and the graph-theoretic explanation is that one cannot generate disjunctive and conjunctive nodes at will. In particular, we can prove from the 'uniqueness', 'exampled' and 'no crosscutting' conditions that there are no conjunctive universals in the Vaiśeṣika graph. For, by 'no crosscutting', the conjunction of two universals must be either empty (a possibility ruled out by the 'exampled' condition) or, if non-empty, then coextensive with and so (by 'uniqueness') identical to one of the conjuncts. We might admit disjunctive universals, however, when two disjuncts are disjoint. For then the disjunction would be a universal higher than either. There are indeed Sanskrit technical terms ('*ubhaya*' and '*anyatara*') with the logical force of this disjunction.

3.5 ABSENCE AS A TYPE OF ENTITY

'Absence' in Vaiśeṣika is not the same as non-existence. Fictional characters, dream-objects and hallucinations are non-existent: they do not exist as it were *by nature* (*cf.* Chapter 2). It would be an absurdity to go in search of Hamlet in order to find out whether he really exists or not – his non-existence is not a merely contingent lack in the world of things. The absence of water on the moon, on the other hand, is a contingent and concrete fact; so too is the absence of colour in my cheeks. Notice the role of the phrases 'of water', 'of colour' here: an absence has an absentee – that which the absence is an absence of. It also has a location (e.g. the moon, my cheeks), and a time. So the proposal is to reparse the sentence '*x* does not occur in *y* at time *t*' as 'an absence-of-*x* occurs in *y* at *t*'. For it is often the case that the absence of something somewhere is more salient than any fact about what is present there (Figure 3.1).

There is one relatively straightforward way to interpret the idea of absence graph-theoretically. If *x* does not inhere in *y*, then there is no edge (**x**, **y**) in the graph. Now for every graph, there is a dual graph. The dual has the same nodes as the original graph, but has an edge between two nodes just in case the original does not. So the dual graph does have an edge (**x**, **y**). Following this idea, one would be led to say that absences are things of a different *type* from any presence because they are edges in the dual graph, rather than edges or nodes in the original.

For various reasons, the Vaiśeṣika do not consider this to be an adequate explanation of the category. One problem is that it makes absences more like relations than 'things', and this does not keep to the spirit of the Vaiśeṣika idea that absences are entities. In fact, absences do display much relation-like behaviour – after all, absence is always the absence of *x* in *y*. Another objection, however, is if absence is a new category, its introduction should result in an extension of the original graph, and not in the introduction of a new graph, let alone a graph completely disconnected from the original. For the connected world of things ought not be represented by a pair of disconnected graphs. A third problem arises if we admit something called 'unpervaded occurrence', as we will see in the next section.

The Vaiśeṣika idea is to represent absences as *nodes*, related in new ways to the nodes of the original graph. Here is how to do it. For each unconnected pair of nodes (**x**, **y**), create a new node **x′** in the original graph. This new node will have edges to **x** and to **y**, but they will be edges of two new types. The edge (**x′**, **x**) is an edge belonging to the extension of the absentee–absence (*pratiyogitā*) relation, which I shall signify as '⇨'. This represents the relation between an absence and what the absence is of. The edge (**x′**, **y**) is an edge belonging to the extension of the 'absential special relation' (*abhāvīya-svarūpa-sambandha*), signified here by '➔'. This represents the occurrence relation between an absence and its location. The relation between an absence and its location is clearly not the same as the relation between a presence and

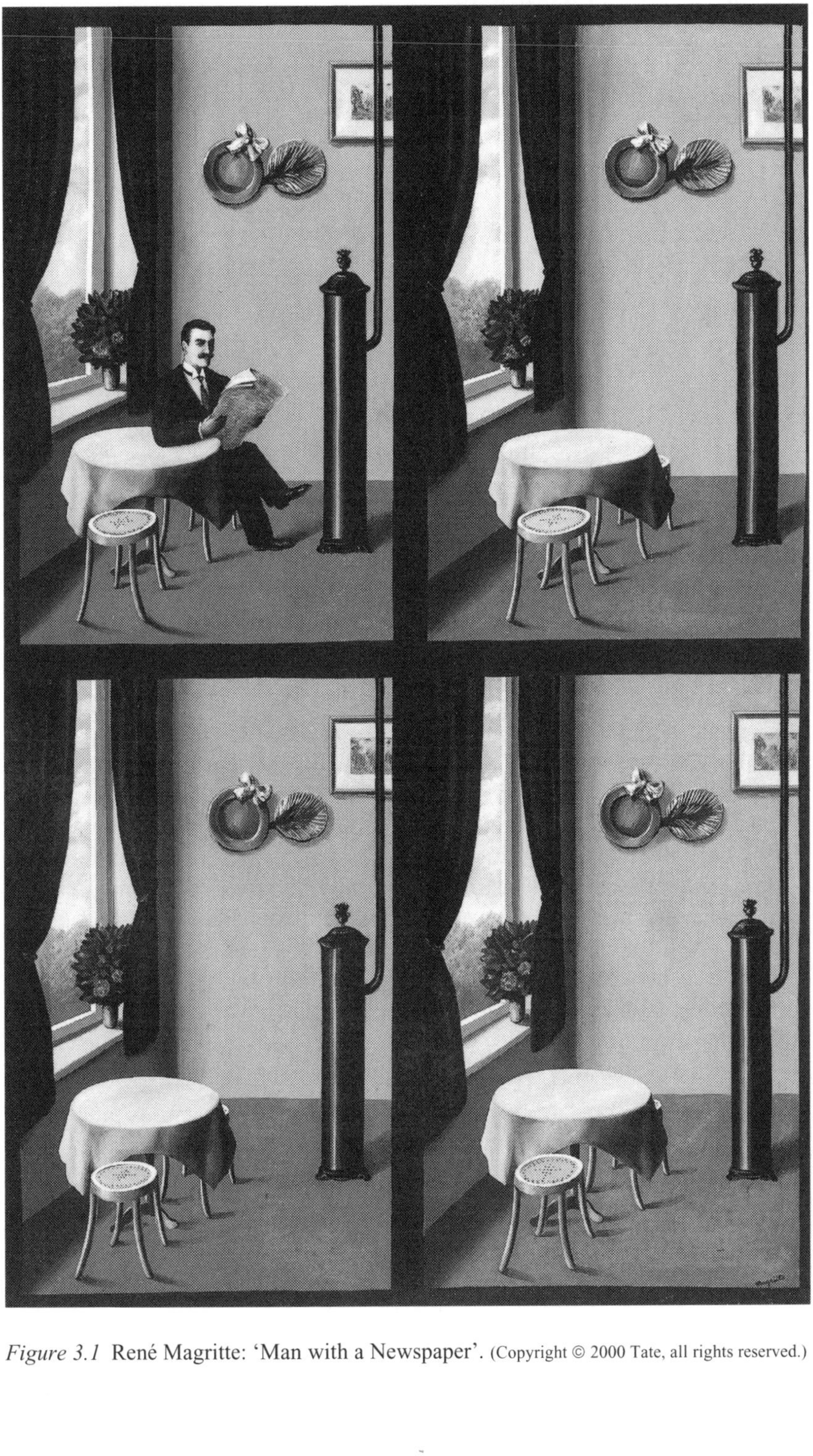

Figure 3.1 René Magritte: 'Man with a Newspaper'.

its location (inherence, contact), for it is clear that, when a person is absent from a room, his absence is not *in* the room in the same sense that the other things *in* the room are.

	Original graph	Modified original
	○ x	○ x
		⇧
ABSENCE		⊙ x′
		↓
	○ y	○ y

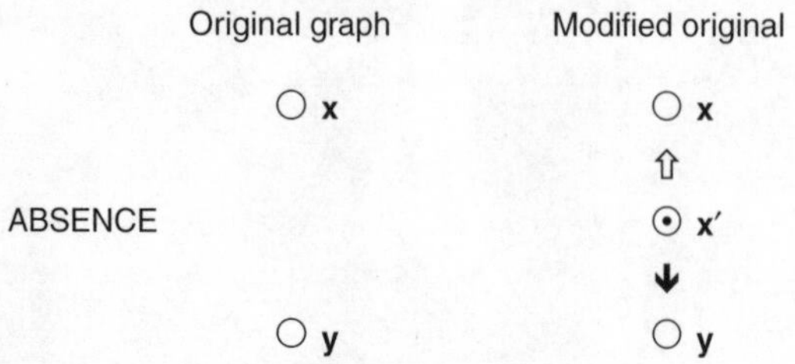

These new nodes belong in a domain outside the system of levels, for they inhere in nothing and nothing inheres in them (inherence, and the whole system of levels, is a structure on presences). The modified graph is instead a concatenation of the original graph of nodes and edges with a new structure of 'absential nodes' and 'absential edges'.

Vaiśeṣika theory of absence draws a type distinction between *simple absence* (*atyantābhāva*) and *difference* (*anyonyābhāva*). Difference is the absence of a relation of identity between two things. Here '$x \neq y$' is paraphrased as 'a difference-from y occurs in x'. Graph-theoretically, the distinction between absence and difference is a distinction between a negation on edges and a negation on nodes in the original graph. For, trivially, every node is such that it is *different* from every other node. One way to represent this would be to introduce a new kind of 'non-identity' edge into the graph, an edge which connects every node with every other node. The Vaiśeṣika, however, wants the category of absence to correspond to a domain of things rather than relations; so in the graph-theoretic representation, differences have to be represented as nodes rather than edges. So let us say that for every node **x** in the original graph, there is a new node **x***. Call it an 'antinode'. The antinode **x*** is connected to *every* node in the graph. It is connected to **x** by an edge of the absentee–absence type, and to every node other than **x** by an absential location edge. There is a one–one correspondence between the new domain of antinodes and the domain of original nodes.

DIFFERENCE

The leading idea behind the graph-theoretic interpretation of the categories is that a type of thing is a type of node, and node-types are determined by patterns of possible valencies in the graph. It was for this reason that we did not need earlier to *label* the nodes. With the introduction of the category of absence, we have two higher-order type distinctions: the distinction between positive and negative nodes, and the distinction among the negative nodes between absential nodes and antinodes. Do these distinctions have a graph-theoretic explanation, or must we allow ineliminable node-labels to demarcate presence nodes, absential nodes and antinodes? What we have now are three different types of edge – corresponding to the relations of inherence, absence–absentee and absential location. So we might hope to distinguish between positive and negative nodes as those which are not and those which are at the end of an absential edge. That is, we make it a requirement that no positive node absentially qualify any other node. Clearly, the suggestion will work only if the absence of an absence is not identical to a presence. We will see in the next section that the graph-theoretically oriented Raghunātha indeed denies that this is so. So as not to beg the question at this point, and for the sake of pictorial clarity, I will continue to mark positive nodes O and negative nodes ⊙ differently.[24]

3.6 HIGHER-ORDER ABSENCE

The above treatment of absence is in effect a procedure for introducing new nodes into the original graph. One set of new nodes fills the 'gaps' in that graph: whenever there is no edge between two nodes, an absential node is introduced between, and linked to, them. Another set of new nodes exactly mirrors the original graph: for each node in the original, there is one and only one antinode, linked to everything the original node is not. But now, having supplemented the original graph with two sets of new nodes, nothing is to stop us from repeating the procedure again – generating new sets of *second-order* absence nodes – and to do this again and again. It seems that we have introduced a procedure for the indefinite recursive expansion of the graph. Fortunately this does not in fact happen. As we will now see, no subsequent recursion of the procedure after the first produces any new nodes.

Prima facie, it seems plausible to reason as follows (as we will shortly see, this reasoning turns out to be subject to an important caveat). If **x** is in **y**, then **x**′, the absence of **x**, is not in **y**, and so **x**″, the absence of **x**′, is in **y**. Conversely: if **x**″ is in **y**, then **x**′ is not in **y**, so **x** is in **y**. Graph-theoretically, we represent this as follows:

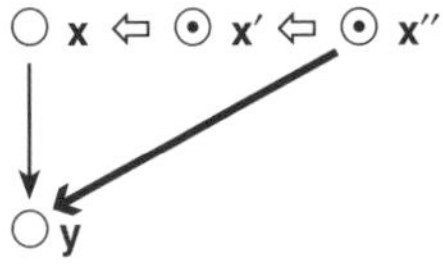

If this is right, then it follows that an entity and the absence of its absence 'occur' in exactly the same set of loci: for all **y**, there is an inherence edge (**x**, **y**) just in case there is an absential location edge (**x″**, **y**). Can we appeal now to an analogue of the uniqueness condition for universals – that two nodes are identical iff they have exactly the same edges – and infer that the absence of an absence of an entity is identical to presence of the entity? The point is controversial, with the majority favouring identification. It is Raghunātha[25] who argues that the identification is unsound, on the ground that nothing can turn an absence into a presence. Here again Raghunātha's intuition agrees with the graph-theoretic reconstruction: the nodes **x** and **x″** are connected to other nodes by means of different types of edge. So they cannot both represent entities of the same type. Moreover, as we shall see in more detail below, the Naiyāyikas do not accept that it is generally valid to infer from the occurrence of **x** in **y** to the occurrence of **x″** there, although they do allow the converse. This is the caveat in the line of reasoning with which I began this paragraph. The implication is that **x** and **x″** need not, after all, share the same set of loci.

Let us repeat the procedure once more. If **x′**, the absence of **x**, is in **y**, then **x″** is not in **y**, and so **x‴**, the absence of **x″**, is in **y**. Conversely: if **x‴** is in **y**, then **x″** is not in **y**, so **x′** is in **y**. Graph-theoretically:

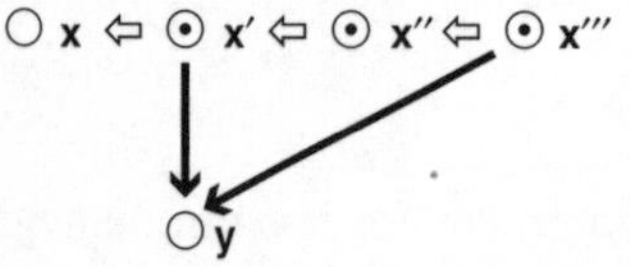

It follows that a first-order absence and the absence of *its* absence reside in exactly the same set of loci. But here we *can* appeal to the uniqueness condition, because the edges are all of the same type. So **x‴** is identical to **x′**, as Raghunātha himself allows.[26] Similarly, **x⁗** is identical to **x″**, and so on. There are no absential nodes of order higher than two. The argument is summed up by Annambhaṭṭa in the *Tarkasaṃgraha*:

> The view of the early thinkers is that the absence of an absence is nothing but a presence; it is not admitted as a new absence for there would then be an infinite regress. According to the new school, however, the absence of an absence is a distinct absence, and there is no regress as the third absence is identical to the first. (TS 89)

Recall that we defined the absence **x′** as a node such that **x′** is absentially located in **y** if there is no edge between **x** and **y**. That definition was adequate for the introduction of first-order absences, because there is only one kind of edge in the original graph, namely the inherence edge. The expanded graph has another sort of edge, however: the absential edge. So the notion of a second-order absence is underdetermined by our original definition. The new definition we need is:

Rule for Absence:
An absence **x′** is absentially located in **y** if **x** does not inhere in **y**.
Rule for Higher Order Absence:
For $i > 1$, an absence $\mathbf{x}^i$ is absentially located in **y** iff $\mathbf{x}^{i-1}$ is not absentially located in **y**.

The second rule implies that absence is a classical negation for $i > 1$, and so, in particular, that an absence of an absence of an absence is identical to an absence. A double negation, however, is a mixture – a negation defined on inherence edges followed by a negation defined on absential qualifier edges – and for that reason behaves non-classically. What I will show in the next section is that Navya-Nyāya logic rejects the classical rule of Double Negation Introduction – the rule that licenses one to infer from p to $\sim\sim p$. What replaces it is a weakened rule – infer from $\sim p$ to $\sim\sim\sim p$. This is because negation is a procedure for filling 'gaps' in the graph: whenever there is no edge between two nodes, the rule for negation licenses us to insert an absential node between them. The classical rule for Double Negation Elimination – the rule that licenses one to infer from $\sim\sim p$ to p – remains valid in Navya-Nyāya logic (i.e. if **x′** is not in **y**, then **x** is in **y**).[27] The effect of this weakening in the rule for Double Negation Introduction is that one is no longer entitled to infer that if **x** is in **y**, then **x′** is not in **x′**. One effect of this is to block the equivalence of a positive entity with the absence of its absence. We can say that **x′** is the absence of **x″**, but we cannot say that **x** is the absence of **x′**. Graph-theoretically, connections of the form ○ **x** ⇒ ⊙ **x′** are prohibited, since a positive entity cannot be the absence of *anything*. Also prohibited are triangles of the form

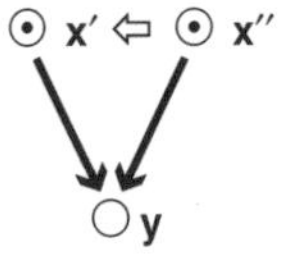

because negation behaves classically within the domain of absences. What is stranger, however, is the effect the weakened rule has of *permitting* a positive entity to be co-located with its absence. For we are no longer in a position to assert that the presence of an entity is inconsistent with its absence. Let us see how the Nyāya philosophers arrive at the conclusion that one must allow for such an unusual possibility.

Whenever something inheres in a compound substance, the question arises: does it also inhere in the parts? An entity is said to be of 'locus-pervading' occurrence just in case it inheres in all the parts of its locus (as well as in the locus itself).[28] It *saturates* its locus. A sapphire is red through-and-through, and sesame oil pervades every part of the seed; but a painted vase is blue only on the outside. Let us say then that *x* is locus-pervading with respect to *y* just in case *x* inheres in *y* and if *z* is a part of *y* then *x* inheres in *z*.[29] The only things that have parts are substances, and substances inhere in their parts and in nothing else. So *x* is locus-pervading with respect to *y* just in case *x* inheres in *y* and if *y* inheres in *z* then *x* inheres in *z*. Certain types of quality pervade their loci, according to the classical Vaiśeṣika authors.[30] Examples include weight, viscosity and fluidity. A thing is heavy just in case every part of it is heavy. Colours, tastes, smells can pervade their loci, but need not do so.[31] And a compound substance is locus-pervading with respect to each of its parts, if 'part of' is a transitive relation.

The notion of a locus-pervading entity has a distinctive graph-theoretic correlate. An edge ($\mathbf{n}_1$, $\mathbf{n}_2$) is locus-pervading just in case there is an edge from $\mathbf{n}_1$ to any node in any path from $\mathbf{n}_2$.

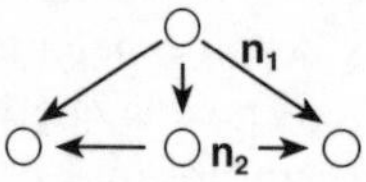

While locus-pervading nodes are straightforwardly definable in the system as so far developed, the concept of 'unpervaded occurrence' (*avyāpya-vṛttitva*) marks a theoretical innovation. The classic Buddhist refutation of realism about wholes is that wholes must be the bearers of contradictory properties. For if some parts of a vase are red and other parts are not red, and if the vase as a whole has a colour in virtue of its parts having colour, then one seems forced to admit either that the whole is both red and not red, or that it has no colour at all.[32] The traditional Nyāya-Vaiśeṣika solution is less than satisfactory – it is to say that the whole has a new shade of colour called 'variegated'! Recognising the *ad hoc* nature of such a response, later Naiyāyikas try instead to make sense of the idea that a property can be co-located with its absence.[33] The idea is to capture the sense in which one says that the vase is red, because its surface is red, allowing at the same time that it is not red, because its inside is some other colour. A favourite Nyāya example involves the relation of contact: the tree enjoys both monkey-contact (there is a monkey on one of its branches) and also the absence of monkey-contact (its roots and other branches are in contact with no monkey). This defence of realism is what motivates later writers to allow there to be such a thing as unpervaded occurrence, defined to be an occurrence that is co-located with its absence. That is, an unpervading node is a node **x** such that there is an edge (**x**, **y**) and an edge (**x′**, **y**). Triangles such as the following are now deemed to be permissible in the graph:

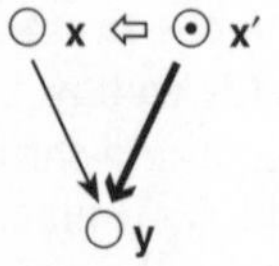

The strangeness of such a possibility is ameliorated if one says, as some Naiyāyikas do, that *x* occurs in *y* as 'delimited' by one part, and its absence occurs in *y* as 'delimited' by another part.[34] Gaṅgeśa nevertheless goes to considerable lengths to reformulate logic and the theory of inference in Navya-Nyāya in a way that permits the co-location of an entity with its absence. The phenomenon of unpervaded occurrence is regarded not as a minor curiosity in Nyāya, but as the occasion for serious revision in their analysis.[35]

3.7 NAVYA-NYĀYA LOGIC

With the introduction of absence, the graph-theoretic ontologies become also semantic models for a propositional language. A sentence 'α' is assigned, let us stipulate, an ordered pair of nodes (**x**, **y**). The sentence is true if that pair is an edge in the graph, false if it is not.[36] The negation of that sentence, '$\sim \alpha$', is true if (**x**′, **y**) is an edge, false if it is not. Again, '$\sim\sim \alpha$' is true if (**x**″, **y**) is an edge, false if it is not. If triangles such as the one above are possible, then the truth of 'α' does not imply the truth of '$\sim\sim \alpha$', since (**x**, **y**) is an edge but not (**x**″, **y**). So the propositional logic being modelled is, as we have already observed, one in which Double Negation Introduction does not hold. In this theory, we still have these correspondences between truth-value and negation:

(R1) if $\sim T\alpha$ then $T\sim \alpha$ from the Rule for Absence
(R2) $T\sim\sim \alpha$ iff $\sim T\sim \alpha$ from the Rule for Higher Order Absence

where 'T' stands for 'it is true that'.

What we no longer have is:

(R3) if $T \sim \alpha$ then $\sim T\alpha$

The reason, as I said before, is that negation is an operation that fills 'gaps' in the graph – it tells us nothing when there is already an edge between two nodes. So the truth of a proposition is consistent, in Navya-Nyāya logic, with the truth of its negation. This element of dialetheism[37] in the theory does not, however, mean that anything is provable or that anything follows from anything else – the correspondences R1–R2 are enough to prevent the system collapsing. Let us see why.

In the modern analysis of valid inference, an inference is valid just in case it is impossible for the premises to be true without the conclusion also being true. In the logic of classical India, validity is a matter of property substitution, and the problem is to determine the conditions under which the occurrence of the reason property at a location warrants the inference that the target property occurs there too. The leading idea is that such property substitutions are valid just in case the reason does not 'wander' or 'deviate' from the target (*avyabhicāra*; see Chapter 1.6–7). In one of the most famous passages in the Indian literature, Gaṅgeśa suggests five ways to make sense of this idea:[38]

> Now, in that knowledge of a pervasion which is the cause of an inference, what is pervasion? It is not simply non-wandering. For that is not:
>
> (1) non-occurrence in loci of the absence of the target, nor
> (2) non-occurrence in loci of the absence of the target which are different from loci of the target, nor
> (3) non-colocation with difference from a locus of the target, nor
> (4) being the absentee of an absence which resides in all loci of absence of the target, nor
> (5) non-occurrence in what is other than a locus of the target,
>
> since it is none of these where the target is maximal.

A 'maximal' property is a property resident in everything (*kevalānvayin*). Gaṅgeśa dismisses the five provisional analyses on the grounds that all are formulated in terms of 'absence of the target', and that that phrase is undefined when the target is maximal (the absence of a maximal property – assumed here not to be of unpervaded occurrence – would occur in nothing and so be 'unexampled', contradicting a basic condition of connectedness). In his preferred definition, Gaṅgeśa exploits a trick to overcome this problem.[39] He says that any property whose absence is co-located with the reason is not identical to the target. This implies that the target is not a property whose absence is co-located with the reason, but the contraposed formulation avoids the use of the troublesome phrase 'absence of the target'.

Consider now the difference between the first and second analyses in the list of five. Graph-theoretically, what the first analysis states is that, if **r** is the node representing the reason, and **t** is the node representing the target, then **r** is present in no node where **t** is absent.

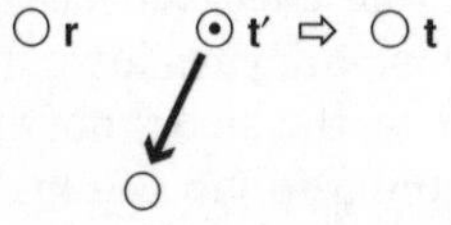

But what happens if the target has unpervaded occurrence? Then the first analysis is too strong.[40] For it is not a necessary condition on valid inference that the reason not be present wherever the target is absent, if there are nodes where the target is present as well as absent. What validity precludes is the presence of the reason without the presence of the target. So the proper definition is that the reason is not present wherever the target is not present (and so also absent). This is exactly what the second analysis states. We can make the point in terms of our earlier definitions of truth and negation. The premise in an inference is the statement that the reason occurs in a certain location, the conclusion the statement that the target occurs in that location. What our first analysis asserts is that the premise is not true if *the negation of the conclusion is true* (= absence of target in the location). The second analysis states instead that the premise is not true if the conclusion is *false* (= denial of presence of target in the location). Ironically, then, it is the very element of dialetheism of the Navya-Nyāya system which forces Gaṅgeśa to disambiguate the definition of validity, and to distinguish the correct definition from the one that had been preferred before.

3.8 NUMBER

The classical Vaiśeṣika theory of number is that numbers are qualities of substances.[41] A quality 'two' inheres in both members of a pair of substances, another quality 'two' inheres in another such pair, and all the qualities 'two' have inhering in them a single universal 'two-hood'.

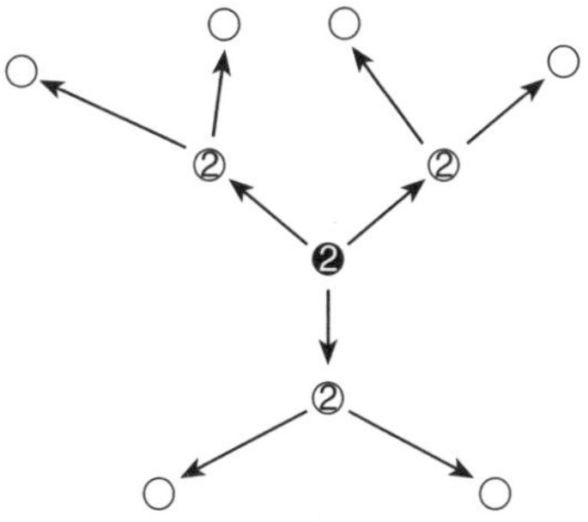

❷ The universal 'two-hood'.
② A quality-particular 'two'.

Bhāsarvajña and Raghunātha, as usual, lead the reforming move. Bhāsarvajña's theory[42] is that numbers are not qualities at all, but relations of identity and difference. Thus the sentence '*a* and *b* are one' means simply that $a = b$, while '*a* and *b* are two' means that $a \neq b$.[43] Bhāsarvajña's analysis is echoed, very much later, in Gadādhara's (*c.* AD 1650) comments on the meaning of the word 'one'.[44] Gadādhara states that the meaning of 'one *F*' is: an *F* as qualified by being-alone, where 'being-alone' means 'not being the absentee of a difference resident in something of the same kind'. In other words, 'one *F*' is to be analysed as saying of something which is *F* that no *F* is different from it. If this is paraphrased in a first-order language as '$Fx \ \& \ \neg (\exists y)(Fy \ \& \ y \neq x)$' then it is formally equivalent to a Russellian uniqueness clause '$Fx \& (\forall y)(Fy \rightarrow y = x)$.' The idea that 'one' expresses uniqueness is in the spirit of Bhāsarvajña's idea that it denotes the identity of a thing. In any case, it is clear that, for Gadādhara, 'one' has a logical role similar to that of the definite article.

Raghunātha is more radical still.[45] The central problem is that things in *any* category in the Vaiśeṣika ontology can be numbered, and Raghunātha concludes that numbers must belong in a new category of their own:

> Number is a separate category, not a kind of quality, for we do judge that there is possession of that [number] in qualities and so on. And this [judgment we make that qualities have number is] not an erroneous one, for there is no [other] judgment which contradicts it.

Raghunātha puts his finger at exactly the right place. The 'is-the-number-of' relation is not reducible to the relation of inherence or any relation constructed out of it, for it is a relation between numbers and *any* type of thing. What is this new relation? Raghunātha points out that while inherence is a distributive relation (*avyāsajya-vṛtti*), the number–thing relation has to be collective (*vyāsajya-vṛtti*). The distinction occurs in the context of sentences with plural subjects. An attributive relation is distributive if it relates the attribute to every subject – if *the trees* are old, then each individual tree is old. A relation is collective if it relates the attribute to the subjects collectively, but not individually – 'the trees form a forest' does not imply that each tree forms a forest. Number attributions are collective; if one says that there are two pots here, one does not imply that each pot is two. Inherence, however, is a distributive relation, and so cannot be the relation of attribution for numbers. This new relation is called the 'collecting' (*paryāpti*) relation by Raghunātha:[46]

> The collecting relation, whose existence is indicated by constructions such as 'This is one pot' and 'These are two', is a special kind of self-linking relation.

His commentator Jagadīśa explains:

> It might be thought that the collecting relation is [in fact] nothing but inherence . . . So Raghunātha states that collecting [is a special kind of self-linking relation]. . . . In a sentence like 'This is one pot', collecting relates the property pot-hood by delimiting it as a property which resides in only one pot, but in a sentence like 'These are two pots', collecting relates the property twoness by delimiting it as a property which resides in both pots. Otherwise, it would follow that there is no difference between saying 'These are two' and 'Each one possesses twoness'.

Thus the number two is related by the collecting relation to the two pots jointly, but not to either individually. Raghunātha's idea is clear in the graph-theoretic context. The introduction of numbers requires one final expansion of the graph. We introduce another new domain of nodes (**1**, **2**, **3**, . . .) and another new type of edge from these nodes. Like ordinary edges, this new type of edge is an ordered pair whose first member is a node, but now the second member is a *set* of nodes. The new edge connects the node **2** with every pair of nodes (**x**, **y**). Likewise, it connects the node **3** with every triple of nodes (**x**, **y**, **z**), and so on. The node **2**, then, is that node from which all edges to pairs begin, the node **3** the node from which all edges to triples begin, and so forth. This is enough to individuate number-nodes graph-theoretically:

Number 2

Number 3

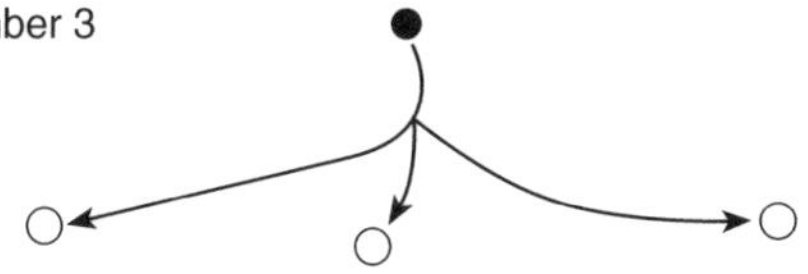

The nodes to which the new edge can connect a number-node can be of any type. In particular, they can themselves be number-nodes. Indeed, the new edge connects **2** with pairs of nodes, one of whose members is **2** itself:

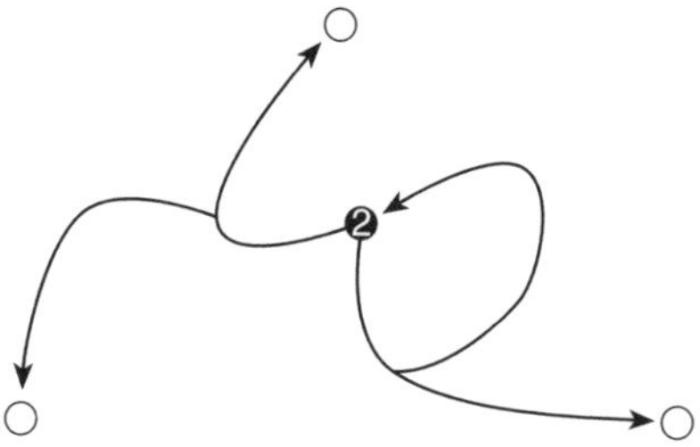

This solves the cross-categorial problem. Number-nodes are related by the new kind of bifurcating edges to nodes of any and every type in the graph, including number-nodes themselves.

The account of number affords an instructive insight into the mechanisms of theory-change and internal criticism in Indian philosophical thinking. The classical Vaiśeṣika theory was modified under pressure from within, through *assimilation* of the categories of quality and motion, *elimination* of the category of individuators or perhaps of differences, and *introduction* of a new category of number. What drove the revision was a perceived explanatory failure in the older theory. The account of numbers as qualities did not seem able to explain their cross-categorial behaviour, nor to give a satisfactory explanation of the relation between numbers and the world of objects. The old theory failed because it supplied no explanation of a range of observed facts about the actual application of the concept of number, in particular that the concept is applicable to objects in any ontological category. The process of rejection and revision was driven, then, by a perceived mismatch between the older theory of a concept and the actual use of that concept in a range of cases. Such a process of theory-rejection might be juxtaposed with another, according to which one looks for inconsistency or incoherence in the basic concepts, and postulates which form the foundation of the theory. This alternative method typically results in or is driven by the discovery of paradox and absurdity. It has been a familiar aspect of philosophical thinking in the West since the Greeks (Zeno, Eubulides), and has had its promoters in India (Sañjaya, Nāgārjuna, Śrīharṣa, see Chapters 1, 2 and 6). However, the idea of rational acceptability as foundational coherence is not the *active principle* behind the rejection or revision of Vaiśeṣika metaphysical theory. The underlying idea in their philosophical theorising is that a theory is rationally acceptable if, or to the extent that, it is in accordance with identified constraints on the construction of ontologies. We have seen, in particular, that such constructions are constrained by conditions of connectedness, redundancy and regress.

The graph-theoretic approach is, I think, full of potential. It offers a new way to read and translate the discussions of the late Nyāya-Vaiśeṣika texts. One might proceed by looking for further situational constraints on what constitutes a permissible graph and applying graph theory to analyse the structure of those graphs. One might also try to establish the relationship between such graphs and classical or non-classical logics. The treatment of negation suggests a comparison with dialetheic logic, and the idea of self-linking nodes perhaps with non-well-founded set theory. My purpose here has been to expose the graph-theoretic basis of Vaiśeṣika theory, and to draw a conclusion about the nature of rational thinking in India. The conclusion is simply this. The idea that nature exemplifies mathematical structure is not remote from the Indian understanding of natural philosophy, contrary to what has generally been believed, but is in fact a fundamental aspect of it.

FURTHER READING

Texts

Bhāsarvajña *c.* AD 950, *Nyāyabhūṣaṇa* (NBhū).
Udayana *c.* AD 1050, *Lakṣaṇāvalī* (LĀ).
Gaṅgeśa *c.* AD 1320, *Tattvacintāmaṇi* (TC), Book II.
Raghunātha *c.* AD 1500, *Padārthatattvanirūpaṇa* (PTN).

The categories (3.1–3)

1 Wilhelm Halbfass, *On Being and What There Is: Classical Vaiśeṣika and the History of Indian Ontology* (Albany: State University of New York Press, 1992), Chapters 1–5.

2 Karl Potter ed., *Indian Metaphysics and Epistemology – The Tradition of Nyāya-Vaiśeṣika up to Gaṅgeśa*, Encyclopedia of Indian Philosophies, Vol. 2 (Delhi: Motilal Banarsidass, 1977), introduction.

3 S. Bhaduri, *Studies in Nyāya-Vaiśeṣika Metaphysics* (Poona: Bhandarkar Oriental Research Institute, 1947).

Universals, cross-cutting (3.4)

1 Bimal Matilal, *Perception* (Oxford: Clarendon Press, 1986), Chapters 11, 12.

2 Kishor Chakrabarti, 'The Nyāya-Vaiśeṣika Theory of Universals,' *Journal of Indian Philosophy* 3 (1975), pp. 363–382.

3 Wilhelm Halbfass, *On Being and What There Is: Classical Vaiśeṣika and the History of Indian Ontology* (Albany: State University of New York Press, 1992), Chapters 6, 7.

4 Sibajiban Bhattacharyya, 'The Navya-Nyāya Theory of Universals,' in his *Gadādhara's Theory of Objectivity*, Part 1: General Introduction to Navya-Nyāya Concepts (New Delhi: Indian Council of Philosophical Research, 1990), Chapter 3.

Absence (3.5–6)

1 Daniel Ingalls, *Materials for the Study of Navya-Nyāya Logic* (Cambridge, Mass.: Harvard University Press, 1951), pp. 54–62, 69–72.

2 Bimal Matilal, *The Navya-Nyāya Doctrine of Negation* (Harvard: Harvard University Press, 1968).

3 Bimal Matilal, 'Double Negation in Navya-Nyāya,' in M. Nagatomi et al. eds., *Sanskrit and Indian Studies: Essays in Honour of Daniel H. H. Ingalls* (Dordrecht: Kluwer, 1980), pp. 1–10; reprinted in *Logic, Language and Reality* (Delhi: Motilal Banarsidass, 1985), pp. 145–154.

4 Prabal Kumar Sen, 'The Nyāya-Vaiśeṣika Theory of Variegated Colour

(*citrarūpa*): Some Vexed Problems,' *Studies in Humanities and Social Sciences* 3.2 (1996) – *Epistemology, Logic And Ontology After Matilal* (Shimla: Indian Institute of Advanced Studies), pp. 151–172.

Navya-Nyāya logic (3.7)

1 Daniel Ingalls, *Materials for the Study of Navya-Nyāya Logic* (Cambridge, Mass.: Harvard University Press, 1951).

2 Bimal Krishna Matilal, 'Gaṅgeśa on the Concept of Universal Property (*kevalānvayin*),' *Philosophy East and West* 18 (1968), pp. 151–161; reprinted in *Logic, Language and Reality* (Delhi: Motilal Banarsidass, 1985), pp. 128–139.

3 J. N. Mohanty, *Gaṅgeśa's Theory of Truth* (Santiniketan, 1966).

4 Cornelius Goekoop, *The Logic of Invariable Concomitance in the Tattvacintāmaṇi* (Dordrecht: Reidel Publishing Co., 1967).

5 Toshihiro Wada, *Invariable Concomitance in Navya-Nyāya* (Delhi: Sri Satguru, 1990).

Number (3.8)

1 Jonardon Ganeri, 'Numbers as Properties of Objects: Frege and the Nyāya,' *Studies in Humanities and Social Sciences* 3.2 (1996) – *Epistemology, Logic and Ontology After Matilal* (Shimla: Indian Institute of Advanced Studies), pp. 111–121.

2 Jonardon Ganeri, 'Objectivity and Proof in an Indian Theory of Number,' *Synthese* (forthcoming).

3 J. L. Shaw, 'Number: From the Nyāya to Frege-Russell,' *Studia Logica* 41 (1982), pp. 283–291.

4 Roy W. Perrett, 'A Note on the Navya-Nyāya Account of Number,' *Journal of Indian Philosophy* 13 (1985), pp. 227–234.

4 Reduction, exclusion and rational reconstruction

4.1 HOW TO PRACTISE POVERTY IN METAPHYSICS

The philosophical quest for unification is ancient and powerful. It is the *leitmotiv* of the Upaniṣads, a dramatic enactment of the search for hidden connections. There are indeed good reasons for seeking unity in a philosophical theory. For any theory which introduces as primitive a distinction between different domains of thing has left at least one thing unexplained – the reason for the distinction. As a methodological principle, the philosopher should not introduce a distinction simply to fix technical problems. We might recall Nāgārjuna's maxim – the special reason for a proposed distinction must be given. We might recall too the nominalist slogan of William of Occam – do not postulate entities beyond necessity. Occam in fact rejected the Aristotelian categories, and argued for simplicity as a constraint on rational theory construction.

The Buddhist philosopher Diṅnāga (*c.* AD 480–540) is uncompromising in his search for unity and simplicity in philosophical explanation. He is an ontological reductionist and a nominalist. It will be instructive to begin our examination of his thought by comparing him with Nāgārjuna. Both are Buddhists, and in this context what that means is that they both reject the ontological commitments of common sense. Common sense commits us to an ontologically rich world, of individuals and properties, of parts and wholes, and most importantly of a concrete connector of 'inherence', which binds everything together in a categorial hierarchy. Nāgārjuna's philosophical method is a debunking one – he wants to undermine common sense (and any other conceptual scheme) by revealing as false the commitments it incurs. In exposing the ontological 'emptiness' of our conceptual schemes, the end of rationality is the elimination of conceptualisation (the end of reason is the *end* of reason).

Diṅnāga's approach is different. His method is one of rational reconstruction. He tries to show that the ontological commitments made by common sense are reducible to a much smaller, more parsimonious set. The basic conceptual scheme of common sense is preserved, but revealed in philosophical analysis to be far less ontologically committed than it represents itself as being. The end of rationality for Diṅnāga is to rebuild our old conceptual superstructures on new, leaner, foundations.

Let us distinguish four basic metaphysical positions – irrealism, reductionism, metaphysical pluralism and additive (non-pluralist) realism. The irrealist denies that things of some type exist, be they belief-states, universals, moral values or entities of another type. He wants to do away with all talk of such things (and either substitute a new vocabulary, or else leave only silence). One variety of irrealism is eliminativism, according to which talk of the kind in question is strictly false. Another variety is non-factualism, a position which maintains that the linguistic role of such talk is not fact-assertive, but rather emotive, prescriptive, or in some other way non-factive. The reductionist's position is perhaps subtler. The existence of things of the type in question is not denied as such, but only their ontological primitiveness. The reductionist's thesis is that statements mentioning those things can, without loss of content, be translated into statements not mentioning those things. A reductionist about universals will translate statements mentioning universals into statements about classes. A reductionist about belief-states translates the statements of intentional psychology into statements about mental events or some other favoured category of basic constituents of the mental. The original statements are still evaluable as true or false, but have been divested of their manifest ontological commitments. Pluralism and additive realism, on the other hand, both take the statements at face value, as really being about (made true by) entities of the type mentioned. Where they differ is in the additive realist's commitment to there being a single proper language of metaphysics, in contrast to the pluralist's commitment to the existence of many irreducible kinds of language use.[1] We have so far encountered a version of irrealism – Nāgārjuna and the Madhyamaka school, and an account of additive realism – the Vaiśeṣika type-hierarchy. In Chapter 5, we will see how the consequences of pluralism are explored by the Jaina metaphysicians. Diṅnāga completes the line-up. He is a reductionist. He wants to preserve the structure of the common-sense scheme, but to divest it of its overt ontological commitments. He wants to translate all talk of universals, wholes, inherence, qualities, motions and absences into a language with only a minimal primitive vocabulary. And the thoroughness with which he executes this programme is nothing short of extraordinary.

4.2 A SKELETAL ONTOLOGY

What is it for an object to *possess* a property? The naive answer – the answer given by common sense and encoded in Vaiśeṣika ontology – is that the object and the property are distinct entities linked together by an entity of a third type, the concrete inherence connector. A state of affairs, an object's having a property, is an ordered triple. Something similar is true for the relationship between a whole and its parts – the whole 'resides' (again by the concrete relation of inherence, or so claim the Vaiśeṣikas) in each and every one of the parts that constitute it.

Here is a way to achieve an ontological gain. The world of individuals and their properties can be reconstrued – following G. F. Stout[2] and D. C. Williams[3] – in terms of 'thin' properties or tropes, e.g. the particular blue of this vase rather than blueness as such. Blueness as such is to be identified with the class of all particular blues. What the particular blues have in common is being 'exactly similar' to one another: a property is a similarity class of tropes under the relation of exact similarity. Another way for two tropes to have something in common is by being tropes of the same object; e.g. the particular blue of this vase and the particular shape of this vase. Let us say that these two tropes stand in a relation of 'concurrence'. Then an object is a similarity class of tropes under the relation of concurrence. The relation of 'possessing a property' is now easily explained: an object possesses a property just in case the class of tropes which is the object *intersects* with the class of tropes which is the property. And the mereological relation 'belonging to a whole' is equally simple: a part belongs to a whole only if the class of tropes which is the whole *subsumes* the class of tropes which is the part.

Our new ontology reduces the world of objects, universals, wholes, parts and inherence to a domain of tropes and two similarity relations. One similarity relation binds tropes into objects, the other along a different dimension into properties. The old idea of a universal – as a class of objects – finds a place here in the notion of a class of classes of tropes. The universal blueness is the class of blue objects; that is to say, a class of classes containing a blue trope. The relations of likeness and unlikeness between objects, which were used in the early Nyāya theory of rational extrapolation (Chapter 1.6), are themselves reducible to the new primitive relation of exact similarity. One object is 'like' another just in case the first has a trope exactly similar to a trope belonging to the second.

The ontology I have just described is very close to the one Diṅnāga is developing in his great classic, the *Collection on Knowing*.[4] At the centre of his system is a new theory of concepts. Diṅnāga rethinks the very nature, role and function of a concept. The traditional theory is that a concept *is* a criterion and *has* a boundary. The criterion '. . . possesses blueness' delimits a region in the space of objects. It marks out a group of objects on the basis of a common shared trait. Diṅnāga's new theory is that a concept *is* a boundary and *has* a criterion. Objects are indeed brought together, but only as groups of essentially disparate things, which happen to be penned in by a single perimeter fence. It is a mistake to think of concepts as bringing objects together on the basis of their sharing a common trait. The function of a concept, like a fence, is rather to keep things out. So Diṅnāga says that the role of a concept is to *exclude*. The boundary of a concept is a line drawn in the space of objects. On one side falls the excluded, and whatever is left falls within the concept. A concept's function is to exclude, to keep things out, to prevent entry. A concept is not a criterion, which some objects meet and others do not (like being red, or living in Paris). It is a pure boundary, a fence, keeping some objects out and leaving the remainder within.

A concept excludes what is other. The relation of 'otherness' here is a relation of *exact dissimilarity*. This is the basic relation in Diṅnāga's system. We have defined a property as a similarity class of tropes. Indeed, from any arbitrary trope, one can construct a property – the class of tropes exactly similar to the arbitrary one. If we take exact *dis*similarity instead as our primitive relation, then what we have now to construct is that property which is the class of tropes *not* exactly *dis*similar to the arbitrary trope. A property is the complement of a dissimilarity class.

The reduction of ordinary statements about objects, qualities and universals is a translation into exclusion-statements. For reasons that I will explain later, I am going to take the exclusion relation to be the relation of non-intersection (so a class of tropes excludes all those other classes which do not intersect with it). Then the task facing us will be to show how an ordinary statement such as 'the lotus is blue', which apparently attributes the universal blueness to an object of a certain type, can be translated into a statement concerning the non-intersection of classes of tropes. If we succeed, we will have shown that the rich ontology of common sense is reducible to a minimal ontology of tropes and two similarity relations.

4.3 MARKING AND SIMILARITY

The key ingredients of Diṅnāga's new ontology are set out in a few sentences in the first chapter of the *Collection on Knowing*:

> There are two means of knowing, perception and inference, because two marks are knowable. (I 2ab)

Apart from the self-marked (*svalakṣaṇa*) and that which is marked by generality (*sāmānya-lakṣaṇa*) there is nothing else. What we shall prove is that perception has the self-marked as its object, and inference has as its object that which is marked by generality.

Among these,

> Perception is that which is free from conceptual construction (*kalpanā*). What then is this conceptual construction? – the association of name, genus, etc. (I 3cd)

In an Abhidharma treatise, too, the following is stated: 'One who has the ability to perceive grasps something blue, but does not grasp "this is blue".' 'One grasps an object in the object, but one does not grasp an element (*dharma*) in the object.' If perception is completely devoid of conceptual construction, then why is it [further] stated that 'the five kinds of sensory cognition have aggregates as their support'? Again, it is mentioned that 'they take as an object a self-marked in so far as it is self-marked by a sensory field not in so far as it is self-marked by a substance.' (*ad* I 4ab)

How is this to be understood?

> Being caused by many objects, [a perception] reaches a whole as its own object. Since it is caused by many substances, it is said, in respect of its field, that it takes the whole as its object; but not by conceptually constructing a unity within that which is many and separate. (I 4cd)
>
> A thing possessing many forms (*rūpa*) cannot be cognised in all its aspects by a sense-faculty. The object of a sense-faculty is the form (*rūpa*) which is indescribable and self-revealing. (I 5)
>
> Illusory cognition, cognition of the conventional truth, inference, that which is inferred, memory and desire are pseudo-perceptions (*pratyakṣābhāsa*), accompanied by obscurity. (I 7cd–8ab)

An illusory cognition is a pseudo-perception because it arises conceptually constructing water, etc. out of such things as vapour floating over sand. Cognition of the conventional truth is a pseudo-perception because it superimposes something extraneous upon things which are only conventionally true, and thus functions through the conceptualisation of forms of these. Inference and that which is inferred are pseudo-perceptions because they arise through the conceptualisation of what formerly has been perceived.

Diṅnāga developed his system out of the Abhidharma in which he had been educated, and in which he had initially written. It is a cardinal doctrine of Abhidharma Buddhism that there is a single kind of thing: the category of *dharma*. A *dharma* is an ingredient, a factor, a fundamental constituent. It is neither a substance nor a property, but that which constitutes both. The Abhidharma literature suggests several different schemes for the classification of *dharma*s. Of these, the chief divisions are those into the five Groups, the twelve Spheres (the six sense-faculties and their six fields), and the eighteen sorts of Base (the six sense faculties, their six fields and six corresponding kinds of mental event).[5] Although there is a strong phenomenalistic bias in these classifications, the fundamental meaning of *dharma* is not 'sense-datum' as such, but 'basic ingredient' of any kind. They are the ingredients out of which ordinary physical objects and their properties, as well as our sense-faculties and mental lives, are all constructed.

Diṅnāga's opening assertion is that there are precisely two sorts of thing. There are the entities which are the 'self-marked' (*sva-lakṣaṇa*), and there are the things which are the 'marked by generality' (*sāmānya-lakṣaṇa*). What are they? An influence, certainly, must be the distinction made in the same terms in the Abhidharmika literature. An architect[6] of the Abhidharma states:

> One examines the body by its own and general marks, as well as sensation, mind and *dharmas*. Their own-mark is precisely [their] own nature (*svabhāva*), while the mark of generality is the non-eternality of the conditioned [*dharmas*], the unhappiness of the defiled [*dharmas*], and the emptiness and non-substantiality of all *dharmas*.

Here the self-mark of a *dharma* is its essence or 'own nature', while its general mark is something that it shares with others. A particular shade of blue – for example, the blue of this vase – has both common and unique qualities. Its common attributes are the things it shares with other *dharmas*, for example, being blue, being a colour. Its unique qualities are things it does not share with others, such as its specific blue shade. The self-mark in Abhidharma is not identical to a *dharma* or trope, but something unique to one.

In Diṅnāga's new system, the self-marked things are characterised in three ways. Diṅnāga says that they are: (1) the objects of perception; (2) free of conceptual construction; and (3) indescribable. How do we explain these three features? One option is to take it that a 'mark' of a trope is a class containing it. Objects and properties are grouped together as classes that are multiply occupied and so 'general', while individual tropes are classified by themselves into singleton classes, and so 'particular'. One can then fit the three features by interpreting conception and language as having only multiply occupied classes of tropes in their field of operation, and by taking perception to be a vehicle for perceiving single tropes. Broadly speaking, this is the interpretation of Diṅnāga preferred, for example, by Richard Hayes[7] and Bimal Matilal.[8]

A second option is to take it that by 'mark' Diṅnāga is referring to a way in which tropes can be grouped. Tropes can be grouped by the relation of concurrence into objects, or else by the relation of exact similarity into properties. Given a particular trope, one can form the class of tropes exactly similar to it, or, along a different axis, the class of concurrent tropes. The property blueness is then said to be 'marked by generality' in the sense that it is the class which collects together all the particular blues. An object such as the vase, on the other hand, can be said to be 'self-marked' in the sense that it is the class which collects together all the tropes that constitute the particular object. The explanation of the three characteristics of the self-marked is now that language and conceptual construction are operations which group tropes by exact similarity into properties, and perception is an operation which groups tropes by concurrence into objects.

This seems to be the interpretation preferred by Masaaki Hattori[9] and Shoryu Katsura.[10] Hattori writes that '[t]he thing in itself, which exists as the indivisible unity of various aspects, is grasped in its totality only by means of perception free from conceptual construction' (1980, p. 62). Katsura's interpretation of Diṅnāga is a development of Hattori's position. He says (1991, pp. 137–8):

> I would like to propose an even more radical version of the framework than Hattori's. Namely,
>
> > There cannot be anything (in the external reality) which possesses either *svalakṣaṇa* or *sāmānyalakṣaṇa* at any time.
>
> I would like to assume that in Diṅnāga's system *svalakṣaṇa* is the object itself which is to be grasped directly by perception, which is neither expressible nor identifiable at that moment, but which is later identified by our conceptual thinking (*kalpanā*) and given a certain name, while *sāmānyalakṣaṇa* is the general feature common to individual objects which is to be grasped by our conceptual thinking, e.g. inference and verbal communication, and which is a concept or a name itself.

I favour this second interpretation. According to it, Diṅnāga's understanding of self-mark and generality-mark differs from the Abhidharmika theory, which follows more closely the first interpretation. This indeed is the innovation in Diṅnāga's new system. The Abhidharmika holds that a *dharma* is the bearer of both specific and general marks. Diṅnāga's view is that the 'marks' are not types of properties of tropes at all, but rather kinds of similarity relation among them. Indeed, it would not be correct to say that a trope 'possesses' an object or a property, as these have here been defined. The relation, rather, is one of constitution. An *object* possesses a property if it intersects with it, and objects and properties are both *constituted* from tropes, but neither stands in the possession relation to its constituents.

Diṅnāga says that self-marked objects are objects of perception, but are not conceptually or linguistically constructed. We need not infer from this that he is introducing a notion of uninterpreted data of pure sensation. The ineffability and unconstructedness of objects might be a simple consequence of the fact that language and conceptual construction are vehicles for the relation of exact similarity. Language and thought group tropes along the axis of generality and not on the axis of concurrence: they 'construct' properties, not objects. As to being the pure objects of perception, this does not imply that tropes are mere sense-data either. The alternative is to take Diṅnāga as asserting that perception is the vehicle for grouping tropes along the axis of concurrence. For as we can see from the passage cited, Diṅnāga thinks that we perceive an aggregate when our perception is caused by a multitude, and that this multiple causation does not involve conceptual construction. Perception is a non-constructive, purely causal, process of grouping tropes via concurrence into objects. Inference is a conceptual process of grouping tropes via exact similarity into properties.

4.4 THE ROLE OF LANGUAGE IN CONCEPTUAL CONSTRUCTION

Diṅnāga's view of conceptual construction is thoroughly linguistic:

> What then is this conceptual construction? – the association of name, genus, etc. (I 3d)
>
> In the case of proper names, a thing is expressed as discriminated by a name; e.g. 'Ḍittha'. In the case of universal-terms, [it is] as discriminated by a universal; e.g. 'the cow'. In the case of quality-terms, [it is] as discriminated by a quality; e.g. 'the white thing'. In the case of action-terms, [it is] as discriminated by an action; e.g. 'the cook'. In the case of substance-terms, [it is] as discriminated by a substance; e.g. 'the staff-bearer' or 'the horned'.
>
> Here, some maintain that what is expressed is a thing discriminated by a relationship. Others hold that a thing is expressed as discriminated by nothing but empty (*arthaśūnya* – 'meaningless') words. [In any case,] that which is devoid of such conceptual construction is perception.

Conceptual construction is the association of an object with a feature in tandem with the application to that object of a noun-phrase. One conceptually constructs whenever one judges that an object possesses a feature. A 'feature' here is any group collected together by a similarity relation; it is a predicative notion spanning all the categories in the Vaiśeṣika type hierarchy.[11] Conceptual construction is a linguistic activity, because features are those classes whose extensions are fixed by noun-phrases. A noun-phrase collects together objects on the basis of an exact similarity relation.

Diṅnāga sometimes writes in a nominalist vein, taking the order of explanation here to run *from* word *to* collection:

> One must necessarily admit that what an object has in common belongs to the particular object. But it is not in the object. Therefore,
>
> the word itself is the thing that objects have in common. (V 10b)
>
> The instantiations such as the pot and so forth are similar owing to their being expressible by the word 'real', but not owing to any intrinsic property of the objects named.

We should then say that objects have exactly similar tropes because denoted by the same noun-phrase. But whichever order one takes the explanation to flow in, the important point is that language is a vehicle for the relation of exact similarity.

We can now see better why *objects* in Diṅnāga's ontology are inexpressible. To denote an object, a word would have to be able to pick out a concurrence class of tropes, but words always and only pick out exact similarity classes. So words never denote objects.

Might not one argue that it is nevertheless just the role of a proper name to denote particular objects? Diṅnāga himself mentions proper names such as 'Ḍittha', which he says express things possessing names. Can we not say that the name 'Ḍittha' picks out that class of concurrent tropes which constitute Ḍittha? If Diṅnāga is a nominalist about the exact similarity relation, why not also about the relation of concurrence? But this is not Diṅnāga's intention. What he has in mind, perhaps, is rather the use of a name to track an object over a period of time. A proper name is semantically akin to a general term in that its denotation spans any *temporal slice* of an object. That is in fact the grammarians' explanation of the function of proper names within a theory that all terms are general,[12] and it is from grammarians that Diṅnāga borrowed in his philosophy of language.[13] Proper names group temporal slices by the exact similarity relation into a diachronically extended object; their function is not to group tropes into an object at a single time.[14]

Might one not denote objects indirectly, via a suitably large conjunction of noun-phrases? The simple noun-phrase 'lotus' denotes the class of lotuses. The compound noun-phrase 'blue lotus' denotes the class of blue lotuses – a smaller class. Surely if one were to conjoin sufficiently many noun-phrase qualifiers, one would eventually construct a compound noun-phrase which denotes a singleton class containing just one object.

Diṅnāga's argument against this possibility rests on what Nicholas Rescher[15] has called the 'cognitive opacity of real things', the fact that an object has more properties than can ever be cognised. Thus Diṅnāga:

> A thing possessing many properties cannot be cognised in all its aspects by the sense. (I 5ad)
>
> An object has many properties. But we do not become aware of them all through the inferential sign. (II 13ab)
>
> Although that which is expressed by a word has many properties, it is not cognised in its entirety through a word. (V 12ab)

To cognise an object *as such* is to cognise it along with all its properties. A sense-faculty, touch say, informs us only about the tactile properties of the object. So through no one sense-faculty can we perceive all the states of affairs involving the object. Likewise, inferential signs and words inform us only about specific properties of the object, the property with which the sign or word is correlated. So if to cognise an object is to cognise it along with all its properties, then objects cannot in this way be constructed in conception.

Rescher makes out the contrast as one between real and fictional things. Fictional particulars, he says in a nice phrase, are of 'finite cognitive depth'. There is a limit to the amount of new non-generic information one can find out about them. But –

> [w]ith real things, on the other hand, there is no reason in principle why the provision of non-generically idiosyncratic information need ever be terminated. On the contrary, we have every reason to presume these things to be cognitively inexhaustible. A precommitment to description-transcending features – no matter how far description is pushed – is essential to our conception of a real thing. Something whose character was exhaustible by linguistic characterization would thereby be marked as fictional rather than real.

For Diṅnāga, the salient contrast is the one between the self-marked and the generically marked – the objects and properties in his system. Properties are conceptual constructs. They are potential contents of conception because it is possible, in principle, to know everything about them. What this means, if the trope-theoretic analysis of the contrast is the correct one, is that one can in principle know every member of a class of exactly similar tropes – the entire set of blues, for example. (Is *this* really possible? See below.) Objects, on the other hand, are not potential constructs of conception because it is not possible, even in principle, to know everything about them. Again, on the trope-theoretic analysis, what this means is that one cannot know every member of a class of concurrent tropes – all the trope-constituents of this vase, for example.

How then *do* objects enter one's mental life, if not by our constructing them in conception? Diṅnāga's answer is that they are non-conceptually made available to us in perception. The concurrent tropes that comprise an object jointly cause a perception of that object (*ad* I 4ab). Such perception is non-propositional: one sees the blue thing, but not *that* it is blue (I 4cd). Perception is the vehicle for apprehending concurrency, conception the vehicle for apprehending exact similarity.

4.5 THE EXCLUSION THEORY OF MEANING

Diṅnāga's fundamental insight is into the nature of concepts. It is that concepts delimit by exclusion. The insight is encoded in his theory of meaning:

> That which is based on words is not a means of knowing separate from inference. Because [a word] expresses its own meaning through the exclusion of others. (V 1)
>
> A word excludes others. (V 11d)
>
> A word indeed speaks about things qualified by the exclusion of others. (*ad* V 36)

The role of a word is to exclude what is other. A more traditional Indian theory of meaning associates terms with 'bases for application' (*pravṛtti-nimitta*). The basis of a term is a universal (or quality or motion), and it is in virtue of an object's possessing that universal that the term is able to denote it. Terms denote basis-possessors. Diṅnāga, the reductionist, does not discard this theory so much as reconstruct it. He finds a new entity, defined in terms of the primitive relations of exclusion and otherness, which can act as a proxy for a universal (*ad* V 36):

> Only under our hypothesis are the properties of a universal established, namely, unity, permanence and the condition of belonging to each member of a class. An exclusion of contrary meanings has unity, because it is undivided. It has permanence, because its substratum is not destroyed. And it has the condition of belonging to each member in a class, because it is cognised in every object in the word's extension. Therefore, since it is free from problems and possessed of excellent virtues, it is only things that are qualified by the exclusion of contrary things that a word denotes.

The universal blueness (U, say) has as its extension the class of blue objects. Trope-theoretically, it is a class of classes – the class of all concurrency classes containing a blue trope. Since the property blue (P, say) is the class of blue tropes, U is the class of all concurrency classes intersecting with P:

$$U = \{X : X \cap P \neq \varnothing\}$$

The challenge is to construct these classes using only the relations of exclusion and otherness. Let us begin by defining a new trope-theoretic property, non-blue – the property comprising what is other than blue. 'Non-' is here a term-forming negation, a functor from terms for things to terms for what is other than those things. Non-blue is the class of all tropes other than any blue trope. Now we form the class of all classes non-blue excludes – the class of all classes non-intersecting with non-blue. This is the class Diṅnāga identifies as the semantic value of the term 'blue'.[16] It is the *anyāpoha*, the exclusion of what is other. If we follow the usual convention of signifying the semantic value of a term by placing that term within double brackets,[17] then Diṅnāga's exclusion theory of meaning for terms is:

$$[\![\text{blue}]\!] = \{X : X \cap \text{non-P} = \varnothing\}$$

According to Diṅnāga, semantic values of this type can replace our talk of universals. What is the relation between a universal and such a semantic value? The trick is to see that the semantic value $[\![\text{non-blue}]\!]$ is now the class $\{X : X \cap P = \varnothing\}$. So, since every class X either does or does not intersect with P, this class is the complement of U. U and $[\![\text{non-blue}]\!]$ exclude each other, and together partition the domain. The universal blueness is that which excludes the semantic value of 'non-blue'. Trope-theoretically, the point is that 'exclusion of others' is a device for switching between classes of objects and classes of properties.

Diṅnāga has to be able to show that his new theory of meaning for primitive terms can sustain a compositional account of the meaning of complex terms. His detailed explanation of the grammatical operations called 'agreement' (*sāmānādhikaraṇya*) and 'qualification' (*vaiśiṣṭya*) is a response to this demand. Suppose we introduce a concatenation of terms, 'B^A'. This stands for 'A-which-is-B': for example 'blue^lotus' stands for 'lotus-which-is-blue'. Here 'B' qualifies or restricts 'A'. Diṅnāga gives the obvious composition rule governing concatenation:

> Although the words 'blue lotus' do differ in the complements that they exclude, the words are in grammatical agreement in virtue of the conjunction of the respective complement-exclusions in one object. This conjunction serves the purpose of pointing out particulars in each word's extension, like a crow standing on a house. (*ad* V 14)

So $[\![B\hat{\ }A]\!] = [\![B]\!] \cap [\![A]\!]$ – 'blue lotus' excludes what is excluded by 'blue' *and* what is excluded by 'lotus'.

What is the relation between the semantic values of 'lotus' and 'blue lotus'? The phrase 'blue lotus' excludes everything the phrase 'lotus' excludes and more – its meaning is *narrower*. So $[\![A]\!] \subseteq [\![B\hat{\ }A]\!]$, and likewise $[\![B]\!] \subseteq [\![B\hat{\ }A]\!]$. Diṅnāga, of course, will express this relationship as an exclusion:

$$[\![A]\!] \cap \text{non-}[\![B\hat{\ }A]\!] = \varnothing$$ [18]

With this relation, one can order terms by extension:

> A term does not exclude terms of wider extension, terms of narrower extension or coextensive terms, even though they differ from it. A wider term does not exclude its narrower terms, because it creates anticipation for them alone. Neither does it entail them, because uncertainty arises concerning which of its narrower terms is applicable. In either case the two terms can apply to the same set of objects. A narrower term precludes the objects denoted by other narrower terms because of hostility. Because particulars of another wider term are contradicted by the word *śiṃśapā*'s own wider term. The one term does not preclude the other directly, because the narrower term is not synonymous with the wider term. If this were the case, then it would not preclude other narrower terms. (V 25–29)

The implication is that there is a branching hierarchy of terms derived from relations of exclusion among their extensions. Indeed, it was to recover this hierarchy that we took exclusion to be a relation of non-intersection. A term excludes another term if it is governed by a branching node also governing

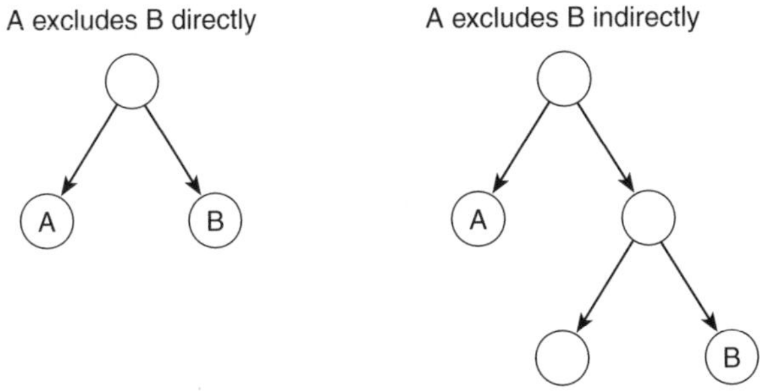

Figure 4.1 Diṅnāga's hierarchy of terms.

the other term, and the exclusion might be direct or indirect (see Figure 4.1).[19]

The progressive addition of more and more qualifiers leads to a honing in of the description onto a narrower and narrower class of objects – the exclusion of more and more of the domain. But although one can continually refine one's description, one can never describe a single object – objects are linguistically obscure. And so the process of description is *asymptotic*, reaching ever nearer, but never actually touching the world of objects.

Diṅnāga, recall, argues that objects cannot be constructed in conception because their properties are unlimited. It might seem, however, that universals are in no better shape than objects in this regard, for universals too are potentially infinite classes. Indeed, Diṅnāga's highly influential criticism of the traditional theory of meaning, again derived from Bhartṛhari, rests on this point.[20] He says that a general term cannot denote merely the objects, because they are potentially 'infinite' in number, and if one thinks that the term's meaning is fixed only with reference to some finite class of objects, one will be unable to explain the potential of that term to 'wander' onto new objects (V 2ab). The new theory needs to be immune to these difficulties:

> If a term expresses its own meaning by excluding other meanings, why do the faults mentioned above not arise?
>
> > Because a term is not observed to apply to objects in the extension of a contrary term, and because it is observed to apply to members of its own extension, it is easy to connect [the term to its meaning], and the term is not errant in its meaning. (V 34)
>
> Association and dissociation are the two ways that a word expresses its object. They consist respectively in applying to what is alike and in not applying to what is unalike. It is not necessary to say that a word applies to every instance of what is alike, because in some cases it is not possible to express an extension that is unlimited. But it is possible to say that it does not occur in the unalike – although it too is unlimited – simply on

the basis of its not being observed to apply to any unalike instance. For this reason, because a term is not observed to apply to anything other than that to which it is related, its expression of its own object is said to be a negative inference.

Diṅnāga's use of the method of association and dissociation (*anvaya-vyatireka*), as well as his concepts of what is alike and what is unalike (*tulya, atulya*) are very important, and we will see them playing a large part in his theory of inference (Chapter 4.7). He concedes that likeness classes cannot be determined directly, but argues that they can be determined via an indirect route. The idea is that unlikeness classes can be determined by mere non-observation, and a likeness class is then fixed as the complement of an unlikeness class. This doctrine has puzzled scholars for understandable reasons. As a principle of inductive reasoning, it looks disastrous. Is Diṅnāga really saying that one is entitled to believe that all *F*s are *G* as long as one has *not* observed an *F* which is non-*G*?

What we need here is a principle of epistemic closure. Such a principle is a rule on what else one knows if one knows some one thing. Knowledge is often said to be deductively closed, meaning that one knows all the deductive consequences of anything one knows. Thus, if S knows that *p*, and *p* entails *q*, then S knows that *q*. Diṅnāga rejects the following closure principle: if S knows that *x* is in the extension of 'A', and *x* is like *y*, then S knows that *y* is in the extension of 'A'. If this were valid, then one would know the extension of 'A' simply by knowing some one member of it. Of course, a stronger rule is valid: if S knows that *x* is in the extension of 'A', and *S knows that x* is like *y*, then S knows that *y* is in the extension of 'A'. The problem with this principle of epistemic closure is that it applies only to objects known to be like *x* – but the whole problem is that the extension of 'A' contains too many objects to be individually known. What Diṅnāga does endorse is the indirect closure principle: if S knows that *x* is in the extension of 'A', and *x* is *unlike y*, then S knows that *y* is *not* in the extension of 'A'. Again, it would not do to require that one *knows that y* is unlike *x* – that is the point of Diṅnāga's insistence that non-observation is the basis of our knowledge of the counter-extension of 'A'. One knows that 'A' does not apply to *y* because *y* is unlike *x*, not because one knows that *y* is unlike *x*. If this indirect closure principle is true, then one can know the counter-extension of 'A', and so by implication (the 'negative inference' of contraposition), know the extension of 'A'.

The problem with all this is that it is difficult to see why the negative epistemic principle should be true, but not the corresponding positive principle. What seems right is one cannot have the capacity to recognise some one instance as blue without thereby having the capacity to recognise any blue instance. Such a person knows what it is to count something as blue. But this does not imply the much stronger thesis, that to be acquainted with one blue instance is to be acquainted with all, or that acquaintance with every instance of blue is necessary for the possession of the concept. The best one can say is that there is a serious lacuna in Diṅnāga's epistemological theory here; indeed, it is a hole later Buddhist epistemologists would attempt to fill (see Chapter 4.9).

4.6 SENTENCE MEANING

Suppose I utter the sentence 'A lotus is blue.' What thereby have I said? The classical Vaiśeṣika answer is that I have described a fragment of the inherence hierarchy, namely, the fragment in which a certain complex substance is inhered in by the universal lotus-hood, and also by a quality blue which in turn is inhered in by the universal blueness:

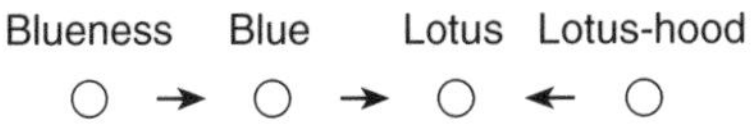

Diṅnāga has a quite different idea. Borrowing again from Bhartṛhari, he asserts that the meaning of a sentence is a *pratibhā* – an immediate consciousness of a single unity, a holistic 'flash of understanding'.[21] One listens to the words being uttered in succession, and suddenly there comes a moment (perhaps even before the whole sentence has been finished) when one 'gets the point' of what is being said. Bhartṛhari says:[22]

> When the [word] meanings are understood by separating [the words from the sentence], there arises a *pratibhā* which is different [from the meanings of the words]. That [*pratibhā*] effected by the word meanings is called the meaning of the sentence.

Bhartṛhari is a sentence-holist. Sentence meanings are, he claims, the fundamental units of meaning. Words, the phonetic constituents of sentences, are assigned meanings by 'extraction' (*apoddhāra*), a process of analysis, synthesis and abstraction, disclosing correlations between recurring sentence-constituents and recurring meaning-ingredients. And Diṅnāga borrows this doctrine without significant modification:

> The meaning of the word has been clarified after extracting the word from the sentence. The meaning of the sentence, which is called *pratibhā*, first arises by dint of that [word meaning]. (V 46)

There is no philosophical tension between the doctrine that words acquire meaning only in the context of sentences, and the doctrine that the meaning of the sentence is a function of the meaning of the parts.[23] The point has already arisen in connection with the relation between simple and compound noun-phrases. Diṅnāga is a compositionalist; indeed he explicitly formulates the relevant composition rule relating the meaning of the compound to the meaning of its components. He sees no tension between this and the doctrine that component meanings are analytical fictions. Referring to the compound 'blue lotus,' he says:

> But given that that which is expressed by the compound 'blue lotus' is neither the quality blue nor the substance lotus, how is it that the expression 'blue lotus' expresses a single object, namely, one that is both blue and a lotus?
>
> > Since the thing expressed is a complex entity, neither blue in isolation nor a lotus in isolation is expressed. (V 15ad)
>
> From the two words, 'blue' together with 'lotus,' one is aware of the two things combined, but one is not aware of them individually. The two words functioning as elements of a complex expression individually
>
> > have no meaning, just as the individual phonetic components of a word have no meaning. (V 15cd)
>
> The situation here is like that of the word *nīla* ['blue'], which is meaningful despite the fact that the individual phonetic components *nī* and *la* are meaningless.

What we want, then, is a composition rule for sentence meaning, a rule which shows how the semantic value of a sentence is a function of the semantic values of the individual words. Diṅnāga, unfortunately, is not very informative here. As Masaaki Hattori[24] has commented, '[i]t is understood that Diṅnāga was primarily concerned with the meaning of a word when he formulated the *apoha* theory. Regarding the meaning of a sentence, he simply accepted Bhartṛhari's doctrine, without discussing the problem how the meaning of a single word is related to the meaning of the sentence.' I do not think, however, that it is too difficult to discover a composition rule of the kind we are looking for.

Diṅnāga thinks that subject–predicate sentences involve a suppressed use of the restrictive particle *only* (Sanskrit: *eva*).[25] The particle *only* can be attached to either the subject or the predicate position, and its explicit insertion in one rather than another place *disambiguates* the sentence. For example, beginning with 'A lotus is blue', we can disambiguate it either as 'Only a lotus is blue' or else as 'A lotus is only blue'. Having (re)inserted the particle *only*, one can appeal to a theory about the semantics of *only* to discover the sentence meaning.

Inserting *only* into a sentence does not add new semantic content. Instead, like brackets or commas, its function is to make manifest and unambiguous a semantic content (the Sanskrit grammarians say that it is a *dyotaka*, a 'manifester' of meaning, not a *vācaka*, an 'expressor' of meaning). Diṅnāga's theory, strikingly, is that *only* constructions are explicit devices for the expression of 'exclusion of others'. Take the sentence 'Only a lotus is blue.' It means that nothing but a lotus is blue, that blueness is excluded from what is other than a lotus. The phrase 'other than a lotus' is a noun-phrase denoting objects that stand in the unlikeness relation with lotuses. As before, let us write such a noun-phrase 'non-lotus'. The equivalence then is between (1a) and (1b):

1a. only S is P.
1b. no non-S is P.

What is the meaning of a statement when *only* is inserted in the predicate position? The natural reading of 'A lotus is only blue' is as stating that no lotus is non-blue:

2a. S is only P.
2b. no S is non-P.

The symmetry between the disambiguations in (1) and (2) is appealing. Indeed, it seems to be implied by the metarule of the pre-Pāṇinian grammarian Vyāḍi: 'restriction should be made to the item other than that which is accompanied by the particle *only*.'[26] It is important, however, to note that constructions such as (1b) and (2b) lack existential import. For example, one can say 'no non-members will be admitted' without saying anything about what will happen to members. The sentence conversationally *implicates*, but does not *state*, that members will be admitted.

There is another reading of (2a). It can be read as asserting that some S is P. I'm not sure that the English word *only* has this emphatic reading, but the Sanskrit particle *eva*, like the Hindi particle *hī*, certainly does. It is often best translated as 'really', 'indeed' or 'just'. This is the reading to take when the sentence does have existential import. If one asserts 'Mosquitoes are indeed malarial,' what one asserts is that mosquitoes are *not non*-malarial. One does not assert that *no* mosquito is non-malarial. So when *eva* takes the predicate position, a second possible reading is:

3a. S is indeed P.
3b. S is not non-P.

If 'non-' is a complement-like negation (so that everything is either P or non-P), then the following equivalencies will hold:[27]

1b.	no non-S is P	all P are S.
2b.	no S is non-P	all S are P.
3b.	S is not non-P	some S is P.

The meaning of a sentence, then, is in general the exclusion of one class from what is other than a second class. Exclusion is the non-intersection relation, a class excluding every non-intersecting class. So (1b) asserts that non-S excludes P, and (2b) that S excludes non-P. (3b) is different – it asserts that S does not exclude P. In set theory, the three truth-conditions are (1) that $S \cap P = P$, (2) that $S \cap P = S$, and (3) that $S \cap P \neq \varnothing$.

Now that we know what the meaning of a sentence actually is, we can go back to our initial question – what is the relationship between word and sentence meaning? The first thing to see is that there is a systematic connection between the meaning of the sentence 'A lotus is blue' and the meaning of the compound noun-phrase 'blue lotus'. Diṅnāga's composition rule for compound noun-phrases is that the semantic value of a compound is the intersection of the semantic values of its constituents. In his terms, 'blue lotus' excludes what is excluded by 'blue' *and* what is excluded by 'lotus'. Now the sentence 'A lotus is blue' makes an assertion about this class of objects. It asserts either that the class is identical to the class of blue objects, or to the class of lotuses, or is non-empty. And so truth-values are assigned to sentences as follows:

1. $[\![\text{only S is P}]\!] = T$ iff $[\![S \wedge P]\!] = [\![P]\!]$.
2. $[\![\text{S is only P}]\!] = T$ iff $[\![S \wedge P]\!] = [\![S]\!]$.
3. $[\![\text{S is indeed P}]\!] = T$ iff $[\![S \wedge P]\!] \neq \varnothing$.

In connection with the third of these composition rules, we may note an expositor's comment that when a word is uttered alone, the verb 'there exists . . .' is understood.[28] So the compound noun-phrase 'blue lotus' uttered alone means the same as 'there exists a blue lotus', and this is the meaning assigned to 'a lotus is indeed blue'. These three truth-clauses discharge the obligation to show how ordinary subject–predicate sentences are reduced in the language of exclusion.

4.7 CONDITIONS ON RATIONAL EXTRAPOLATION

Diṅnāga uses his new theoretical framework in a fundamental restructuring of the early Nyāya analysis of reasoned extrapolation and inference. Recall that analysis (Chapter 1.6–7). It is an inference from likeness and unlikeness. In the one case, some object is inferred to have the target property on the grounds that it is 'like' a paradigmatic example. The untasted grain of rice is inferred to be cooked on the grounds that it is in the same pan as a test grain which is found to be cooked. In the other case, the object is inferred to have the target property on the grounds that it is 'unlike' an example lacking the target property. Likeness and unlikeness are matters of sharing or not sharing some property, the reason property or evidence grounding the inference. Examples are either 'positive' – having both the reason and the target property, or 'negative' – lacking both. Extrapolation is the process of extrapolating a property from one object to another on the basis of a likeness or unlikeness between them.

The difficulty is that not every such extrapolation is rational or warranted. The extrapolation of a property from one object to another is warranted only when the two objects are *relevantly* alike or *relevantly* unalike. (In what follows, 'alike' and 'unalike' are used when the adjectives occur in the predicate – the statement 'A and B are alike' is synonymous with 'A is like B'.) That two objects are both blue does not warrant an extrapolation of solidity from one to the other; neither can we infer that they are different in respect to solidity because they are of different colours. What one needs, then, is a theory of *relevant* likeness or unlikeness, a theory, in other words, of the type of property (the reason property) two objects must share if one is to be licensed to extrapolate another property (the target property) from one to the other.

This is exactly what Diṅnāga does in his celebrated theory of the 'reason with three characteristics'. Diṅnāga's thesis is that relevant likeness is, once again, an exclusion relation. Two objects are relevantly alike with respect to the extrapolation of a property S just in case they share a property excluded from what is other than S. In other words, a reason property H for the extrapolation of a target property S is a property no wider in extension than S (assuming again that 'non-' is such that $H \cap \text{non-}S = \varnothing$ iff $H \subseteq S$). Here is the crucial passage in the *Collection on Knowing*:

> The phrase [from II 1b] 'through a reason that has three characteristics' must be explained.
>
> > [A proper reason must be] present in the site of inference and in what is like it and absent in what is not. (II 5cd)
>
> The object of inference is a property-bearer qualified by a property. After observing [the reason] there, either through perception or through inference, one also establishes in a general manner [its] presence in some or all of the same class. Why is that? Because the restriction is such that [the reason] is present *only* in what is alike, there is no restriction that it is *only* present. But in that case nothing is accomplished by saying that [the reason] is 'absent in what is not'. This statement is made in order to determine that [the reason], absent in what is not [like the site of inference], is not in what is other than or incompatible with the object of inference. Here then is the reason with three characteristics from which we discern the reason-bearer.

Diṅnāga's important innovation is to take the notions of likeness and unlikeness in extrapolation to be relative to the *target* property rather than the *reason* property. Two objects are 'alike' if they both have, or both lack, the target property. Two objects are 'unalike' if one has and the other lacks the target property. We want to know if our object – the 'site' of the inference – has the target property or not. What we do know is that our object has some other property, the reason property. So what is the formal feature of that reason property, in virtue of which its presence in our object determines the presence or absence of the target property? The formal feature, Diṅnāga claims, is that the reason property is present only in what is like, and absent in whatever is unlike, our object.

This can happen in one of two ways. It happens if the reason property is absent from everything not possessing the target property and present only in things possessing the target property. Then we can infer that our object too possesses the target property. It can also happen if the reason property is absent from everything possessing the target property and present only in things not possessing the target property. Then we can infer that our object does not possess the target property.

Call the class of objects which are like the site of the inference the 'likeness class', and the class of objects unlike the site the 'unlikeness class' (Diṅnāga's terms are *sapakṣa* and *vipakṣa*). Interpreters have traditionally taken the likeness class to be the class of objects which possess the target property, and the unlikeness class to be the class of objects which do not possess the target property. I read Diṅnāga differently. I take his use of the terms 'likeness' and 'unlikeness' here at face value, and identify the likeness class with the class of things *in the same state vis-à-vis* the target property as the site of the inference. We do not know in advance what that state is, but neither do we need to. The pattern of distribution of the reason property tells us what we can infer – that the site has the target property, that it lacks it, or that we can infer nothing. My approach has several virtues, chief among which is that it preserves the central idea of likeness as a *relation* between objects rather than, as with the traditional interpretation, referring to a *property* of objects. I think it also avoids many of the exegetical problems that have arisen in the contemporary literature with regard to Diṅnāga's theory.

One of the traditional problems is whether the site of the inference is included in the likeness class or not.[29] If the likeness class is the class of objects possessing the target property, then to include it seems to beg the question the inference is trying to resolve: does the site have that property or not? But to exclude it implies that the union of the likeness and unlikeness classes does not exhaust the universe (the site cannot, for obvious reasons, be unlike itself). So one is left with two disjoint domains, and an apparently insuperable problem of induction – how can correlations between the reason property and the target property in one domain be *any* guide to their correlation in another, entirely disjoint, domain?[30]

If we take Diṅnāga's appeal to the idea of likeness at face value, however, the problem simply does not arise. The site of the inference is in the likeness class on the assumption that likeness is a reflexive relation – but that begs no question, for we do not yet know whether the likeness class is the class of things which possess the target property, or the class of things which do not possess it. It is the class of things which are in the same state *vis-à-vis* the target property as the inferential site itself. We can, if needs be, refer to objects 'like the site but not identical to it'; or we can take likeness to be non-reflexive, and refer instead, if needs be, to 'the site *and* objects like it' – but this is a matter only of semantics, with no philosophical interest.

Another of the traditional problems with Diṅnāga's account is an alleged logical equivalence between the second and third conditions.[31] The second condition states that the reason property be present *only* in what is alike. The third condition states that it be absent in what is not. But if it is present *only* in what is alike, it must be absent in what is not; and if it is absent in what is not alike, it must be present *only* in what is. Now it is clear that Diṅnāga's reason for inserting the particle *only* into his formula is to prevent a possible misunderstanding. The misunderstanding would be that of taking the second condition to assert that the reason property must be present in all like objects. That would be too strong a condition, ruling out any warranted inferences in which the reason property is strictly narrower than the target. Recalling our discussion of the meaning of the particle *only*, we can see that it is also one of the two readings of the statement:

> In what is alike, there is only the presence [of the reason]

where the particle *only* is inserted into the predicate position. Diṅnāga eliminates this unwanted reading of the second condition, but he does so in a disastrous way. He eliminates it by inserting the particle into the subject position:

> Only in what is alike, there is the presence [of the reason].

The reason this is disastrous is that it makes the second condition logically equivalent to the third. Recall, however, that when *only* is in predicate position, there are still two readings. The reading one needs to isolate is the second of these two readings:

> In what is alike, there is *indeed* the presence [of the reason].

That is, the reason is present in *some* of what is alike.

Accordingly, the theory is this. The extrapolation of a property S to an object is grounded by the presence in that object of any property X such that X excludes non-S but not S. A reason property for S is any member of the class

$$\{X : X \cap S \neq \emptyset \ \& \ X \cap \text{non-S} = \emptyset\}$$

The clause 'but not S' (the second of Diṅnāga's three conditions) has a clear function now. It is there to rule out properties which exclude *both* non-S *and* S. Such properties are properties 'unique' to the particular object which is the site of the inference, and Diṅnāga does not accept as warranted any extrapolation based on them. I will look at his motives in the next section.

Reason properties are non-empty subsets of the properties whose extrapolation they ground. If two objects are 'alike' in sharing a property, and one has a second property of wider extension than the first, then so does the second. Inductive extrapolation, in effect, is grounded in the contraposed universal generalisation 'where the reason, so the target.' A difficult problem of induction remains – how can one come to know, or justifiably believe, that two properties stand in such a relation without surveying all their instances? Diṅnāga has no adequate answer to this problem. Dharmakīrti, Diṅnāga's brilliant reinterpreter, does. His answer is that when the relation between the two properties is one of causal or metaphysical necessity, the observation of a few instances is sufficient to warrant our belief that it obtains (Chapter 4.9). Diṅnāga, however, is not interested in such questions. For him, the hard philosophical question is that of discovering the conditions for rational extrapolation. It is another, for him quite secondary, issue whether those conditions can ever be known to obtain.

To sum up, Diṅnāga's three conditions on the reason are:

(1)	Presence in the site *a*	attachment	*(pakṣadharmatā)*
(2)	Presence (only) in what is like *a*	association	*(anvaya)*
(3)	Absence in what is unlike *a*	dissociation	*(vyatireka)*

If we take these conditions to be independent, it follows that there are exactly seven kinds of extrapolative inferential fallacy – three ways for one of the conditions to fail, three ways for two conditions to fail, and one way for all three conditions to fail.[32] So the new theory puts the concept of a fallacy on a more formal footing. A fallacy is no longer an interesting but essentially *ad hoc* maxim on rationality. It is now a formal failing of the putative reason to stand in the correct extrapolation-grounding relation. One way for the reason to fail is by not attaching to the site at all, thereby failing to ground any extrapolation of other properties to it. This is a failure of the first condition. Another way for the reason to fail is by 'straying' onto unlike objects, thereby falsifying the third condition. The presence of one property cannot prove the presence of another if it is sometimes present where the other one is not. (It can, however, prove the absence of the other if it is present *only* where the other is not – and then the *absence* of the first property is a proof of the *presence* of the second.) We might then think of the third condition as a 'no counter-example' condition, a counter-example to the extrapolation-warranting relation of subsumption being an object where the allegedly subsumed property is present along with the absence of its alleged subsumer. An extrapolation is grounded just as long as there are no counter-examples.

4.8 REASONING FROM SPECIFICS

I have said that an extrapolation-grounding property is a non-empty subproperty – a property narrower in extension than the property being extrapolated, and resident at least in the object to which that property is being extrapolated. The sweet smell of a lotus is a ground for extrapolating that it has a fragrance; its being a blue lotus is a ground for extrapolating its being a lotus. Extrapolation is a move from the specific to the general, from species to genus, from conjunction to conjunct. Extrapolation is a move upwards in the hierarchy of kinds (the hierarchy which the Vaiśeṣikas explained in terms of their partial order in the level of universals, Chapter 3.4). This model of extrapolation works well in most cases, but what happens at the extremes? The extreme in one direction is a most general property of all, a property possessed by everything. Existence or 'reality', if it is a property, is a property like this, and the theory entails that existence is always extrapolatable – the inference '*a* is, because *a* is *F*' is always warranted. Diṅnāga's theory faces a minor technical difficulty here. Since everything exists, then everything is 'like' the site of the inference (in the same state as the site with respect to existence), and the unlikeness class is empty. So Diṅnāga has to be able to maintain that his third condition – absence of the reason property in every unlike object – is satisfied when there are no unlike objects. The universal quantifier must have no existential import. His innovative distinction between inference 'for oneself' (*svārthānumāna*) and inference 'for others' (*parārthānumāna*) is a help here. It is the distinction between the logical preconditions for warranted extrapolation and the debate-theoretic exigencies of persuasion. While it might be useful, even necessary, to be able to cite a supporting negative example if one's argument is to carry conviction and meet the public norms on believable inference, there is no corresponding requirement that the unlikeness class be non-empty if an extrapolation is to be warranted.

What happens at the other extreme? Extrapolation is a move from the more specific to the less specific, and the limit is the case when the reason property is entirely specific to the site of the inference. There is no doubt that Diṅnāga thinks that extrapolation breaks down at this limit. He calls such reason properties 'specific indeterminate' (*asādhāraṇānaikāntika*), and classifies them as bogus reasons.[33] Indeed it is the entire function of his second condition to rule out such properties. That is why the second condition insists that the reason property must be present in an object like the site. This condition is an addition to the first, that the reason property be present in the site – it demands that the reason be present in some other object like, but not identical to, the site. Diṅnāga's example in the *Collection on Knowing* (II 7d) is:

> [Thesis] Sound is non-eternal.
> [Reason] Because it is audible.

In the *Chart of Reasons* (5cd–7a), he gives another example:

> [Thesis] Sound is eternal.
> [Reason] Because it is audible.

What is the difference? In fact, the difference between these two examples holds the key to what Diṅnāga thinks is wrong. The property audibility, something specific to sound, does not determine whether sound is eternal or non-eternal. In either case, audibility is absent from what is unlike sound (because it is unique to sound), but also from what is like sound (except for sound itself). This symmetry in the distribution of the reason property undermines its capacity to discriminate between truth and falsity. To put it another way, if we take the universal quantifier to range over everything except the site of the inference, sound, then it is true both that everything audible is eternal and that everything audible is non-eternal – both are true only because there are no audibles in the range of the quantifier.

This seems to be Diṅnāga's point, but it is not very satisfactory. Sound *is* either eternal or non-eternal, and so audibility *is* a subproperty of one or the other. One and only one of the above universal quantifications is true when the quantifier is *unrestricted*. In any case, just why is it that we should not reason from the specific properties of a thing? We do it all the time. Historical explanations are notoriously singular – unrepeated historical events are explained by specific features of their context. Diṅnāga, it seems, is like the follower of the deductive-nomological model in insisting on repeatability as a criterion of explanation. What about mundane cases such as this one: the radio has stopped because I have unplugged it? Being unplugged by me is a property specific to the radio, and yet the form of the explanation seems unapproachable. Perhaps, however, what one should say is that the explanatory property is 'being unplugged', and not 'being unplugged by me', and the explanation rests on the generalisation 'whenever a radio is unplugged, it stops.' So then the restriction is not to any property specific to the site, but only to those which are not merely tokens of some more general explanatory property. And yet there are still intuitively rational but specific inferences – that salt is soluble in water because it has a certain chemical structure, that helium is inert because it has a certain atomic number, flying creatures fly because they have wings. Why shouldn't the specific properties of a thing be implicated in inferences of its other properties?

What we see here is Diṅnāga's adherence to a strictly inductivist model of extrapolation. The specific property audibility does not ground an extrapolation of eternality or non-eternality because there can be no inductive evidence for the extrapolation. Inductive evidence takes the form of objects in the likeness and unlikeness classes known to have or not to have the reason. One might think that one does have at least 'negative' evidence, for one knows that audibility is absent from any object in the unlikeness class. So why can one not infer from the fact that audibility is absent in unlike objects that it must be present in like objects? The answer is that one can indeed make that inference, but it does not get one very far. For we must recall again the way these classes are defined – as classes of objects like or unlike the site with respect to eternality. We do not know whether the site is eternal or non-eternal, and in consequence we do not know whether unlike things are things which are non-eternal or eternal. So while we have plenty of examples of eternal inaudibles and non-eternal inaudibles, we still do not know which are the 'like' ones and which the 'unlike'.

The explanation of salt's solubility by its specific chemical structure exemplifies a quite different model of explanation. It is a theoretical explanation resting on the postulates of physical chemistry. It is from theory, not from observation, that one infers that having an NaCl lattice structure is a sub-property of being soluble. Similarly, within the context of suitable theories about the nature of sound and secondary qualities, one might well be able to infer from sound's being audible to its being non-eternal. Diṅnāga, in spite of his brilliance and originality, could not quite free himself from the old model of inference from sampling. His inclusion of the second condition was a concession to this old tradition. He should have dropped it. Later Buddhists, beginning with Dharmakīrti, did just that – they effectively dropped the second condition by adopting the reading of it that makes it logically equivalent to the third.

4.9 ARE REASON–TARGET RELATIONS LAW-LIKE?

Dharmakīrti (AD 600–660) offers a substantive account of the conditions under which the observation of a sample warrants extrapolation. His claim is that this is so if the reason property is one of three types: an 'effect' reason (*kārya-hetu*), a natural reason (*svabhāva-hetu*), or a reason based on non-observation (*anupalabdhi-hetu*).[34]

In each case, the presence of the reason in some sense *necessitates* the presence of the target. An effect reason is a property whose presence is *causally* necessitated by the presence of the target property – for example, inferring that the mountain has fire on it, because of smoke above it. The reason–target relation is a causal relation. Clearly one can, and later philosophers[35] indeed did, extend this to cover other species of causal inference, such as cases when reason and target are both effects of a common cause. The generalisation 'night follows day' is true, not because day causes night, but because both day and night are caused by the rotation of the earth. An example often cited is the inference of lemon-colour from lemon-taste, when both are products of the same cause, viz. the lemon itself. Still another example is the inference of ashes from smoke: ashes and smoke are both effects of fire. Such an inference has two steps. First, fire is inferred from smoke; second, ash is inferred from fire. The second step, in which we infer an effect from its cause, is possible only because ash is a necessary effect of fire.

A natural reason is one whose presence *metaphysically* necessitates that of the target property, for example the inference that something is a tree because it is a *śiṃśapā* (a species of tree). Dharmakīrti appears to regard the law 'all *śiṃśapā*s are trees' as necessarily true, even if its truth has to be discovered by observation, and thus to anticipate the idea that there are *a posteriori* necessities.[36] He states, surprisingly, that the reason–target relation in such inferences is the relation of identity. Why? Perhaps his idea is that the two properties being-a-*śiṃśapā* and being-a-tree are token-identical, for the particular tree does not have two distinct properties, being-a-*śiṃśapā* and a separate property being-a-tree, any more than something which weighs one kilogram has two properties, having-weight and having-weight-one-kilogram. The properties as types are distinct, but their tokens in individual objects are identical. Trope-theoretically, the point can easily be understood. The very same trope is a member of two properties, one wider in extension than the other, just as the class of blue tropes is a subset of the class of colour tropes. But a blue object does not have two tropes – one from the class of blue tropes and one from the class of colour tropes. It is the self-same trope.

Is absence of evidence evidence of absence? According to Dharmakīrti, non-observation sometimes proves absence: my failure to see an object, when all the conditions for its perception are met, is grounds for an inference that it is not here. The pattern of argument such inferences exemplify was known to the medievals as *argumentum ab ignorantiam*, or an 'argument from ignorance'. The pattern occurs whenever one infers that *p* on the grounds that there is no evidence that *p* is false. Dharmakīrti states that the argument depends on the object's being perceptible, i.e. that all the conditions for its perception (other than its actual presence) are met in the given situation. Douglas Walton, in a major study of arguments from ignorance,[37] claims that they depend for their validity on an implicit conditional premise – if *p* were false, *p* would be known to be false. The characteristics of an argument from ignorance are then a 'lack-of-knowledge' premise – it is not known that not-*p*, and a 'search' premise – if *p* were false, it would be known that not-*p*. The underlying hidden premise mentioned by Dharmakīrti seems to be exactly the one Walton gives: if the object were here, one would see it. The necessity here is *subjunctive*. The argument has a presumptive status – one has a right to presume the conclusion to be true to the extent that one has searched for and failed to find counter-evidence. It is this idea that is strikingly absent in Diṅnāga. Warranted extrapolation depends not on the mere non-observation of counter-examples, but on one's failing to find them in the course of a suitably extensive search.

In each of the three cases, the universal relation between reason and target is a relation not of coincidence, but of necessity – causal, metaphysical or subjunctive. Dharmakīrti's solution to the problem of induction, then, is to claim that observation supports a generalisation only when that generalisation is law-like or necessary. In this, I think he anticipates the idea that the distinction between law-like and accidental generalisations is that only the former support the *counter-factual* 'if the reason property were instantiated here, so would be the target property'. In such a context, let us note, the observation of even a single positive example might sometimes be sufficient to warrant the extrapolation: I infer that any mango is sweet having tasted a single mango; I infer that any fire will burn having once been burnt.

Extrapolation from a number of observed instances is warranted when the reason–target relation is law-like. What Dharmakīrti has succeeded in doing is to describe the conditions under which extrapolation *works* – the conditions under which one's actions, were they to be in accordance with the extrapolation, would meet with success. It is a description of the type of circumstance in which extrapolation is rewarded (i.e. is *true* – if, as it seems, Dharmakīrti has a pragmatic theory of truth[38]). As to how, when or whether one can know that one is in such a circumstance, that is another problem altogether and not one that Dharmakīrti has necessarily to address. For a general theory of rationality issues in conditions of the form 'in circumstances C, it is rational to do ϕ,' or 'in circumstances C, it is rational to believe *p*.' And this is precisely the form Dharmakīrti's conditions take.

4.10 THE PROBLEM OF GROUNDING

The idea of a 'support' or 'ground' (*ālambana*) is a very significant one. We have already seen that Nāgārjuna's philosophical method consists in an attempt to prove the supportlessness of thought. A thought is supported if it has empirical content, if it makes a claim about some objective state of affairs. Supportless thoughts are empty fictions – like the magician's illusion, the dream or the hologram. So an explanation of the notion of 'support' is an account of what it is for mental states to have informational content. Now Diṅnāga, in an early work entitled *The Examination of Supports*,[39] offered an astute definition of the notion of a support for a perceptual experience. He said that the support is both the cause and the content of a thought. An entity is a support

> because it has the form of the awareness itself and because it is the causal condition of the awareness. (ĀP 6cd)

Something is the support of a thought only if it satisfies the following 'matching' condition:

> An entity *x* supports a thought *y* iff
>
> (i) *x* is among the set of causes of *y*, and
> (ii) *x* is in the representational content of *y*.

A hallucination has a representational content (for example, dagger-like), but is caused, not by any dagger, but by aberrances of the perceptual system. The same is true of a perception of a rainbow – it is caused, not by great arcs of colour in the sky, but by droplets of water. If a thought is to be supported, there must be a *match* between its cause and its content. The object mentioned in the causal explanation of a thought's occurrence must be alike in form with what is represented in its content.[40]

In the *Examination of Supports*, Diṅnāga's aim is to defend the Abhidharmika thesis that thought is not supported by anything external, but by 'internal' objects of awareness. While Mādhyamika argues that nothing of the sort which appears *in* thought is relevant to the causal explanation *of* thought (the notion of a support is supportless), the Abhidharmika argues for an explanatory closure within the domain of thought. An adequate causal explanation of the arrangement and succession of thoughts can be given without reference to anything external to thought itself. Diṅnāga's double criterion seemed to allow him to draw the same conclusion:

> Those who believe that the supports of the types of awareness such as the visual are external objects propose either that the supports are atoms, since atoms are the material cause of the awareness, or that the supports are collections of atoms, since awareness occurs with the appearance thereof. About that view, I say first of all
>
> > even if atoms are the material cause of the sensory phenomenon, the atoms are not its field of operation (*viṣaya*), because the phenomenon no more has the appearance of atoms than it has the appearance of the sense-faculty. (ĀP 1 a–d)
>
> The so-called 'field of operation' is that whose character awareness ascertains, because it is what causes awareness to arise. But atoms, although they are the material cause of awareness, are not that whose character awareness ascertains, in the same way that the sense-faculty is not that whose character awareness ascertains. And so, to begin with, atoms are not the supports. As for the collection, although it is that whose appearance awareness has,
>
> > the phenomenon does not come from that whose appearance it has. (ĀP 2a)
>
> It is correct that the support is whatever object generates the awareness of its own appearance, for it was taught thus as a causal condition of the occurrence [of awareness]. But the collection is not what generates the awareness of its own appearance,
>
> > because, like the second moon, it does not really exist. (ĀP 2b)
>
> In seeing a second moon, owing to a deficient sense-faculty, although there is the appearance of a second moon, that is not its field of operation. Similarly, a collection, although it is the material cause of awareness, is not the support, because it does not exist.
>
> > Thus neither external object can be the field of operation of awareness. (ĀP 2cd)
>
> The support is neither the external object called the atoms nor the external object called the collection of atoms, because each of these is deficient in some respect.

Cause, but not content, content, but not cause – nothing external can meet the matching condition. An object such as a vase or a table is in composition merely an aggregate of atoms. The atoms no doubt cause the perception as of a vase, but what we *see* is not a cluster of atoms. What we *see* is a solid, extended body, but no such thing is the cause of the perception. But, Diṅnāga goes on to argue, something *internal* can satisfy both conditions simultaneously, namely, that 'internal cognisable form which represents itself as external'. This is how, in his early period, he tries to defend the Abhidharma phenomenalism.

What becomes of the problem of grounding in Diṅnāga's new system, the system of the *Collection on Knowing*? The factorisation of content into non-conceptual perceptual content and non-perceptual conceptual content – and a corresponding factorisation in the domain of things – seems to result in a trivialisation of the notion of a support. Perception is of an object (= a class of concurrent tropes), and caused by the means of apprehending concurrence, viz. multiple sensory contact. Conception is of a property (= a class of exactly similar tropes), and caused by the means of apprehending exact similarity, viz. inference. The new system is structured from the very outset in such a way that there is no substantive problem of matching cause and content. One could be forgiven for thinking that the problem of grounding has been solved (or dissolved) only at the expense of introducing an unbridgeable gap between the domains of perception and conception, domains in order to relate which one would need some notion akin to Dharmakīrti's 'perceptual judgment', a post-perceptual cognition which makes a perceived object *available* to conceptual content.[41]

Diṅnāga, however, is emphatic that there is no special problem of combining objects and properties in judgment, or of repeatedly recognising one and the same object; nor is any new means of knowing needed.[42] And I think he is right to be adamant about this. For we must be careful to distinguish between the claim that perceptual objects are not *constructed* by conception, and the different claim that they are not *available* as contents of conceptual thought. Objects are non-conceptual only in the sense that they are not classes of exactly similar tropes, and so not constructed by conceptual or linguistic operations. It would follow that they are not available to thought only if one thinks of them as being something along the lines of an uninterpretable 'given'. In fact, however, the trope-theoretic analysis shows that we should not think of the objects and properties in Diṅnāga's system as belonging to distinct ontological domains at all. They are simply groupings along different axes in a single two-dimensional space of tropes. Regions in this space are marked out in different ways by perception and conception, but once marked out, they are equally available as contents of judgment.

Between the additive realism of Nyāya-Vaiśeṣika and Diṅnāga's Buddhist reductionism, it would seem that there is profound philosophical disagreement. On the old and intractable problem of persistence and change, especially, there is a strong divergence in inclination, intuition and emphasis. Nyāya-Vaiśeṣika conceives of a stable world whose objects persist by being wholly present at different times and change in the gain, loss and replacement of qualities and motions. Quite different is the world of Diṅnāga's Buddhism, a world of change in which objects are merely tropes gathered into sums, and persistence is a matter only of sequence. In this clash of opposites, can it really be true that one is right and the other wrong? Surely there must be a grain of truth in the intuitions that drive both, a real insight that exaggeration has turned into dogma. This belief in the possibility of philosophical rapprochement is what drives the Jaina search for a rationality of reconciliation. Not least for this reason, Jaina theory has an ineliminable place in Indian philosophical theory. I examine the Jaina analysis in Chapter 5, before turning in Chapter 6 to the problem that has lain before so much of our discussion – is any form of rational activity itself rationally justified? Is the pursuit of reason a reasonable pursuit?

FURTHER READING

Texts

Diṅnāga *c.* AD 480–540, *Pramāṇasamuccaya* (PS, *Collection on Knowing*).
Diṅnāga, *Hetucakraḍamaru* (HC, *Chart of Reasons*).
Dharmakīrti *c.* AD 600–660, *Pramāṇavārttika* (PV, *Commentary on Knowing*).
Dharmakīrti, *Nyāyabindu* (NB).

Metaphysics and epistemology (4.1–3)

1 Masaaki Hattori, *Dignāga, On Perception, being the Pratyakṣa-pariccheda of Dignāga's Pramāṇasamuccaya from the Sanskrit fragments and the Tibetan versions* (Cambridge, Mass.: Harvard University Press, 1968).

2 Richard Hayes, *Dignāga on the Interpretation of Signs* (Dordrecht: Kluwer Academic Publishers, 1988).

3 B. K. Matilal and J. G. D. Evans eds., *Buddhist Logic and Epistemology: Studies in the Buddhist Analysis of Inference and Language* (Dordrecht: Reidel Publishing Company, 1982).

4 Bimal Matilal, *Perception* (Oxford: Clarendon Press, 1986), Chapters 7, 10.

Language, meaning, exclusion (4.4–6)

1 Katsura Shoryu, 'Dignāga and Dharmakīrti on *apoha*,' in E. Steinkellner ed., *Studies in the Buddhist Epistemological Tradition* (Vienna: Österreichische Akademie der Wissenschaften, 1991), pp. 129–146.

2 Hattori Masaaki, 'The Sautrāntika Background of the *apoha* Theory,' in Leslie S. Kawamura and Keith Scott eds., *Buddhist Thought and Civilization: Essays in Honour of Herbert V. Guenther on his Sixtieth Birthday* (Emeryville: Dharma Press, 1977), pp. 47–58.

3 Hattori Masaaki, 'Apoha and Pratibhā,' in M. Nagatomi et al. eds. *Sanskrit and Indian Studies: Essays in Honour of Daniel H. H. Ingalls* (Dordrecht: Reidel Publishing Company, 1980), pp. 61–74.

4 Bimal Matilal, *Perception* (Oxford: Clarendon Press, 1986), Chapter 12.

5 Jonardon Ganeri, 'Dharmakīrti's Semantics for the Particle *eva (only),*' in Shoryu Katsura ed., *Dharmakīrti's Thought and Its Impact on Indian and Tibetan Philosophy* (Vienna: Österreichische Akademie der Wissenschaften, 1999), pp. 101–116.

Extrapolation, the triple condition (4.7–9)

1 Katsura Shoryu, 'Dignāga on *trairūpya*,' *Journal of Indian and Buddhist Studies* 32 (1983), pp. 15–21.

2 Bimal Matilal, 'Buddhist Logic and Epistemology,' in B. K. Matilal and R. D. Evans eds., *Buddhist Logic and Epistemology: Studies in the Buddhist Analysis of Inference and Language* (Dordrecht: Reidel Publishing Company, 1982), pp. 1–30; reprinted in his *The Character of Logic in India* (Albany: State University of New York Press, 1998), Chapter 4.

3 Tom F. Tillemans, 'On sapakṣa,' *Journal of Indian Philosophy* 18 (1990), pp. 53–80.

4 Claus Oetke, *Studies on the Doctrine of trairūpya* (Vienna: Wiener Studien fur Tibetologie und Buddhismuskunde, 1993).

5 Motoi Ono, 'Dharmakīrti on *asāsāraṇānaikāntika*,' in Shoryu Katsura ed., *Dharmakīrti's Thought and Its Impact on Indian and Tibetan Philosophy* (Vienna: Österreichische Akademie der Wissenschaften, 1999), pp. 301–316.

6 Richard Hayes, 'On the Reinterpretation of Dharmakīrti's *svabhāva-hetu*,' *Journal of Indian Philosophy* 15 (1987), pp. 319–332.

5 Rationality, harmony and perspective

5.1 A RATIONALITY OF RECONCILIATION

The rationality of the debating hall is confrontational. It is a winner-takes-all rationality. In the purest form of debate, victory consists in adducing such a reason as proves the truth of one's thesis and so the falseness of one's opponent's. To be sure, in the debating model, the end of reason is the resolution of a conflict. But there are limits on the extent to which that end is in practice achieved. The ancient philosophical controversies – is there permanence or only change? is the soul immortal? is the world finite or infinite? – seem to persist through all argument. They represent a deeper, more embedded level of commitment, intractable to the up-front reasoning of debate and argument. If the end of reason is harmony, then a new model of rationality is required.

The search for a rationality of reconciliation is the programme of the Jaina philosophers in India. There is, they say, a core of truth in every deeply held metaphysical belief. But what more dogmatic philosophers fail to realise is that there are hidden parameters in belief and assertion. The conflict that arises when thesis and antithesis are opposed is a spurious one. It is a conflict based on a failure to recognise that the thesis is true when certain hidden parameters have one set of values, the antithesis true when they have another. Failure to recognise that all assertion is parameterised is now to be exposed as a deep philosophical error. It leads to dogmatism and one-sidedness. It is an error embedded in the ordinary concept of assertion. A new model of rationality is needed, a new method whose function is to subvert the way ordinary language works, a technique which makes explicit the hidden parameters in assertion and so enables the reasoner to harmonise apparently conflicting beliefs. Harmony, the proper goal of reason, follows when we realise that most of the time there is no genuine conflict.

5.2 THE MANY-SIDED NATURE OF THINGS

How does one construct an ontology which begs no metaphysical question? It must be an ontology flexible enough to respect the core of truth in all – even opposing – metaphysical theories. Objects in Jaina ontology are held, first and foremost, to be 'many sided' (*anekānta*). We have already seen how Diṅnāga exploits the idea that an object has many properties in his argument that no process of cognising which grasps an object through its properties can grasp the object *in its entirety* (Chapter 4.4). There was, though, no implication there that a single object could be the bearer of both members of a pair of conflicting properties. Indeed, for the Buddhist, conflicting properties must have different loci – the dissolution of contradiction is a dissolution of the object itself as a single bearer of multiple properties. That is not rapprochement, but separatism.

Haribhadra[1] (*c.* AD 800) sheds considerable light on the nature of the doctrine of many-sidedness when he redescribes it as a theory of the manifoldness of *every* real entity, as a theory of *integration*, and as a theory of the *entanglement* and *intermixture* of conflicting aspects. The goal of reason is harmony, and harmony consists in an integration of information from a diversity of sources. The Jainas will say that, at the limit, integration leads to the acquisition of *complete* knowledge of things. What is not yet clear is whether completeness must imply totality – knowledge of everything about the object – with the problems attendant upon such an idea of omniscience, or if not, where the epistemic boundaries of integration lie. This is a question we shall be able to answer only when the mechanics of rapprochement are understood.

Persistence and change are twin poles in the concept of an object. An object is something that persists through change, and something that changes even though persisting. The view that objects exist *only* in a state of change is as one-sided as the view that they are *only* stable and enduring. The truth is that things are both constants and variables. Identifying the stable and enduring nature of a thing with its 'substance' (*dravya*) aspect, and the changing nature of a thing with its 'modification' (*paryāya*) aspect, the Jaina analysis is that an object is a thing whose nature is to be both substance and modification. An object is an inextricable mixture of being and becoming. Hemacandra (AD 1089–1172), a versatile philosopher and biographer[2] of the Jaina elders, invents an etymology to bring out the intended contrast:[3]

> The domain of a means of knowing is an object, the nature of which is to be substance and modification. (PM 1.1.30)
>
> (para. 118) . . . The word 'substance' (*dravya*) is derived from [the verb] 'to run' (*dru*) – it is that which runs through the modifications. It is thus the head commonality running through and grounding the connection between earlier and later changing states. Modifications are states of change. They are what change and they exist in the two properties of arising and ceasing. An object, the nature of which is to be substance and modification, is one whose nature is that [running through] and those two [arising and ceasing]. This is what is meant by 'objectively real'

> (*paramārthasat*). As it is said in the canonical text of Vācaka, 'the real is what is linked with persistence, origin and decay.'

The reference is to sūtra 5.29 of Vācaka Umāsvāti's *Tattvārthasūtra*. Y. J. Padmarajiah[4] has said with justifiable exaggeration that sūtra 5.29 is '[t]he most celebrated text the implications of which form almost the entire theoretical foundation of the Jaina philosophy of being.' The juxtaposition of the twin polarities of persistence and change in a single definition is meant to confront all one-sided definitions. Hemacandra again:

> Here, by including the phrase 'substance and modification', the ideas of those who have a one-sided substance theory and those who have a one-sided modification theory are blocked. By including the phrase 'nature of which', the belief of the Yauga [=Vaiśeṣika] school of Kaṇāda that substance and modification are completely different is blocked. As it is said by Siddhasena,[5] 'Ulūka [=Kaṇāda] has built his system in pursuance of both respects, yet it is vitiated by falsity, because he has advocated that substance and modification are mutually independent and that each is supreme in its own sphere.' (PM 1.1.30, para. 119)

The idea is that an object is neither that whose nature is to persist, nor that whose nature is to change – it is something in which persistence and change are intertwined. It is a centre of origin, endurance and decay. This integration of opposites within a single entity is what blocks one-sided views of the nature of a thing and sustains an inclusive conception in which different partial views can be reconciled.

5.3 DISAGREEMENT DEFUSED

If the theory really is that a single object is the bearer of conflicting properties (such as origin and decay, stability and flux, generality and specificity), does it not fall into contradiction? The criticism is pressed by Śaṃkara[6] and by the Buddhist Śāntarakṣita.[7] The thoroughness of the Jaina philosophers leads them to consider contradiction as but one of a list (usually of eight) potential defects in their theory. Let me follow Hemacandra once more:

> [Opponent:] The *syādvāda* [= Jaina] theory, rejecting as one-sided both the identity and the non-identity of [an object with] substance and modification, allows somehow both identity and non-identity. But this is not reasonable, for there are faults such as that of contradiction (*virodha*).
>
> (1) There cannot be both the assertion and denial [of identity or non-identity] with respect to a single object, just as [it cannot be both] blue and non-blue.

(2) Suppose the identity is [asserted] in some respect, and the non-identity is [asserted] in some respect – then the identity has one locus and the non-identity a different locus; so there is the fallacy of a division of loci.
(3) One-sidedness is granted otherwise than if those two things, one in which identity has been placed and the other in which non-identity has been placed, are [themselves said to be] both identical and different – that being so, the fallacy of a regress [follows].
(4) The respect in which there is non-identity is one of both identity and non-identity, and the respect in which there is non-identity is also one of both identity and non-identity – [this is] a fallacy of cross-mixing.
(5) Non-identity is the respect in which there is identity, and identity is the respect in which there is non-identity – [this is] a fallacy of reciprocal dependence.
(6) Since it is impossible to determine a distinct respect for an object whose nature is one of both identity and non-identity, [there will occur] the fallacy of doubt.
(7) Then too follows the fallacy of non-ascertainment.
(8) Then the fallacy of no establishment of an object [also follows]. (PM 1.1.32, para. 130)

The most serious problem is contradiction, of which indeed the others are merely corollaries. Thus objects as bearers of contradictory properties lack determinate identity conditions (a fault perhaps akin to the medieval logicians' doctrine that 'anything follows from a contradiction'). The faults are countered by an appeal to common sense. Hemacandra continues:

> [Reply:] This is not so, for an object actually brought to mind cannot be contradictory. One thing is the contradictory of another when, if present, the other is not found – this is well attested. When an object is actually found, what space is there for even a whiff of contradiction? Even as regard blue and non-blue, if [indeed] found in one place, then there is no contradiction. For the Buddhists do not admit there to be a contradiction between blue and non-blue in a cognition of a cloth's mixed colours in one and the same place, while the Vaiśeṣikas admit there to be a single, mixed, colour. And if contradictory properties like moving and non-moving, red and non-red, covered and non-covered are found in a single cloth, is there even a whiff of doubt about [the presence of] a contradiction? By this means, the fault of division of loci is set aside, for as has already been said, the two are cognised in a single locus. . . . [The other faults too are set aside in a similar way] . . . and so our claim that an object has the nature of both substance and modification is not contradicted either by what is perceived or by what is wished for. (PM 1.1.32, para. 130)

The problem of a cloth with mixed colours embarrassed the Buddhist and Nyāya-Vaiśeṣika metaphysicians alike. The problem is to say what colour is *the cloth*, when some parts are one colour and others another, without attributing to the cloth contradictory colours. The Buddhist solution is to deny that one can meaningfully ascribe any colour to the cloth at all. Some threads have one colour, other threads have the other, and nothing has both. There is no common substratum of different colours (Chapter 4.2–3). The standard Nyāya-Vaiśeṣika solution is that the cloth has a single new colour, produced by the mixing together of the pure colours of its parts (Chapter 3.6). The cloth is coloured, but has just one mixed colour, not two contradictory ones. Hemacandra reasons differently. One colour contradicts another only if the first is never found where the second is present. We do find different colours in one and the same piece of cloth. So the different colours cannot be contradictory! The moral seems to be that extreme views falsify common sense. It is better to follow common sense and let the problems fall where they will. Objects *are* by nature subject to both stability and instability, to modification and non-modification – these are the facts which cannot be denied. So stability and instability cannot after all be contradictory properties, appearances notwithstanding.

At stake is the notion of contradiction itself. When are two properties in contradiction? The Jaina answer is that two properties are in contradiction just in case one is 'not found' where the other is. Two properties are not in contradiction simply because one is truly assertible of an object and the other is truly deniable. We will see, however, that denial for the Jaina is assertion of the negation (Chapter 5.5). So the claim is that the statements '*Fa*' and '*not-Fa*' are not contradictory, even though the statement '*Fa & not-Fa*' is a contradiction! One can truly assert that the pot exists and, without contradiction, truly assert that it does not exist. But one cannot truly assert that the pot exists *and* does not exist. What we need is a way to make sense of this idea.

Two strategies for analysing out contradictions are disallowed by the integrationist. One is to break apart the object into plural subjects of predication, so that no one object has both properties. The other is to merge the properties into a single new predicate. In both of these approaches, the metaphysics is revisionary rather than reconciliatory. The Jainas want a new technique for the dissolution of contradictions, one which remains true to common sense. The new idea is that there are hidden parameters in assertion. It is then possible both to assert and deny that an object has a certain property, because the hidden parameters have different values in each case. The basic idea can be seen already in the way Mahāvīra, the founder of Jainism, explains the questions the Buddha refused to answer:[8]

> According to substance, the world has an end; according to space, the world has an end; according to time, the world has no end; according to state, the world has no end.

The world has an end and does not have an end. Why is this not a contradiction? It is because the assertion 'the world has an end' is not yet complete – it requires for completion one of the four 'determinants' that constitute a canonical *nikṣepa*, viz. substance (*davva*), place (*khetta*), time (*kāla*) and state (*bhāva*). The substance of the world is not endless, neither is its spatial extent; but it has no beginning or end in time and has endless states or properties. The point to stress is that the idea is not that an expression such as 'end' is ambiguous. A possible strategy for defusing the apparent contradiction would be to say that 'an end' means 'a spatial boundary' and 'no end' means 'no temporal boundary'. The apparently contradictory statement would not, after all, ascribe conflicting properties to a single object. This is another inadmissible way of defusing the contradiction – it is a sort of incommensurability thesis, in which one denies that the two parties are in genuine conflict on the ground that their uses of the terms have different meanings. There is no disagreement here, but there is no agreement (common subject matter) either.

The Jaina idea is rather that an expression has a hidden indexical element *within* its meaning. The idea is semantically respectable and the phenomenon has been studied in detail both by classical Indian[9] and modern[10] semantic theorists. If one wants to say that the term 'today' is unambiguous, even though its reference changes from one day to the next, what one has to do is to find some constant element in the meaning, an element that determines the reference on any occasion of use. A natural way to think of the common element is as a function from contexts or indices to referents. Thus the constant meaning of the term 'today' is the function expressed by 'the referent of an utterance of "today" is the day on which the utterance is made.' Of course, there is nothing hidden about the indexicality of 'today'. But the indexicality of other expressions is disguised. Incomplete definite descriptions are an important case.[11] A description such as 'the house' is not ambiguous, even though it denotes different houses on different occasions – there is a hidden indexicality in its meaning.

The paradigmatic idea, that contradictions can be defused by discovering a hidden parameterisation in their statement, is encoded in the post-canonical literature in two specific theories. One is the theory of standpoints (*nayavāda*), the other the theory of the conditionalisation of assertion (*syādvāda*). The first gives the epistemology, the second the semantics. I will examine each technique in detail, but one thing is already clear. The source of conflict and disagreement lies in the use of language. It is not that the parties to a controversy talk at cross-purposes or mean different things by their assertions. The point of the Jaina dialectic is that the language used by each party is *underspecific* – it fails fully to specify the proposition being expressed. What each party states is not false but incompletely specific. Rationality, in the hands of the Jaina, is a method for exposing the underspecification implicit in ordinary language use. When this is properly done, conflict and contradiction drop away of their own accord.

5.4 THE EPISTEMOLOGY OF PERSPECTIVE

Tattvārthasūtra 1.6 is another fundamental verse: 'acquiring [knowledge] is through a means of knowing (*pramāṇa*) or a perspective (*naya*)'. The traditional epistemic processes – perception, inference, testimony and so on – are not the only methods of acquiring knowledge. There is another way. A *naya* is a perspective, a point of view, a standpoint, an angle, a take, an attitude. The intended contrast is between a method that gives complete (*sakalādeśa*) knowledge of the object and a method that gives only partial (*vikalādeśa*) knowledge. There may be ways of acquiring complete knowledge of an object, knowledge of every fact about it. If such there be, they are not the ways of acquiring knowledge normally employed. For if an object has many facets, how can one know the whole truth about it? Siddhasena:[12]

> An object whose nature is to be many-sided is the content of complete knowledge.
>
> The field of a *naya* is a thing qualified by one aspect. (NA 29)

Complete knowledge is knowledge of everything about the object, partial knowledge the knowledge of something about it. As a metaphor from the *Tattvārthaślokavārttika*[13] has it, just as a part of the ocean is not the whole of the ocean, but neither is it something other than the ocean, so too a *naya* is not a *pramāṇa*, but neither is it something other than a *pramāṇa*.

Crucial to the Jaina concept of a *naya* (a perspective, a method of acquiring partial knowledge) is the idea that the knowledge of one aspect of the object does not exclude knowledge of its other aspects. The traditional philosophical systems, to be sure, encode partial knowledge about the nature of things, but each does so in a way that implies the others are wrong. That makes each of them a 'pseudo-method' (*nayābhāsa*). The intended distinction concerns the validity of the following epistemological principle: 'If one knows that *a* is *F* then one does not know that *a* is *not F*.' This principle states that the knowledge that an object has a property entails knowledge that it does not have the contrary property. But if one can truly assert and deny *F* of an object, because there are hidden parameters on assertion and denial, then this principle must be invalid. Knowing that an object has a certain property does not imply that one is not in a position to know that it also does not have the property. The theory of standpoints is a doctrine of epistemic openness. The philosophical error to which the traditional schools are prone is one of mistaking methods of acquiring partial knowledge for methods of acquiring complete knowledge, and so of failing to recognise the nature of the knowledge they have. The way to complete knowledge is through the accumulation and integration of partial knowledge – collating all the facts about a single object and defusing apparent contradictions by an evaluation of the hidden parameters.

There are traditionally said to be seven different types of standpoint. They are: (1) *naigama*, the indiscriminate; (2) *saṃgraha*, the collective; (3) *vyavahāra*, the practical; (4) *ṛjusūtra*, the straight to what is manifest; (5) *śabda*, the verbal; (6) *samabhirūḍha*, the subtle; (7) *evambhūta*, the actual. It is usual to group the first three together as substance-affirming, and the remainder as modification-affirming. One type relates to a level at which we emphasise general, universal features, the other to a level at which particulars and differentiations are highlighted. Another grouping is also found, in which the first four are classified together as metaphysical (*artha-naya*), while the last three are linguistic (*śabda-naya*). Paul Dundas[14] has summarised the traditional division:

> The first three relate to the fact that entities must in ontological terms be interpreted as being conjoined either with both general and specific properties, or with general properties only, or with specific properties only. The fourth *naya* relates to entities as necessarily rooted in the present when judgements are being made about them, while the last three demonstrate the manner in which language is implicated in ontological analysis. Thus, according to the fifth and sixth *nayas*, verbal statements have to be carefully differentiated on the basis both of an understanding of the way in which their sense can be modified through tense and grammatical inflection, and through a consideration of the etymology of words as a means of gaining information about their meaning or nuance. The seventh *naya* delimits individual words to one particular meaning: that is, a word only has its proper meaning when something is carrying out the function designated by it.

Let us look in more detail. The 'indiscriminate' reflects a broad level of metaphysical description in which all the features of an object, general or particular, are represented and ordered. No distinction is made between substance and attribute, or between an attribute and an attribute of that attribute. It is the position, perhaps, of someone who is concerned merely to catalogue what there is, without worrying about the different kinds of thing. Such a position becomes misguided only when turned into a dogmatic assertion that such categorial distinctions are bogus. The 'collective' is a level of description at which we pay attention only to the most general commonalties between things. We ignore the specific properties which distinguish one thing from another, but note, for example, that everything shares the property of being an existent. When adopted dogmatically, not as just one possible standpoint, this attitude leads to monistic metaphysics of, for instance, Advaita Vedānta. The 'practical' is the complement of the 'collective', stressing the special distinguishing features of things, and classifying them under a variety of headings suitable for practical activities. It becomes a dogmatic pseudo-standpoint when bogus distinctions are invented, or real distinctions are denied. The Jainas place the Cārvāka 'materialists' in the latter group.

The 'straight to what is manifest' is a level of metaphysical description which pays attention only to what is present, or what is perceived in the present time. It takes as primitive the immediate givens, such as presently occurring pleasure or pain sensations. When such a view is taken to be the correct method, it leads to a typically phenomenalist stance, an attempt to reduce talk of enduring substances, etc. to talk about sense-data or the logical atoms of present experience. As a dogmatically held pseudo-standpoint, it is the doctrine adopted by two Buddhist factions, the Sautrāntikas and the Yogācārins.

The previous four standpoints have all been concerned with the question of what sorts of object we should take as basic in our metaphysics. The last three standpoints concern instead their proper linguistic expression. Each picks out certain syntactic categories which, it is claimed, reflect underlying semantic distinctions. The 'verbal' standpoint is one in which differences in grammatical inflection (tense, number and gender) are held to have a semantic basis. Thus a sentence such as 'The Sumeru mountain used to exist' means something different from 'The Sumeru mountain will exist'. Clearly, taking tense, gender and number to be indicators of semantic distinctions will have consequences for the sort of metaphysics we construct. In the standpoint called the 'subtle', we make a 'subtle' etymological distinction between the meanings of words, even if they refer to the same object. For example, 'Indra' (so-called because possessing sovereign authority) and 'Śakra' (so-called because possessing mighty power) both refer to the lord of the gods. The 'subtle' attends to the difference in their meanings; the 'verbal' to the identity in their referents.

Finally, the 'actual'. Many words have 'functional' meanings – they refer to objects on the basis of a kind of capacity the object instantiates, or function which the object can perform. For example, 'cook' refers to someone who has the capacity to cook, 'swimmer' to someone who has the capacity to swim. According to this standpoint, we should use such terms only when the object is actually performing its function, and not at other times. If we wish to construct a metaphysics in which objects are picked out by means of the capacities and powers they possess, we use here names which pick out the objects when they are *actually* exercising the capacity. Thus, we only call someone 'a cook' when that person is actually cooking.

What is interesting is to see how later Jainas rationalise the list. Here is the proposal endorsed by the systematising Yaśovijaya (*c.* AD 1650).[15] Thought of as levels of description, the order is one of increasing specificity. The first describes everything, whether existent or non-existent. The second describes only existents, but describes all existents. The third describes only the existence of a single particular, but does so at all times. The fourth describes only the existence of a particular at the present time, but allows any name of that particular. The fifth describes only the existence of a particular at the present time under a name, but under any co-referring name. The sixth describes only the existence of a particular at the present time under a single specific name. The seventh describes only the existence of a particular at the present time under a single name of a specific sort, one which denotes via the actions the thing is capable of performing.

The move, I think, is in the direction of a discourse pluralism, an acceptance that there is a plurality of irreducible kinds of language use, organised into a vertical hierarchy.[16] The descriptions are neither incompatible nor incommensurable, but represent different levels of talk about the same domain of things.

5.5 THE LOGIC OF ASSERTION

Two models of assertion have been in play in the earlier chapters of this book. On one model, the primary assertoric force of a statement in the declarative mode is inclusive. To say of a thing that it is an *F* is to include that thing in the class of things satisfying some condition. This is the classical model, developed by the Nyāya-Vaiśeṣika philosophers. The other model is Diṅnāga's. A concept delimits a class by exclusion. Its extension is a class of objects not failing some condition. Denial, not assertion, is the primary assertoric force of a statement. To say of a thing that it is *F* is to exclude it from what is other than *F*. The difference between these two models lies in their respective ontological commitments – only the first, allegedly, is committed to the existence of a real property all *F*s share. The two models nevertheless rest on a common assumption. This is the assumption that assertion and denial are exclusive. One cannot consistently both assert and deny that the thing is *F*.

This assumption is the target of the Jaina integrationist meaning theory. For if one can develop a theory in which assertion does not exclude denial, then one can make respectable the leading Jaina insight, that one philosophical truth does not exclude its rival. Vādideva Sūri (twelfth century AD) presents the developed Jaina theory:[17]

> A word, always expressing its own meaning through assertion and denial, follows a seven-fold division. (PNTĀ 4.13)

The formal similarity between this statement and Diṅnāga's celebrated thesis (Chapter 4.5) is striking:[18]

> Because [a word] expresses its own meaning through the exclusion of others.

It is clear that the intention is to develop a theory of meaning parallel to Diṅnāga's, but without commitment to the troublesome presupposition that assertion and denial are exclusive. Assertion and denial are non-exclusive because of the hidden parameters with respect to which each is made, in virtue of which one can consistently assert that the object is *F* (with respect to one set of parameter-values) but deny that it is *F* (with respect to another set). But what is this 'seven-fold division' (*saptabhaṅgī*)? Vādideva Sūri again:

> A seven-fold division is the use of a statement in seven ways, [each] marked by the particle 'somehow' (*syāt*), made without contradiction out of assertion and denial, either combined or separated, with respect to an inquiry about just one property in a single object. (PNTĀ 4.14)

It might seem at face value that, even if one accepts the non-exclusiveness thesis, there are still only three ways of combining an assertion and a denial: (1) asserting that the object is *F*; (2) denying that it is *F*; or (3) both asserting and denying that it is *F* (with different values of the hidden parameters). Suppose, however, that there is a way of combining assertion and denial 'in the same breath' into a new kind of speech-act *assert-deny*. Whether or not this is a genuine possibility requires careful examination. But if it is possible, then there are seven ways of combining an assertion and a denial: (1) asserting that the object is *F*; (2) denying that it is *F*; (3) assert-denying that it is *F*; (4) both asserting and denying that it is *F* (with different values of the hidden parameters); (5) both asserting and assert-denying that it is *F* (with different values of the hidden parameters); (6) both denying and assert-denying that it is *F* (with different values of the hidden parameters); and (7) asserting, denying and assert-denying that it is *F* (with different values of the hidden parameters). The simple combinatorial point of the Jainas seven-fold division is that there are $2^n - 1$ ways to choose at least one thing from a group of *n* (here $n = 3$ and 'thing' = type of speech-act).

Let me postpone discussion of the viability of 'assert-deny' as a speech-act (Chapter 5.6). It is not vitally important anyway – if it is not viable, then the division ought really to be three-fold rather than seven-fold. Of much greater interest and importance is the introduction of the conditionalising particle 'somehow' (*syāt*) before any statement. Grammatically, *syāt* is the third person singular of the optative form of the verb √*as*, 'to be'. Semantically, it is a modal operator on a par with 'possibly', and, like 'possibly', can be treated as an existential quantifier, ranging here not over possible worlds, but over possible valuations of the hidden parameters. So in Jaina theory it comes to mean 'in some respect', 'in some way', 'for some value of the parameters substance, place, time and state'. The effect of inserting 'somehow' into a statement is precisely to suspend the normal implicative force of an assertion, and so to free the assertion from the troublesome presupposition. R. C. Pandeya[19] has put the idea well: '*syādvāda* represents a formal programme whereby you can distinguish an exclusive statement from a non-exclusive statement, and it is a recommendation to use all statements in a non-exclusive sense. The scheme of *saptabhaṅgī* is therefore to be taken as a device for converting an exclusive statement into a non-exclusive statement.'

How does this happen? The formal structure of an assertion is now:

(1)	*syāt*	*ghaṭaḥ*	*asti*	*eva*
	somehow	the pot	exists	indeed.

Notice again the use of the restrictive particle *eva* (we have seen it before in Chapter 4.6). Here it attaches neither to the subject nor to the predicate, but to the verb, and its force is emphatic: the pot indeed exists. Malliṣeṇa (twelfth century AD) explains the construction in (1):[20]

> '*syāt*' – somehow, through its own substance, place, time and state, the pot and all indeed exists, not through another substance, place, time and state. So a pot exists as regards substance by being made of earth, but not by being made of water. As regards place, [it exists] by being in Pāliputra, not by being in Kānyakubja. As regards time, [it exists] by being in the winter, not by being in the spring. As regards state, [it exists] by being black, not by being red. Otherwise, its own nature would be lost on account of its having the nature of another.

Assertions are evaluated only with respect to values of the four hidden parameters. Simply to say 'the pot exists' is not yet to say anything. It would be like the sentence written on a piece of paper 'I will be coming back today', but with no indication as to which day the note was written or who wrote it. The sentence is not false, but it is underspecific – it makes no *statement*.[21] One way to eliminate the underspecification would be to give actual values to the hidden parameters. Another way is to quantify over those parameters. This is the effect of the insertion of the particle 'somehow'. The incomplete assertion 'the pot exists' is now transformed into the complete assertion 'with respect to some substance, place, time and state, the pot exists.' And of course, once we have made clear that this is the logical form of the assertion, it is obvious that the assertion might be true with respect to one set of parameter-values and false with respect to a different set.

One can think of 'somehow' as a kind of assertion sign. The unmodified statement 'the pot exists' expresses a dummy proposition 'the pot exists at s, x, t, p'. There are many different sorts of assertion one can make with this dummy proposition. One can assert that it is true for *some* set of parameter-values, without saying anything about its truth or falsity at other values. This is the assertoric force carried by the 'somehow' sign. A different sign might have indicated a different assertoric force – that the proposition is true for *every* set of parameter-values, that it is true for *only some* set, and so on.

What about denial? The second member of the seven-fold division is a denial that the pot exists. It is represented by the construction:

(2)	*syāt*	*ghaṭaḥ*	*na*	*asti*	*eva*
	somehow	the pot	not	exists	indeed.

Denial, then, is assertion of a sentential negation – to *deny* that an object is *F* is to *assert that it is not the case* that the object is *F*. The denial-negation has narrow scope with respect to the assertion sign 'somehow'. Because this is a quantifier over parameter-values, it is possible both to assert and to deny that the object is *F*, giving the third construction:

(3)	*syāt*	*ghaṭaḥ*	*asti*	*eva*	*syāt*	*ghaṭaḥ*
	somehow	the pot	exists	indeed,	somehow	the pot
	na	*asti*	*eva*			
	not	exists	indeed.			

There is a set of values at which it is *F* and a set of values at which it is not the case that it is *F*. The difference between the second and third positions in the seven-fold division is this. The assertoric force of a straight denial is that the proposition is false for some set of values without saying anything about its truth or falsity at other values. The assertoric force carried in the third position is that the proposition is true for some, but only some, set of values – true at some, false at others. The point is that it is possible to assert that the pot exists, to deny that it exists, and both to assert and to deny that it exists, and that these are three different speech acts with different assertoric forces. Each says something not said by either of the other two.

We find reading (3) of the third construction in the later Jainas, such as Vādideva Sūri, Hemacandra and Malliṣeṇa. But in some earlier Jaina writings (and following them unfortunately in a good deal of the contemporary literature), we find the third position represented as:

(3*)	*syāt*	*ghaṭaḥ*	*asti*	*na*	*asti*	*eva*
	somehow	the pot	exists	not	exists	indeed.

What this would assert is that there is a set of parameter-values with respect to which the pot both exists and does not exist. That is genuinely contradictory, and so makes no assertion at all.

The move to the proper formulation is an important advance in the Jaina understanding of the logic of assertion. It brings the Jaina theory into line with the idea behind non-adjunctive logics of discourse. Graham Priest et al.[22] conjecture that 'the Jains anticipate contemporary discursive logic, initiated by Jaśkowski.' I believe this conjecture is correct. A single quotation from Jaśkowski[23] will be sufficient for our present purposes:

> To bring out the nature of the theses in such a system it would be proper to precede each thesis by the reservation: 'in accordance with the opinion of one of the participants in the discourse' or 'for a certain admissible meaning of the terms used'. Hence the joining of a thesis to a discursive system has a different intuitive meaning than has assertion in an ordinary

> system. *Discursive assertion* includes an implicit reservation of the kind specified . . .

The adjunction rule states that 'A & B' is entailed by 'A' and 'B'. But as we have seen, what we need is to be able to assert '*Fa*' and assert ' not *Fa*' without being committed to asserting '*Fa* & not *Fa*'. Embedding assertion within a modal operator is a standard way to get this result in a non-adjunctive logic, and 'somehow' has exactly the same function in the Jaina theory.

5.6 ASSERTION AND THE UNASSERTIBLE

Is it possible to assert that the pot exists and in the same 'breath' or speech-act (*sahārpaṇa*) deny that it exists? According to the Jainas, this represents a genuine possibility. Since denial is defined to be the assertion of negation, the possibility envisaged is one of asserting that the pot exists and asserting 'in the same act' that it does not exist. We have already seen that the alleged possibility cannot be that of asserting that there is a set of parameter-values with respect to which the pot both exists and does not exist. The Jainas say that what one asserts in an 'assert-deny' speech-act is that the pot is unassertible! They represent the new possibility with the construction:

(4)	*syāt*	*ghaṭah*	*avaktavyam*	*eva*
	somehow	the pot	unassertible	indeed.

Matilal[24] expresses a popular view when he says that 'the direct and unequivocal challenge to the notion of contradiction in standard logic comes when it is claimed that the same proposition is both true and false at the same time in the same sense. This is exactly accomplished by the introduction of the third value "inexpressible", which can be rendered also as paradoxical.' But it can't really be true that the Jainas are deliberately setting out to introduce paraconsistency in so strong a sense into their system, for they say quite clearly that all seven of the modes of assertion are meant to be combinations of assertion and denial *without contradiction*, and we have seen Hemacandra responding to the charge that the Jaina system is contradictory with a firm rebuttal.

Is there any non-paraconsistent understanding of the simultaneous assertion and denial of a proposition, given that denial is assertion of the negation? The only suggestion I have found is one in the late (seventeenth century AD) Jaina philosopher Yaśovijaya. Yaśovijaya's aim is to redescribe the Jaina system in the technical language of Navya-Nyāya, a precise formal language developed in order to eliminate ambiguity from philosophical discourse. What Yaśovijaya says is that what one asserts when one asserts a thing to be simultaneously both existing and non-existing is in the form of an 'alternation' (*anyataratvādinā*). The term 'alternation' is a technical one in Navya-Nyāya.

It is defined as 'that which possesses a difference to which the absenteeness is limited by both differences'. The alternation of fire and water is that which is different from what is both different from fire and different from water. Daniel Ingalls[25] identifies this with the standard definition for the inclusive 'or': $p \vee q$ iff $\sim(\sim p \,\&\, \sim q)$. If he is right, then Yaśovijaya's point is that a simultaneous assertion and denial is an assertion that the pot *either* does *or* does not exist. It is an assertion of ignorance. The fourth position is one in which one asserts that, with respect to certain parameter-values, the object is one of the two: *F*, *not-F*. This is identical neither to an assertion that it is *F* there, nor an assertion that it is *not-F* there, nor an assertion that it is *F* with respect to some values, but *not-F* with respect to others. Nor is it an attempt to assert that it is both. It is a speech-act with a distinctive assertoric force.

Let us take Σ to be the totality of points in the four-dimensional space whose coordinates are the parameters on assertion. A description of the object distributes values for the proposition '*x* is *F*' at points in Σ. It does so by determining a function from points in the parameter space to values in the set {true, false, unassertible}. The proposition '*x* is *F*' is assigned the value 'true' at a point if the description specifies that the object is *F* at that point, with respect to those parameters. It is assigned the value 'false' at the point if the description specifies that the object is *not-F* at that point.[26] The third value, 'unassertible', is assigned if the description does not specify which of *F* and *not-F* the object is at that point.[27] Perhaps there are 'optimal' descriptions, descriptions that specify whether the object is *F* or *not-F* at every point in the parameter space (for example, the description of the number 4 as the sum of 3 and 1). Admitting the new value 'unassertible' is a way of recognising that most descriptions are not optimal, but simply fail to specify whether the object is *F* or not at many points in the parameter space. They admit ignorance.

Why is it that one is said to be asserting the *unassertible*? Let me quote Yaśovijaya:[28]

> The fourth is made when assertion and denial have predominance at the same time – thus, 'somehow it is indeed unassertible.' [It is called 'unassertible'] because it is impossible to assert both at the same time through a single word. Even a convention-based term like *śatṛ–śānac* [a term in Pāṇini's grammar for the two sorts of present participle affix] denotes its two meanings consecutively. Even when both are somehow understood through alternation, it would be difficult even for God to understand both from a single word having its own unique character.

A simultaneous assertion *about* both existence and non-existence is not necessarily an assertion *of* both existence and non-existence. It could be the assertion that one or the other obtains (but we do not know which). This is an assertion which can only be made by a succession of uttered terms. An analogy might be the way one can build up a single idea of an object from a succession of tactual experiences. Sequential order in the *vehicle* of thought (tactual experience, language) does not imply sequential order in the *content* of thought. In our case, although the content of the thought is a single disjunction, the vehicle by which it is expressed is, necessarily, a sequential statement of the disjuncts.

The point is made clearly by Malliṣeṇa, from whom Yaśovijaya derives his '*śatṛ–śānac*' example:[29]

> An object such as the soul is [said to be] unassertible because it is impossible for a word to denote a single object giving predominance at the same time to both existence and non-existence in the same act. For the two qualities of existence and non-existence cannot be asserted at the same time by the word 'exists', for it lacks the capacity to denote non-existence. Thus too by the word 'non-exists', for it does not have the capacity to denote existence. Nor can it be denoted by a single conventional term such as *puṣpavant* [meaning 'sun or moon'], because it too can denote both meanings only in succession. This is like the conventional term *śatṛ–śānac*. Whether a conjunctive or a descriptive determinative compound, the sentence does not denote it. So the object is unassertible because there is no expression denotative of the whole. Even when simultaneous existence and non-existence have equal prominence, the ordering cannot be passed over. But it is not totally unassertible, because then it would not be asserted by the word 'unassertible'! Thus the fourth.

The remaining three of the seven modes of assertion now follow in the same non-adjunctive pattern as the third. The point to stress is that it is possible to make all seven kinds of assertion about the same object and the same property. Each one carries a distinctive type of information about the distribution of truth and falsity of 'x is F' over the space whose co-ordinates are the parameters (substance, place, time, state).

An ancient and rather obscure group of Jainas known as the Trairāśikas ('followers of the doctrine of the three heaps') were so-called because they admitted only a three-fold division. Their view is reported in a commentary on the *Nandisūtra*,[30] where it is assimilated with that of the heretical Ājīvikas:

> The Ājīvika heretics founded by Gośāla are likewise called Trairāśikas, since they declare everything to be of triple character, viz. living, not living, and both living and not living; world, not world, and both world and not world; existent, non-existent, and both existent and non-existent. In considering standpoints (*naya*) [they postulate that a standpoint may be] substance-affirming, modification-affirming, or both-affirming. Thus, since they maintain three heaps (*rāśi*), they are called Trairāśikas.

The Trairāśikas, perhaps, are worried that no sense can be made of a speech-act with the force of 'assert-deny' other than as a paraconsistent assertion of simultaneous existence and non-existence. In this, they may be right. My suggestion, following Yaśovijaya, is that the introduction of the new kind of speech-act is a device for allowing there to be descriptions which are less than optimally specific. A little more can be said, but first let us take a look at the consequences of the non-exclusiveness thesis for the classical theory of extrapolative inference.

5.7 THE MARK OF A GOOD REASON

The doctrine that objects are many-faceted has important ramifications for the theory of inference. Diṅnāga had argued that there are three marks individually necessary and jointly sufficient for the warranted extrapolation from reason to target (Chapter 4.7). They are: (1) that the reason be present in the site of the extrapolation; (2) that the reason be present (only) in what is similar to the target; and (3) that the reason be absent in what is dissimilar to the target. The second of these conditions is, arguably, equivalent to the third, which asserts that the reason property is absent when the target property is absent. That was supposed to capture the idea of a 'no counter-example' condition, according to which an extrapolation is warranted just in case there is nothing in which the reason is present, but not the target. What happens to this account if one allows, as the Jainas do, that a property and its absence be compossible in a single object? What happens is that the three marks cease to be sufficient for warranted extrapolation. In particular, the third mark no longer captures the idea behind the 'no counter-example' condition. For now the absence of the reason property in a place where the target is absent does not preclude its *presence* there too! So the third mark can be satisfied and yet there still be counter-examples – cases of the presence of the reason together with the absence of the target.

The Jainas indeed claim that the three marks are neither necessary nor sufficient for warranted extrapolation. Their response is to substitute for the three marks a new, single, mark. It is clear that, if the presence and absence of a property are compossible, then a distinction needs to be drawn between absence and non-presence. The first is consistent with the presence of the property; the second is not. Early post-Diṅnāga Jainas such as Akalaṅka and Siddhasena described the new mark in quasi-Buddhistic terms, as 'no presence without' (*avinābhāva*) – i.e. no presence of the reason without the target. Thus Akalaṅka:[31]

> An extrapolation is a cognition of what is signified from a sign known to have the single mark of no presence without the target (*sādhyāvinābhāva*). Its result is blocking and other cognitions.

The relata of the causality and identity relations cannot be cognised without the suppositional knowledge (*tarka*) of their being impossible otherwise, [which is] the proof that this is the single mark even without those relations. Nor is a tree the own-nature (*svabhāva*) or the effect (*kārya*) of such things as shade. And there is no disagreement here.

There is an obvious reference to and criticism of Dharmakīrti here,[32] and also a mention of the important idea, to which we shall return in Chapter 6, that suppositional reasoning (*tarka*) is what gives us knowledge of the universal generalisations grounding extrapolations. The crucial difference from the Buddhists is in the meaning of 'no presence'. For the Jainas, it has to stand for non-presence and not for absence. That led them to reformulate the reason–target relation as a relation of necessitation. Siddhasena:

> The mark of a reason is 'being impossible otherwise' (*anyathānupannatva*). (NA 22)

Vādideva Sūri gives the developed Jaina formulation:

> A reason has a single mark, 'determined as impossible otherwise'. It does not have three marks, for fallacies are then still possible. (PNTĀ 3.11–12)

The idea is that the reason *cannot* be present if the target is not. It is impossible for the reason to be present otherwise than if the target is present. The presence of the reason necessitates the presence of the target. The necessity introduced by the new definition is in fact a universal quantification over parameter-values. What the new definition states is that there is no set of parameter-values for which the reason is present, but not the target. That rules out the worrisome case – the case where the target is non-present, but the reason is both absent and present. For a property is absent if it is not present at *some* set of values, and it is non-present if it is not present at *any* set of values. And if we read 'no presence without' as 'non-presence without' then what the definition states is that there is no set of parameter values at which the reason is present, but not the target.

The problem is discussed in detail by Prabhācandra (eleventh century AD). While commenting on the definition provided by Siddhasena, he probes the proper logical form of the extrapolation relation:[33]

> [Opponent:] And again, is it that smoke is impossible when some one fire is absent or when all fire is absent? Not some one, because even when one fire is absent the presence of smoke is possible if another fire [is present]. Nor all, for it is impossible to comprehend [every absence of fire] without comprehending a condition [qualifying the absences generally]. A condition (*upādhi*) for the absence of smoke is the absence of fire in general, and that cannot be comprehended when every fire is not comprehended, since to comprehend an absence it is necessary to comprehend the locus of the absentee.
>
> And also, even when the absence of a certain fire is absent, an opposition (*virodha*) is seen between the presence of smoke and the absence of smoke. So the condition for opposition to the presence of smoke is not the absence of fire but the absence of smoke . . .

> [Reply:] Whatever was said on the lines of 'is it that smoke is impossible when some one fire is absent or when all fire is absent,' that is not right at all. For the extrapolation relation (*vyāpti*) is understood in dependence on all, as in 'any particular smoke is impossible when all fire is absent', and not by mentioning each and every locus, as in 'smoke is impossible when fire is absent on the mountain or in the house or in the forest.' For if that were required no extrapolation relation could be proved even with an infinite amount of time, since there are infinitely many loci. And because an extrapolation would be useless, since the time of comprehending the extrapolation relation would be the same as that of comprehending the loci of fire and smoke together.
>
> Now one should not say that, if the qualifying condition for the impossibility of smoke concerns all fire, and this is not comprehended, then neither can one comprehend its absence. For the absence of the [fire] is it's presence at other places, etc. [i.e. other parameter values], and because the absence is being present at other presences, which [in turn] is because presence expels absence. That is how a place, etc. is cognised perceptually as disjoined from all fire . . .
>
> And whatever was said on the lines of 'even when the absence of a certain fire is absent, an opposition is seen between the presence of smoke and the absence of smoke,' that too is mere words. For when fire is absent, the presence of smoke is necessarily ruled out. This is because both the absence of fire and the absence of smoke can be the bases of an opposition to [smoke]. That which is necessarily ruled out when something is present is a basis of an opposition to it. For example, cold touch in the presence of hot touch. The presence of smoke is necessarily ruled out when fire is absent; so it is the basis of an opposition to smoke . . .

The distinction between some fire being absent and all fire being absent is just the one between fire being absent (not present with respect to some parameter) and non-present (not present with respect to any parameter). Prabhācandra is emphatic that it is the latter that we need. One property contradicts another if its presence 'necessarily rules out' the presence of the other. The absence of fire does not contradict its presence, but its non-presence does. And the logical form of the extrapolation relation is: if there is no set of parameter values for which fire is present, then there is no set of parameter values for which smoke is present. Non-presence of target implies non-presence of reason. We can also now understand the point of the negative formulation of the extrapolation relation by the Buddhists and Jainas – the essential contrast between absence and non-presence could not be made out if the formulation were attempted solely in terms of presence.

I said that Diṅnāga's three marks are, for the Jainas, neither necessary nor sufficient. They are not sufficient because they permit extrapolation when the reason is both present and absent, and the target non-present. On what grounds are they thought not to be necessary? The theory of extrapolation as developed first by the early Naiyāyikas and then by Diṅnāga has a built-in simplifying assumption (Chapter 1.6). The assumption is that extrapolation is always a matter of inferring from the presence of one property in an object to the presence of a second property *in that same object*. But that assumption excludes many intuitively warranted extrapolations. The main examples considered by the Jainas are: (1) the *śakaṭa* star-group will rise because the *kṛttikā* star-group has risen; (2) the sun is above the horizon because the earth is in light; (3) there is a moon in the sky because there is a moon in the water.

These examples are said to prove that the first of Diṅnāga's three marks, that the reason property is present in the site, is not a necessary condition on warranted extrapolation. And yet, while it is certainly desirable to broaden the reach of the theory to cover new patterns of extrapolative inference, it is not very clear what these examples show. What is the underlying generalisation? What are the similar and dissimilar examples? In the first case, the extrapolation seems to be grounded in the universal generalisation 'whenever the *kṛttikā* arises, so too does the *śakaṭa*.' But then there is indeed a single site of extrapolation – the present time. The inference is: the *śakaṭa* will rise *now* because *kṛttikā* has *now* risen. A similar point could be made about the second example. There seems indeed to be an implicit temporal reference in both of the first two cases, an extrapolation grounded in a universal generalisation over times.

The third case is more convincing, yet here too one might try to discern a common site. For the true form of the extrapolation is: the moon is in the sky because *it* is reflected in the water, an extrapolation grounded in a universal generalisation of the form 'objects cause their own reflections'. Certainly, however, there are patterns of extrapolation for which the 'single site' condition does not hold. If, for example, one can find a universal generalisation of the form '$\forall x\, \exists y\, (Fx \rightarrow Gy)$', then from '$\exists x\, Fx$' one can infer '$\exists x\, Gx$'. Perhaps *this* is the pattern of extrapolation the Jainas intend to exemplify with their example of a sky-moon and a water-moon. If so, it represents an important criticism of a simplifying, but in the end also restricting, assumption in the classical theory of extrapolation.

5.8 INTEGRATION AND COMPLETE KNOWLEDGE

The means and methods of acquiring knowledge are perspectival. Each gives knowledge of a part or aspect of the object, but none gives knowledge of the whole. The Jainas, however, are not sceptics but syncretists. There *is* a way of knowing the whole – it is through the integration of one's knowledge of the parts. Akalaṅka:[34]

> A scriptural statement is of two sorts – a somehow-statement (*syād-vāda*) and that called a perspective (*naya*). A somehow-statement is complete; a perspective is a partial statement.

> A somehow-statement is a statement the nature of whose meaning is to be many-sided. For example, 'the person, [his] matter, principle of motion and rest, space and time'. Here, the person is many-sided, marked in a way common [with other sorts of thing] by being the bearer of qualities and of properties, having equal status, being knowable and being existent; and marked in a way both common and uncommon by being subtle, having non-denumerably many spatial atoms, being intangible; and marked in an uncommon way by happiness, exertion, perception and belief. As this is the whole of a person, the somehow-statement is a complete means of knowing (*pramāṇa*). According to some, they have the capacity for transformation. A perspective is a partial statement, for instance 'a person is a thinker, because known to be happy, unhappy and so on.'. . . Here, the word 'person', [governed by] a convention resting on the notion of capacity, denotes, through exclusion of what is other, [only] a state. . . . Now because the use of 'somehow' destroys all one-sided assertion, the person is denoted as qualified by the four sorts of qualifier, like own-nature, etc. . . . Even so a perspective is precisely a single side. When one says 'somehow the person indeed [exists]', the word 'somehow' has many sides as its scope. When one says 'the person somehow exists indeed', the word 'somehow' has one side as its scope.

Akalaṅka tells us that the name must occur *within* the scope of the modal operator 'somehow', and that when it does the statement is many-sided. I have chosen this passage because it counters a common misconception of the Jaina theory. The misconception is that we should understand a statement conditionalised by 'somehow' as a statement of how things are from a particular perspective. But, as this passage makes clear, the fundamental *contrast* is between statements from a certain perspective and statements conditionalised by the 'somehow' operator. Embedding a statement within the scope of the operator quantifies over the values of the four hidden parameters (substance, place, time, state). A *complete* description of an object is a description with explicit reference to the state of the object at each of the values of those parameters. What the insertion of 'somehow' allows us to do is to begin to build up such a pointwise description of the object, each somehow-conditionalised statement carrying information along a line of sight of points. As more statements are added, a picture gradually builds up of the whole object, just as (to use a favourite metaphor of Sukhlalji Sanghvi) we build up a picture of the whole house by inspecting it from different sides, inside and out.

I have said that each new statement adds new information about the object. But a question still remains – can we ever, by this means, reach a *complete* description of the object? A complete description is a truth-value specification at each of infinitely many points, but we do not have infinitely many conditionalised statements. In fact, we have only seven, or rather only seven *types*, of statement. Perhaps then the contrast is this: a statement conditionalised by 'somehow' gives one partial knowledge of the full object, while a perspectival statement gives one full knowledge of part of the object. Siddhasena:

> Since scriptural statements occur as *naya*s, which reside in one [aspect].
>
> A scriptural statement ascertaining the full object is called a 'somehow-statement'. (NA 30)

One frequent suggestion is that description in all the modes of the seven-fold division (*saptabhaṅgī*) is a method for reaching a complete description. The seven-fold division is a division into seven types of partial statement about the whole. Given any partial description of the object, we can classify the description according to the type of speech-act it is and so the type of information it conveys. What is the effect of adding further new descriptions? Do we ever attain, by this method, a specification of truth-value at every point? This is a common understanding of the Jaina position. 'The Jainas,' Matilal[35] says, 'contend that one should try to understand the particular point of view of each disputing party if one wishes to grasp completely the truth of the situation. The total truth . . . may be derived from the *integration* of all different viewpoints.' The contention, however, is non-trivial. Perhaps it can be done, but it is far from clear. The Jaina rationality of reconciliation certainly leads to ever more complete descriptions, but does the description ever become complete? The attainment of the 'total truth' does not seem obviously to follow from the Jaina method of integrating different viewpoints (the parameterisation of assertion, the use of 'somehow' as a quantifier over parameters). It *may* follow, if by the 'total truth' one means something less than optimal truth, or if there exist simplifying constraints on the distribution of a property in parameter space, or if there are parameter-specific correlates of 'somehow'.

Mahāvīra is reported to have said that it is only when 'one understands the true nature of all substances by all the means of knowing and all the perspectives that one's knowledge is complete.'[36] Another possibility is that 'complete knowledge' is knowledge of everything *that can be known* about things, not necessarily knowledge of everything about them. The goal of rational harmonisation would then be to acquire complete knowledge of the truth, and not knowledge of the complete truth. Knowledge of the complete truth (*kevalajñāna*) is the sole preserve of the omniscient.

FURTHER READING

Texts

Siddhasena Divākara *c.* AD 700, *Nyāyāvatāra* (NA).
Hemacandra AD 1089–1172, *Pramāṇamīmāṃsā* (PM).
Vādideva Sūri *c.* AD 1150, *Pramāṇanayatattvālokālaṃkāra* (PNTĀ).

Many-sidedness (5.1–3)

1 Sukhlalji Sanghvi, '*Anekāntavāda*: The Principal Jaina Contribution to Logic,' in his *Advanced Studies in Indian Logic and Metaphysics* (Calcutta: Indian Studies Past and Present, 1961), pp. 15–28.

2 Y. J. Padmarajiah, *Jaina Theories of Reality and Knowledge* (Bombay: Jain Sahitya Vikas Mandal, 1963).

3 Jayandra Soni, 'Dravya, Guṇa and Paryāya in Jaina Thought,' *Journal of Indian Philosophy* 19.1 (1991), pp. 75–88.

4 Frank Van Den Bossche, 'Jain Relativism: An Attempt at Understanding,' in R. Smet and K. Watanabe eds. *Jain Studies in Honour of Jozef Deleu* (Tokyo: Hon-No-Tomosha, 1993), pp. 457–474.

5 Frank Van Den Bossche, 'Existence and Non-Existence in Haribhadra Sūri's *Anekāntajayapatākā*,' *Journal of Indian Philosophy* 23 (1995), pp. 429–468.

Standpoints, logic of assertion (5.4–6)

1 Pradeep Gokhale, 'The Logical Structure of *Syādvāda*,' *Journal of Indian Council of Philosophical Research* 8 (1991), pp. 73–81.

2 R. A. Kumar, T. M. Dak and A. D. Mishra eds., *Anekāntavāda and Syādvāda* (Landun: Jain Visva Bharati, 1996).

3 B. K. Matilal, '*Anekānta*: both yes and no?,' *Journal of Indian Council of Philosophical Research* 8 (1991), pp. 1–12; reprinted as 'The Jaina Contribution to Logic,' in *The Character of Logic in India* (Albany: State University of New York Press, 1998), pp. 127–139.

4 Piotr Balcerowicz, 'The Logical Structure of the *naya* Method of the Jainas,' unpublished typescript.

Logical theory (5.7)

1 Sukhlalji Sanghvi, 'On Problems of Inference,' in his *Advanced Studies in Indian Logic and Metaphysics* (Calcutta: Indian Studies Past and Present, 1961), pp. 77–110.

2 Atishi Uno, 'Vyāpti in Jainism,' in N. K. Wagle and F. Watanabe eds., *Studies on Buddhism in Honour of Professor A. K. Warder* (Toronto: University of Toronto, 1993), pp. 160–167.

3 Muni Shri Nyaya-vijayaji, *Jaina Philosophy and Religion*, trans. Nagin J. Shah (Delhi: B. L. Institute of Indology and Motilal Banarsidass, 1998), chapter 5.

6 Reason in equilibrium

6.1 REASON AND THE MANAGEMENT OF DOUBT

Reason is imperfect – there is a permanent possibility of error. Knowledge is achieved through the elimination of doubt, and what eliminates doubt is the existence of a compelling reason. But doubt is more infectious than it first appears, for one might doubt whether one's reason really is compelling, doubt whether the reason for thinking that it is compelling is itself compelling, and so on forever along a familiar evidential regress. Doubts cascade, and truly compelling reasons are scarce. Even when they are to hand, their value is limited – for not even psychological certainty can exclude the logical possibility of error. So it transpires that the hard question is not how to free one's inner space from all doubt (an impossible project of dubious value), but how to live with the uncertainty with which it is necessarily infused.

What is reason's role in the management of doubt? Later Nyāya epistemologists develop a theory of what they call 'suppositional reasoning' or *tarka*. It is a theory about the burden of proof and the role of presumption, about the conditions under which even inconclusive evidence is sufficient for warranted belief. That the term *tarka* is used in this context is significant in itself. For in the canonical and early literature, *tarka* is virtually synonymous with reasoned thinking in general. The free-thinkers so derided in the epics, we have seen, were called *tārkika*s or 'followers of reason' (Chapter 1.1). Even later on, when the fashion was to adorn introductory surveys of philosophy with such glorious names as *The Language of Reason* (*Tarkabhāṣā*, Mokṣākaragupta), *Immortal Reason* (*Tarkāmṛta*, Jagadīśa), *Reason's Moonlight* (*Tarkakaumudī*, Laugākṣi Bhāskara), it was usual to confer on a graduate of the medieval curriculum an honorific title such as Master or Lord of Reason (*tarkavāgīśa*, *tarkatīrtha*). Such a person is a master in the art of evidence and the management of doubt, knowing when to accept the burden of proof and also when and how to deflect it. In its popular use, *tarka* is the nearest one gets to a Sanskrit synonym for 'rationality'.

Extrapolative inference rests on the knowledge of universal generalisations, and it is the possibility of such knowledge that some of the most troubling forms of scepticism call into question. How can one be entitled to believe that something is true of every member of a domain without inspecting each member individually? How does one cope with the ineliminable possibility that an unperceived counter-example exists in some distant corner of the domain?[1] The difficulty here is with the epistemology of negative existentials. We have seen Diṅnāga's formulation of the extrapolation relation as a 'no counter-example' relation (Chapter 4.7). For him, x extrapolates y just in case there is no x without y (*y-avina x-abhāva*). The Navya-Nyāya logicians of the New Epistemology prefer a different negative existential condition, one derived from the reflexivity and transitivity of the extrapolation relation. Given transitivity, if x extrapolates y then, for any z, if y extrapolates z, so does x. The converse of this conditional holds too, given that the extrapolation relation is reflexive (proof: let $z = y$). So let us define an 'associate condition' (*upādhi*) as a property which is extrapolated by y, but not x. Then x extrapolates y just in case there is no associate condition.[2] One can infer fire from smoke, but not smoke from fire, for there is an associate condition, dampness-of-fuel, present wherever smoke is, but not wherever fire is. Tinkering with the definition, though, does not affect the epistemological problem; it remains the one of proving a non-existence claim.

As if the justification of extrapolation were not problem enough, it turns out that the sceptical worry cuts deeper still. It threatens the very tenability of the *pramāṇa*-theoretic conception of an epistemic agent as someone endowed with generally truth-conducive processes of belief-acquisition. For a person is not merely a belief-forming automaton, but is able to reflect upon (revise, reject, overrule) the epistemic processes with which they are endowed. Ernest Sosa[3] appropriately calls the state of being a rational epistemic agent one of having an 'epistemic perspective' on the deliverances of one's epistemic faculties. There is a distinction to be drawn between mere 'animal knowledge', knowledge produced by one's epistemic faculties in direct response to one's environment, and 'reflective knowledge', something that involves an understanding of the place the deliverances of the epistemic faculties have in a 'wider whole that includes one's belief and knowledge of it and how these came about'. An explanatory inference sustains the epistemic perspective, the reflective justification of the beliefs produced by a certain faculty being derived from the inference that attributes those beliefs to the faculties from which they derive.

The problem then is that an epistemic perspective itself rests on a knowledge of generalities. Like Sosa, the Nyāya understanding of reflective knowledge sees it as derived from an explanatory inference. The epistemic agent is entitled to have confidence in her beliefs and belief-acquisition procedures because, or to the extent that, actions performed in agreement with the beliefs so produced meet with successful outcomes. The accord between belief and success in action is the basis of a perspective on one's global epistemic 'set-up', and it is also the warrant for local belief in the truth of individual beliefs. One infers from success to truth – success in action *confirms* truth in belief. A perspective on one's own epistemic capacities is gained in the reflective justification of one's beliefs based on an inference from their behavioural effects or an inference from the epistemic 'likeness' of one belief with another.[4] And so the reflective equilibrium of the rational epistemological agent rests on their entitlement to believe in a *general* relation between success in action and truth in belief. Scepticism about the possibility of general knowledge hits not merely first-order belief-acquisition processes, but the very possibility of achieving epistemic stability.

6.2 THE BURDEN OF PROOF

Suppositional reasoning, *tarka*, is a device for appropriating a presumptive right – the right to presume that one's own position is correct even without conclusive evidence in its support. One is, let us imagine, in a state of doubt as to which of two hypotheses A and B is true. A and B are exclusive (at most one is true), but not necessarily contradictory (both might be false). Technically, they are in a state of 'opposition' (*virodha*).[5] The doubt would be expressed by an exclusive disjunction in the interrogative – Is it that A or that B? Uncertainty initiates inquiry (Chapter 1.2), and at the beginning of any inquiry the burden of proof is symmetrically distributed among the alternative hypotheses. A piece of suppositional reasoning shifts the burden of proof by adducing a *prima facie* counter-factual argument against one side. The form of the argument is the same in all cases. It is that one alternative, supposed as true, would have a consequence in conflict with some set of broadly defined constraints on rational acceptability. The existence of such an argument gives one the right to presume that the other alternative is true, even though one has no conclusive proof of its truth, and even though the logical possibility of its being false remains open. In the psychologised language of the Naiyāyika, a suppositional argument is a 'blocker' (*bādhaka*) to belief in the supposed alternative, and an 'eliminator' (*nirvartaka*) of doubt. The Naiyāyika Vācaspati (ninth century AD) comments:[6]

> Even if, following a doubt, there is a desire to know [the truth], the doubt still remains after the desire to know [has come about]. This is the situation intended for the application of suppositional reasoning. Of two theses, one should be admitted as known when the other is rejected by the reasoning called 'suppositional'. Thus doubt is suppressed by the application of suppositional reasoning to its subject matter. . . . A method of knowing is engaged to decide a question, but when there is a doubt involving its opposite, the method of knowing fails [in fact] to engage. But the doubt concerning the opposite is not removed as such by the undesired consequence. What makes possible its removal is the method of knowing [itself].

Vācaspati stresses that a thesis is not itself *proved* by a suppositional demonstration that the opposite has undesired consequences; one still needs evidence corroborating the thesis. But there is now a presumption in its favour, and the burden of proof lies squarely with the opponent. Suppositional reasoning 'supports' one's means of acquiring evidence, but is not itself a source of evidence. Its role is pragmatic and situational: to change the standard of evidence required for proof in the specific context.

A radical sceptical hypothesis is a proposition inconsistent with ordinary belief, but consistent with all available evidence for it. The aim of the radical sceptic is to undermine our confidence that our beliefs are justified, to introduce doubt. The New Epistemology's response to scepticism is not to deny that there is a gap between evidence and belief, or to deny the logical possibility of the sceptical hypothesis. It is to draw a distinction between two kinds of doubt, the *reasonable* and the *reasonless*. A doubt is reasonable only when both alternatives are consistent with all the evidence *and the burden of proof is symmetrically distributed* between them. One paradigmatic example is the case of seeing in the distance something that might be a person or might be a tree-stump (recall the clause in the *Nyāyasūtra* definition of perception as 'definite in nature', a clause specifically inserted to rule out such doubt; Chapter 1.4). Udayana gives the epistemology of such a case: it is a case in which one has knowledge of common aspects, but not of specific distinguishing features. What we can now see is that the example gets its force only on the assumption that there is a level epistemic playing field, with both hypotheses carrying the same *prima facie* plausibility. Suppositional reasoning has the potential to break the impasse – imagine, for example, that the unidentified lump is just one of ten in an orderly row known not to be there an hour ago. The perceptual evidence remains the same, but the burden of proof is on anyone who wants to maintain in this situation that the lump is a stump.

The other paradigm is knowledge of extrapolation relations. The problem here is that the thesis is one of such high generality that the burden of proof is already heavily against it! How can a few observations of smoke with fire ground a belief that there is fire *whenever* there is smoke? Suppositional argument has a different supportive role here. Its function is to square the scales, to neutralise the presumption *against* the belief in generality. It does so by finding *prima facie* undesirable consequences in the supposition that an associate condition or counter-example exists. Then sampling (observation of only confirmatory instances in the course of a suitably extensive search for counter-examples), though still weak evidence, can tilt the scale in favour of the generalisation.

Gaṅgeśa (*c.* AD 1320), the definitive systematiser of the New Epistemology, distinguishes two kinds of doubt as relevant to the problem of justifying extrapolation.[7] The two kinds are the sort of doubt produced by a worry over whether an associate condition is present, and the sort of doubt produced by an awareness of some general feature (lumpiness) in the absence of any identified distinguishing mark (arms, branches). Of course, there are plenty of other sources of doubt in so far as a doubt is just a mental state, but not every such doubt is reasonable, and it is only reasonable doubt that need trouble the constructive epistemologist. Gaṅgeśa admits that mere observation of confirming examples is an insufficient basis on which to rest belief in general relations. What he insists on is observation in tandem with the principled absence of doubt, and, since reasonable doubt is a product of evidential balance between rival alternatives, its elimination consists in finding a presumption in favour of one side.

6.3 CRITERIA FOR RATIONAL REJECTION

A suppositional argument moves from conjecture to unacceptable consequence. Modern writers often identify it with the medieval technique of *reductio ad absurdum*, but in fact its scope is wider. The 'unacceptable consequence' *can* be an out-and-out contradiction, but need not be so. For we are not trying to prove that the supposition is false, but only to shift the burden of proof onto anyone who would maintain it. And for this it is enough simply to demonstrate that the supposition comes into conflict with well-attested norms on rationality or deeply held beliefs. Udayana, the first to offer any systematic discussion, does not even mention contradiction as a species of unacceptable consequence. He says[8] that suppositional reasoning is of five types:

1	self-dependence	*ātmāśraya*
2	mutual dependence	*itaretarāśraya*
3	cyclical dependence	*cakraka*
4	lack of foundation	*anavasthā*
5	undesirable consequence	*aniṣṭaprasaṅga*

The last of these is really just the generic case, what distinguishes suppositional reasoning in general. The first four form a tight logical group. If the supposition is the proposition A, then the four types of unacceptable consequence are: (1) proving A from A; (2) proving A from B, and B from A; (3) proving A from B, B from C, and C from A – or any higher number of intermediate proof steps eventually leading back to A; and (4) proving A from B, B from C, C from D, . . ., without end. So what suppositional reasoning must show is that the supposition is ungrounded, its proof being either regressive or question-begging.

Two points are noteworthy about Udayana's list. First, rational unacceptability bears upon the proof adduced for the supposition, not the supposition itself. The underlying implication is that one has the right to presume that one's thesis is correct if one can find fault with the opponent's proof of the antithesis. Principles of this sort are familiar from discussion of the informal logic of arguments from ignorance[9] in which one claims entitlement to assert

A on the grounds that it is not known (or proved) that $\neg$A. In general such a claim must be unfounded – it amounts to the universal appropriation of a presumptive right in all circumstances.

The second point to notice about Udayana's list, however, is that it is very narrow. Udayana places strict constraints on what will count as an unacceptable consequence, constraints which are more formal than broadly rational. Conflict with other well-attested belief is not mentioned, for instance. Udayana severely limits the scope of suppositional reasoning. His motive, perhaps, is to disarm the sceptic. For suppositional reasoning is the favoured kind of reasoning of the sceptic-dialecticians (and indeed the term Udayana uses is *prasaṅga*, the same term Nāgārjuna had used for his dialectical method). Sceptics typically will want to loosen the conditions on what constitutes an unacceptable consequence of a supposition, so that the scope for refutation is expanded. So what Udayana seems to be saying is that one does indeed have the right to presume that one's thesis is correct when the argument for the counter-thesis commits a fallacy of a particularly gross type – not mere conflict with other beliefs, but formal lack of foundation. If the best argument for the antithesis is that bad, then one has a prima facie entitlement to one's thesis.

Śrīharṣa (*c.* AD 1140) is an Advaita dialectician, a poet and a sceptic.[10] He expands the notion of unacceptable consequence, noticing several additional types unmentioned by Udayana.[11] One is 'self-contradiction' (*vyāghāta*). It was Udayana himself[12] who analysed the notion of opposition as non-compossibility, and cited as examples the statements 'My mother is childless,' 'I am unable to speak,' and 'I do not know this jar to be a jar.' In the first instance, the non-compossibility is in what the assertion states, in the second it is in the speech-act itself, while in the third the propositional attitude self-ascription is self-refuting (a case akin to the Cartesian impossibility of thinking that one is not thinking).

Another refutation-exacting circumstance is the one called 'recrimination' (*pratibandī*). This is a situation in which one's opponent accuses one of advancing a faulty proof, when his own proof suffers exactly the same fault! There is a disagreement about what this state of equifallaciousness does to the burden of proof. The practice of Naiyāyikas is to take the circumstance as tilting the balance against the opponent – the opponent discredits himself in pressing an accusation without seeing that it can be applied with equal force to his own argument. But Śrīharṣa quotes with approval Kumārila's assertion that 'all things being equal, where the same fault afflicts both positions, *one* should not be censured [and not the other]'.[13]

Śrīharṣa, qua sceptic, would like to see *both* parties refuted by this circumstance. The same point underlies his mention as an unacceptable consequence the circumstance of 'lack of differential evidence' (*vinigamanāviraha*), when thesis and antithesis are in the same evidential situation. Again, what we see is a jostling with the burden of proof. Here Śrīharṣa is saying that absence of differential evidence puts a burden of proof on both thesis and antithesis – doubt itself refutes. It is the sceptic's strategy always to seek to maximise the burden of proof, and so to deny that anyone ever has the right to presume their position to be correct. That is, as Stanisław Schayer observed a long time ago, a difference between the *tarka* of the Naiyāyika and the *prasaṅga* of a sceptic such as Śrīharṣa or Nāgārjuna.[14] For the latter, the demonstration that a thesis has an allegedly false consequence does not commit the refuter to an endorsement of the antithesis. Nāgārjuna, as we saw in chapter 2, wants to maintain instead that thesis and antithesis share a false existential precommitment.

Simplicity (*laghutva*) is, Śrīharṣa considers and the Naiyāyikas agree, a *ceteris paribus* preference-condition. Of two evidentially equivalent and otherwise rationally acceptable theses, the simpler one is to be preferred. The burden of proof lies with someone who wishes to defend a more complex hypothesis when a simpler one is at hand. The Nyāya cosmological argument appeals to simplicity when it infers from the world as product to a *single* producer rather than a multiplicity of producers. Here too the role of the simplicity consideration is to affect the burden of proof, not itself to prove. Cohen and Nagel[15] make a related point when they diagnose as the 'fallacy of simplism' the mistake of thinking that 'of any two hypotheses, the simpler is the *true* one.' In any case, simplicity can be a product not of the content of a hypothesis, but only of its mode of presentation – the distinction is made by the Naiyāyikas themselves.[16] And it is hard to see how it can be rational to prefer one hypothesis to another only because it is simpler in *form*.

We have assumed that the rival hypotheses are both empirically adequate, that is to say, they are both consistent with all known facts. Śrīharṣa mentions an unacceptable consequence involving empirical evidence (*utsarga*). It is an objection to the usual idea that if there is empirical evidence supporting one hypothesis, but not the other, then the first is confirmed. Śrīharṣa's sceptical claim is that a hypothesis must be considered refuted unless it is conclusively proved; non-conclusive empirical evidence does nothing to affect this burden of proof. Likewise, he says, a hypothesis must be considered refuted if it is incapable of being proved or disproved – this at least seems to be the import of the unacceptable consequence he calls 'impertinence' (*anucitya*) or 'impudence' (*vaiyātya*).

Other varieties[17] of suppositional refutation have been suggested along lines similar to the ones we have reviewed. Different authors propose different sets of criteria for rational non-acceptance. What we have seen is that there is, in the background, a jostling over the weight and place of the burden of proof. The sceptic presses in the direction of one extreme – that a thesis can be considered refuted unless definitively proved. The *pramāṇa*-theoretic epistemologist tries to press in the direction of the opposite extreme – that a thesis can be considered proved unless definitively disproved. The truth lies somewhere in between, and it is the role of suppositional reason to locate it.

6.4 SUPPOSITION AND PRETENCE

Suppositional reasoning is counter-factual – were the supposition to be true, so would the unacceptable consequence. What then is the status of a supposition? It cannot be a state of knowledge, for the whole point of suppositional reasoning is that it is a means for the elimination of doubt in A by showing the unacceptibility of ~A. Udayana's proposal[18] is that a supposition is an 'imaginary imposition' (*āhāryāropa*), a pretence. The term *āhārya*, let us note, also means an actor's costume, and *āhārya-śobha* is a made-up beauty produced by ornamentation and paint. The state of affairs with respect to which the counter-factual is evaluated is a pretend state, a product of the imagination. The new logicians[19] define the mental act of pretence as a thought whose qualifier is contrary to that property which specifies the qualificand – the thought, for example, that the fiery mountain is without fire. So it is not so much counter-factual, as counter to what one believes to be actual. It is the state of mind in which one pretends that an object is something other than what one believes it to be, as, for example, in the child's game where a rock is imagined to be a boat. Pretence is said by an eighteenth-century Nyāya poetician[20] to be what governs metaphor (*rūpaka*) – one imagines a face to *be* the moon, knowing all the time that it is not. It is a 'willing suspension',[21] a 'deliberate self-deception',[22] in which one attempts to think of a thing as something other than what one believes it to be, and to trace the consequence of so doing. Udayana maintains that a pretence is a species of false belief, but this does not seem right. It is better thought of either simply as the antecedent of a true counter-factual,[23] or as not truth-apt at all.[24] The imaginary imposition is an act of mental simulation, the re-creation in imagination of a fictitious world, and such acts are fundamentally different in character from states of belief. Another Nyāya suggestion is that the state of pretence is quasi-perceptual, somewhat akin to the state one is in when experiencing a perceptual appearance one knows to be illusory. But there is no reason to suppose the domain of pretence to be limited to possible objects of perception alone, as indeed is shown by the case of pretending that an extrapolation relation obtains.

A necessary condition for doubt – Is it that A or that B? – is the possibility of being able to imagine A and to imagine B, without yet knowing which one is actual. Doubt is impossible, therefore, if one of the putative alternatives is unimaginable. Gaṅgeśa will say (see below) that the absence of doubt is sometimes 'self-established', and one meaning, perhaps, is that it is impossible to imagine the alleged alternative hypothesis. The limits of imaginary supposition are the limits of doubt. Where then do those limits lie? Presumably one cannot imagine what is logically contradictory. Other limits too follow from the Nyāya definition. It is an axiom in the Nyāya theory of content that the constituents of content (the qualificand, the qualifiers, the relation) are real entities. All error is the *misascription* of a real qualifier to a real qualificand.[25] Even one's belief in fictitious objects, such as monsters with three heads, is explained this way – the fictitious monster is nothing but a monstrous miscombination of real animal parts. An implication of this theory of error is that one can never be mistaken about the qualificand; all thought, no matter how erroneous, must have a real 'nucleus' to which the qualifiers are attributed. It follows that even if one can, in imagination, counterfactually ascribe qualifiers, one cannot, even in imagination, pretend that the qualificand does not exist. The Nyāya principle of acquaintance is that every basic thought-constituent is real. All thought is the arrangement and rearrangement of those basic constituents. So even pretence is limited to an available domain of fundamental thought-constituents. Pretence can only invent new order in an old world.

The implication of this is that not every metaphysically possible world is imaginable. Imaginative imposition is limited to worlds sufficiently similar to ours (or to the way we believe ours to be), in the sense of being made out of the same basic constituents. This then is a more stringent limit on the possibility of doubt. We can doubt which of a domain of possible worlds is actual, but the domain is restricted to worlds constitutively like our own.

It follows that the sceptic is not entitled to formulate the sceptical doubt in terms of a propositional negation, but must use an internal negation. For the propositional negation '~A' is true in many worlds *inaccessible* to thought, worlds constitutively quite unlike our own. In attempting to imagine ~A, what we in fact imagine is that the constituents of 'A' have some non-actual arrangement; if 'A' is the proposition '*Fa*', its imaginable negation is the totality of propositions '*Ga*', where '*G*' is a qualifier opposite to (non-compossible with) '*F*'. So a Nyāya response to scepticism is to allow the possibility of sceptical doubt about the arrangement of the fundamental constituents of thought, but to deny the possibility of sceptical doubt about those constituents themselves. There are resonances here with modern treatments of scepticism.[26] To know that A, one's evidence must exclude every imaginable possibility that one knows to be incompatible with A, but not every possibility that ~A simpliciter.

6.5 A NEW DOXASTIC ASCENT

Let us return again to the extrapolation problem, which is the problem of knowing when or whether one property proves another (Chapters 1.6, 4.7). Suppositional reasoning was meant to level the playing field and defuse the initial presumption against beliefs of such generality. In an often-quoted and sometimes parodied couplet, Udayana says:

> If there be doubt, there is inference indeed
> All the more if doubt does not occur.
> Doubt has its limit in opposition
> Suppositional reasoning is regarded as the limit of doubt.[27]

In his commentary on this couplet, Udayana first argues that a global scepticism about extrapolation – as advanced, allegedly, by the 'perceptualist' Cārvāka – is self-refuting. Those who doubt that extrapolation is *ever* warranted, on the grounds that the purported inferential relation might fail at future times or unobserved places, commit themselves to a belief in unobserved times and places, and that commitment can only be grounded in an extrapolation from past times and observed places! The possibility of global doubt about extrapolation presupposes the possibility of extrapolation. This is not quite the Humean point that extrapolation rests on a belief that nature is uniform, a belief that itself presupposes extrapolation from past to future uniformity. For Hume's intention is to show that inductive justifications of induction are self-defeating, while Udayana's aim is to show that it is global scepticism about induction that is self-defeating.

The second half of the couplet refers to the threatened infinite regress. A doubt (about the obtaining of an inferential relation) is resolved by a piece of suppositional reasoning, but does not that piece of suppositional reasoning itself rest on one's knowing a general relation, being an inference from supposition to unacceptable consequence? And since a doubt might arise in connection with this second general relation, is there not a regress in the making? It is far from clear that this line of thought ought to worry Udayana, for counterfactual statements are not in general true in virtue of corresponding universal generalisations and so it is not necessarily correct to say that pieces of suppositional reasoning are themselves extrapolative. Udayana's response is different. He argues that there is a practical contradiction in basing one's actions on a set of beliefs and at the same time doubting whether those beliefs are true. The beliefs upon which one's actions rest are a practical limit to doubt. So an infinite regress of doubt is impossible. The idea is clarified by Gaṅgeśa, in his response to Śrīharṣa's criticism of Udayana. So let us see first of all what Śrīharṣa has to say.

Śrīharṣa[28] seeks, of course, to switch the burden of proof:

> You are not able to establish an extrapolation relation as the basis of inference by arguing that when doubt should arise about a failure of extrapolation then by suppositional reasoning an opposition would be revealed in the 'deviating' option of an opposed pair that the doubt would presuppose. For suppositional reasoning of this sort brings about (according to you) an understanding of an opposition, and since this reasoning may not be well-founded, you would still face the problem of not being able to rule out the possibility of merely ostensible suppositional reasoning (*tarkābhāsa*).
>
> Since such reasoning can lead to what you would call an opposition when the reasoning is fallacious, you face the problem of possible opposition equally on each side, i.e., on both sides of the option and the opposing pair, one of which the reasoning is undertaken to eliminate. Because of the possibility of fallacious suppositional reasoning, opposition

on the side that you, sir, wish to establish (as opposed to eliminate) could occur as (fallaciously) deduced.

Then if it is held that the suppositional reasoning has its foundation in an extrapolation relation, that won't help. When there is doubt about deviation from a true extrapolation relation, there will be an infinite regress. In trying to prove another opposition with respect to the unwanted option that the new doubt involves, the difficulty arises *ad infinitum*.

Therefore, on this topic it is not difficult for us to read your couplet with the words ever so slightly altered:

> If there is opposition, there is doubt
> If none, there is doubt all the more.
> Opposition includes doubt within its borders;
> How then can suppositional reasoning be the limit of doubt?

We have seen the sceptical use of doxastic ascent before (Chapter 2.5). Śrīharṣa's application is in connection with the distinction between true and false counterfactuals. Suppositional reasoning eliminates a doubt 'Is it that A or is it that B?' by means of a counterfactual 'if B were true, then there would be an opposition (with accepted fact or attested behaviour).' As a piece of reasoning, it is persuasive only if one can be assured that the counterfactual on which it is based is true – otherwise, the reasoning would be at best unpersuasive and at worst fallacious. So the claim that the alternative hypothesis B would lead to an opposition, far from eliminating doubt, only produces more.

Gaṅgeśa's solution is to reclaim a presumptive right. It is not always necessary to prove that an extrapolation relation obtains in order to be justified in making extrapolations on its basis. One needs further proof (i.e. a piece of suppositional reasoning) only when there is a reasonable doubt about the obtaining of the relation. In all other cases, one is entitled to extrapolate without involving oneself in a proof regress. It is, of course, always possible to doubt whether the extrapolation relation obtains – but not every such doubt is a reasonable one. In particular, when the doubt is in conflict with the doubter's actual beliefs, as attested by their actions, then their doubt is merely capricious. Gaṅgeśa:[29]

> When there is doubt, there is no regular pattern of behaviour. When there is a regular pattern, doubt does not occur. Thus it has been said (by Udayana): 'That is doubted concerning which as doubted there occurs no opposition with the doubter's action.' For it is not possible at once to resort regularly to fire for smoke and to doubt that fire causes it. This is how we should understand (Udayana's) saying. Thus we may reject the argument that contradiction, understood as opposition, governing precisely which *x* cannot occur along with precisely which *y*, cannot block an

> infinite regress. It is the doubter's own behaviour that proves the lie to the doubt, that blocks it. Therefore, the view that [Śrīharṣa,] the author of the *Khaṇḍanakhaṇḍakhādya* expresses [in his parody of Udayana's couplet] may be rejected.

Gaṅgeśa's point is clear. A person's actions are explained by attributing to them a set of beliefs and desires. If people nevertheless claim to doubt one of these beliefs, or even actually to get themselves into a mental state of doubt, that mental state will still be an inoperative one in their psychological life, and as such need not be taken seriously.

6.6 EPISTEMIC EQUILIBRIUM

What is the function of reason? Reason's proper work, it is sometimes said, is to provide us with a maximum of explanatory coherence and comprehensiveness in our body of beliefs. That is the role assigned by Gaṅgeśa to suppositional reasoning. It is an 'incoherence-seeking' reason, testing a putative belief or principle for coherence-failure against a background of other beliefs, principles and theories. It might seem as if incoherence-seeking reason has no place in the justification of belief. For the claim of the *pramāṇa* epistemology is that a belief is justified when it is the product of a truth-conducive belief-forming process or method. The justification attaching to any particular belief is defeated, however, by reasonable doubt as to the truth-conduciveness of the process or method that produced it. The epistemic function accorded to incoherence-seeking reason, then, is to eliminate potential justification-defeaters. It does so by showing that belief in alternatives to the principles sustaining the belief-forming processes – fundamentally the relations that ground ampliative inference – has unacceptable consequences, unacceptable, that is, by the standards of incoherence-seeking reason itself.

Gaṅgeśa's thesis is that justification is the result of an equilibrium in a person's beliefs, actions, principles and background theories. He concludes his examination of our knowledge of extrapolation relations with a summing up of his considered view:[30]

> [It seems that] doubt persists through repeated observation, and suppositional reasoning only generates an infinite regress – how then is the inferential relation to be proven?
>
> Here's what to say. The proof of an extrapolation relation is the observation of co-existence [of reason and target] without 'cognition' of any counter-examples. 'Cognition' means both definite belief as well as doubt. That [doubt] results sometimes from a worry concerning the existence of an associate condition, and sometimes from the observation of a general characteristic without any observed distinguishing mark. And its

> absence is sometimes the result of a suppositional reason blocking the alternative, and sometimes [the absence of doubt] is given by nothing but itself (*svataḥ siddha eva*).
>
> Might it not be said that since suppositional reasoning is grounded in the proof of an[other] general relation, an infinite regress will ensue? No, because one follows a line of suppositional reasoning [only] when there is a doubt. So where, thanks to some opposition, no doubt falls, the extrapolation relation is proven even without suppositional reasoning.

Particular extrapolative judgements are justified if licensed by general extrapolation relations. Those general relations are themselves justified just as long as there is no reasonable doubt concerning their validity. The state of being free from such doubt is created and sustained by suppositional arguments, the effect of which is to shift the burden of proof in favour of the putative principle of extrapolation. It does this by showing that alternatives fail to match some standard of coherence with one's wider beliefs, principles and theories.

What Śrīharṣa questions is the justification of suppositional reason itself. The problem is to distinguish justified from merely ostensible suppositional reasoning (*tarkābhāsa*). On what grounds can I be sure that my capacity to detect incoherence is itself reliable? Might it not be a merely ostensible piece of reasoning, not a genuine inference? My capacity to derive the consequences of counterfactual suppositions is what removes the defeaters of the justification induced by the belief-forming methods and processes with which I am endowed. Śrīharṣa's scepticism brings into question my right to place my trust in that very capacity.

Shall we then say that specific acts of suppositional reasoning are themselves justified by principles of extrapolation – not, to be sure, the very same principle that the piece of suppositional reasoning is meant to justify, but another, higher-order, principle, relating suppositions and unacceptable consequences? The new principle is, in its turn, justified just in case there is a principled absence of doubt, and the absence of such doubt is created and sustained by still another intervention of coherence-seeking, suppositional reason. The chain of justification threatens to be regressive.

Nelson Goodman's influential proposal is that there is a virtuous circle of justification:[31]

> Principles of deductive inference are justified by their conformity with accepted deductive practice. Their validity depends upon accordance with the particular deductive inferences we actually make and sanction. If a rule yields unacceptable inferences, we drop it as invalid. Justification of general rules thus derives from judgements rejecting or accepting particular deductive inferences.
>
> I have said that deductive inferences are justified by their conformity to valid general rules, and that general rules are justified by their conformity

> to valid inference. But this circle is a virtuous one. . . . A rule is amended if it yields an inference we are unwilling to accept; an inference is rejected if it violates a rule we are unwilling to amend. The process of justification is the delicate one of making mutual adjustments between rules and accepted inferences; and in the agreement thus achieved lies the only justification needed for either.
>
> All this applies equally well to induction. An inductive inference, too, is justified by conformity to general rules, and a general rule by conformity to accepted inductive inference.

The idea is that an iterated process of adjustment leads eventually to a situation in which the specific inferences and the principles of inferences are in 'reflective equilibrium'.[32] From an initial set of intuitively compelling inferences, one formulates those principles that give a best fit. Some of the initial inferences cannot be made to fit, and these we now revise in line with our newly discovered principles. The eventual state of complete accord is one in which the principles best explicate the inferences, and the inferences explicate the principles (Figure 6.1).

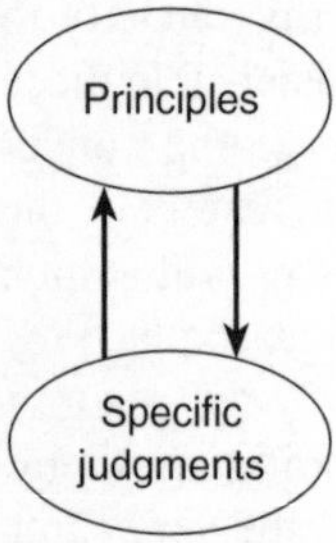

Figure 6.1 The virtuous circle

There is a serious difficulty with this proposal.[33] It is that the method at best leads to a characterisation of a person's inferential *skills*, but is unable to determine if the person is inferentially *competent*. The method of best fit is conservative, justifying with only minor scope for revision the rules of inference actually instantiated by the person's inferential practice. It seems from the empirical studies of Stich and Nisbett[34] that most people reason in accordance with some version of the gambler's fallacy when dealing with games of chance. Applying the reflective equilibrium test here would lead to the certification of a wholly unacceptable principle of inference.

Gaṅgeśa, as we saw, *does* endorse a reflective equilibrium between specific inferences and principles of inference. One the one hand, extrapolation relations are what justify specific extrapolations. On the other hand, Gaṅgeśa insists that certain principles of extrapolation are justified by actual behaviour. It is not possible for someone rationally to doubt the principle 'where there is smoke, there is fire,' and at the same time to seek out the fire whenever they encounter smoke. The principle is justified because it cannot reasonably be doubted, and the absence of such doubt is sustained by the person's inferentially grounded behaviour.

What saves the account is that there are other ways for principles of inference to be revised. The equilibrium is 'wide' rather than 'narrow'.[35] Principles of inference are revised in a process of reflecting, more or less *a priori*, on possible alternatives. Being the rule that best fits actual inferential practice is not sufficient. A principle of inference must also be found on reflection to cohere with other beliefs, principles and theories. The principle underlying inference in accordance with the gambler's fallacy coheres poorly with probabilistic theory, and a person who knows this will at least attempt to revise their rules of inference accordingly. The role of suppositional reasoning in Gaṅgeśa's theory, like that of philosophical argument in standard accounts of wide reflective equilibrium, is to render any partial or local reflective equilibrium liable to disruption under the pressure of broad reflective analysis (Figure 6.2).

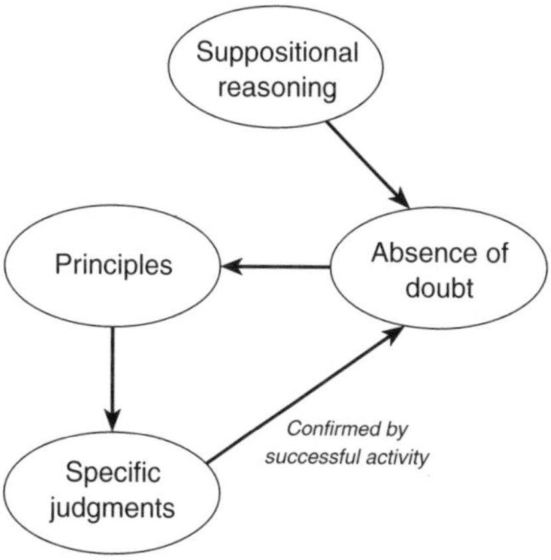

Figure 6.2 Reason in balance

Śrīharṣa's point is that suppositional reasoning itself depends for its justification on further, higher-order, *principles* of inference, and those principles too require justification. Gaṅgeśa blocks the regress by observing that even if the use of suppositional reasoning is the main way to justify principles of inference, those principles can also be justified in other ways. They can be justified pragmatically, with reference to practice and specific judgments – that is the way of narrow equilibrium. In addition, however, some principles are, at least in part, *self-certifying*, in the sense that they themselves prevent any doubt as to their veracity arising. These are principles to doubt which itself eliminates the doubt. A strong contender must be the principle of non-contradiction – for any doubt of the form 'is it that A or ~A?' presupposes that, at most, one of 'A' and '~A' is true. The use of coherence-seeking reason is itself justified by this principle, and so the spiral of doubt and doxastic ascent is turned in upon itself.

These self-doubt-eliminating principles are foundational elements in an otherwise coherentist theory. The claim is not that they are necessarily or self-evidently true: a logical possibility remains open that they are false. The claim is rather that a revision of these principles would catastrophically perturb the equilibrium of reflective justification. All other principles can be revised under the pressure of suitably compelling philosophical arguments, but these are preconditions for there to be a stable rational structure, and so form a group of principles independent of the others.[36]

Suppositional reasoning, Gaṅgeśa claims, is not always needed in the justification of general principles, for there are cases when to doubt a principle would result in a practical contradiction with one's own actions. True, reflective or suppositional reasoning alone will never bring the chain of justification to an end, but, nevertheless, and as a matter of contingent fact, our belief-forming processes are reliable. It is the fact that they do actually yield largely true beliefs, that our actions in accordance with their deliverances do actually meet with success, that belies any doubt concerning them. Suppositional rationality is an epistemic virtue – it is that which maintains our beliefs, principles and theories in a virtuous circle of mutual justification. But rationality by itself provides no guarrantee that our beliefs are generally free from error, or even free from massive error. The world must cooperate – we must happen to live in a world in which our belief-forming processes are generally reliable, so that they are epistemic virtues too. Reflective or suppositional reasoning by itself is of little epistemic value – the victim of an evil demon might be entirely rational, in respect of the internal coherence of their beliefs and principles. Their epistemic failing is not one of internal rationality, but lies rather in the contingent fact that their external belief-forming processes are unreliable followers of the truth. But suppositional reasoning is an epistemic virtue *for us*, nevertheless, because it works in tandem with our reliable belief-forming processes to give us a comprehensive understanding of ourselves as truth-seekers and an assurance that we have beliefs that cohere with our deep intellectual standards.

In a penetrating study of the place of reason in Indian thought, J. N. Mohanty has raised a foundational problem for Indian epistemological theories.[37] Each of the Indian schools selects certain means and methods of belief-formation (*pramāṇa*), and asserts that beliefs derive warrant when acquired from those preferred methods. The problem is to explain the basis for selection:

> [I]t appears as though the laying bare of the rationality of our beliefs and cognitions, of moral rules and artistic creations, confronts, in Indian thought, an absolute limit. The *pramāṇa*s establish them, consciousness evidences this act of establishment, but the judicative authority of the

*pramāṇa*s is not, and cannot be, traced back to their origin in the structure of that consciousness. The concept of rationality as operative – even if not thematized – in Indian thought depends upon our answer to this question.

This is rather similar to Roderick Chisholm's 'problem of the criterion' – is it that beliefs are justified because they meet criteria that are given in advance, or that criteria are justified because they sanction particular well-attested beliefs?[38] Gaṅgeśa, it seems to me, is proposing a solution. He describes a structure of epistemic support in which one's beliefs, rules and actions are brought together into a single body of mutual justification. The selected methods of acquiring evidence and principles of extrapolation are justified because they are what we end up with after a process of mutual revision and adjustment, a process which includes both reflective consideration of the alternatives (*tarka*) and empirical testing against the patterns of regular success in one's behaviour. Reason alone cannot eliminate all uncertainty: we must also be in a relation of nonaccidental contact with the external world. Rationality in Gaṅgeśa's epistemology involves the use of imagination and hypothetical supposition to bring our beliefs and principles into a state of reflective equilibrium. Reason alone, contra Descartes, cannot be used to eliminate all uncertainty; rather, the proper work of reason is in making ourselves epistemically more virtuous in a cooperative world. Reason is in *a fine balance*.[39]

FURTHER READING

Texts

Jayarāśi *c.* AD 800, *Tattvopaplasiṃha* (TUS).
Śrīharṣa *c.* AD 1140, *Khaṇḍanakhaṇḍakhādya* (KhKh).
Gaṅgeśa *c.* AD 1320, *Tattvacintāmaṇi* (TC).

Suppositional reasoning (6.1–4)

1 Sitansusekhar Bagchi, *Inductive Reasoning: A Study of Tarka and its Role in Indian Logic* (Calcutta: Munishchandra Sinha, 1953).

2 Vijay Bharadwaja, *Form and Validity in Indian Logic* (Shimla: Indian Institute of Advanced Study, 1990), Chapter 5.

3 Esther Solomon, *Indian Dialectics* (Ahmedabad: B. J. Institute of Learning and Research, 1976), Chapter 12 (Vol. 1), Chapter 13 (Vol. 2).

Scepticism, doxastic ascent (6.5)

1 Phyllis Granoff, *Philosophy and Argument in Late Vedānta: Śrīharṣa's Khaṇḍanakhaṇḍakhādya* (Dordrecht: Reidel Publishing Company, 1978).

2 Stephen Phillips, *Classical Indian Metaphysics* (La Salle: Open Court, 1995), Chapter 3.

3 Bimal Matilal, *Logical and Ethical Issues in Religious Belief* (Calcutta: University of Calcutta Press, 1982), Chapter 4.

4 Bimal Matilal, *The Logical Illumination of Indian Mysticism*, inaugural lecture (Oxford: Clarendon Press, 1977).

5 C. Ram–Prasad, 'Immediacy and the Direct Theory of Perception: Problems from Śrīharṣa,' *Studies in Humanities and Social Sciences* 3.2 (1996) – *Epistemology, Logic and Ontology After Matilal* (Shimla: Indian Institute of Advanced Studies), pp. 33–56.

Epistemic equilibrium, the new epistemology (6.6)

1 Stephen Phillips, *Classical Indian Metaphysics* (La Salle: Open Court, 1995), Chapter 4.

2 Mrinalkanti Gangopadhyay, 'Gaṅgeśa on *vyāptigraha*: The Means for the Ascertainment of Invariable Concomitance,' *Journal of Indian Philosophy* 3 (1975), pp. 167–208.

3 Bimal Krishna Matilal, *Perception: An Essay on Classical Indian Theories of Knowledge* (Oxford: Clarendon Press, 1986), Chapters 4, 5.

Notes

Introduction

1 *Taittirīya Upaniṣad* 2.4.

2 Max Müller, *The Six Systems of Indian Philosophy* (Oxford, 1899); Sarvepalli Radhakrishnan, *Indian Philosophy* (London: George Allen and Unwin, 1923); in the same vein is M. Hiriyanna, *Outlines of Indian Philosophy* (London, 1932). The origin of 'six system' doxographies goes back in fact to Haribhadra's eighth-century *Ṣaḍdarśanasamuccaya*.

3 J. N. Mohanty, *Essays on Indian Philosophy*, Purushottama Bilimoria ed., (Delhi: Oxford University Press, 1993), p. 261. See also J. N. Mohanty, *Reason and Tradition in Indian Thought* (Oxford: Clarendon Press, 1992). Robert Solomon, in 'Existentialism, Emotions, and the Cultural Limits of Rationality,' *Philosophy East and West* 42 (1992), pp. 597–621, cautions against Mohanty's 'intellectualisation' of the notion of rationality, an upping of the ante to the point where only philosophers satisfy their definition of a rational agent. In pressing the point, however, one must distinguish carefully between practices and norms. A philosophical theory of rationality describes an ideal against which actual rational practices are to be judged.

4 See his papers in the section entitled 'Dharma, Rationality and Moral Dilemmas,' in B. K. Matilal, *Philosophy, Culture and Religion: Collected Essays*, Vol. 2: Ethics and Epics (Delhi: Oxford University Press, 2001).

5 A. K. Ramanujan, 'Is There an Indian Way of Thinking?' *Contributions to Indian Sociology* 23 (1989), pp. 41–58.

6 Another endorsement of the type-difference hypothesis is to be found in the earlier work of Max Weber. For anthropological evidence against the hypothesis, see Jack Goody, 'East and West: Rationality in Review,' *Ethnos* (1992), pp. 6–36. For an argument in favour of the idea that judgments of rationality can be made cross-culturally, see Charles Taylor, 'Rationality,' in his *Philosophy and the Human Sciences: Philosophical Papers 2* (Cambridge: Cambridge University Press, 1985), pp. 134–151.

7 Lakshmi Ramakrishnan, 'On Talk of Modes of Thought,' *Journal of the Indian Council of Philosophical Research* 13.2 (1996), pp. 1–17. Quotation at p. 17. The criticism is pressed in the first instance against views J. N. Mohanty expresses in his *Reason and Tradition in Indian Thought* (Oxford: Clarendon Press, 1992).

8 For the Indian solutions: Jonardon Ganeri, *Semantic Powers: Meaning and the Means of Knowing in Classical Indian Philosophy* (Oxford: Clarendon Press, 1999), Chapter 5.

9 See Gary Gutting, *Michel Foucault's Archaeology of Scientific Reason* (Cambridge: Cambridge University Press, 1989), Chapter 1.

10 David Seyfort Ruegg, 'Does the Mādhyamika have a Thesis and Philosophical Position?,' in B. K. Matilal and R. D. Evans eds., *Buddhist Logic and Epistemology* (Dordrecht: Kluwer, 1986), p. 236.
11 David Hume, *Dialogues Concerning Natural Religion*, Part VII.

1 The motive and method of rational inquiry

1 *Manusaṃhitā* 2.11.
2 J. W. McCrindle, *Ancient India as Described by Megasthenes and Arrian: Being a Translation of the Fragments of the Indika of Megasthenes and the First Part of the Indika of Arrian* (Calcutta, 1926); Allan Dahlquist, *Megasthenes and Indian Religion: A Study in Motives and Types* (Uppsala: Almquist & Wiksell, 1962).
3 Hermann J. Jacobi, 'A Contribution Towards the Early History of Indian Philosophy,' translated by V. A. Sukthankar, *The Indian Antiquary* XLVII (1918), pp. 101–109.
4 Paul Hacker, 'Ānvīkṣikī,' *Wiener Zeitschrift für die Kunde Süd- und Ost-Asiens* 2 (1958), pp. 54–83. For a detailed discussion: Wilhelm Halbfass, 'Darśana, Ānvīkṣikī, Philosophy,' in his *India and Europe: An Essay in Understanding* (Albany: State University of New York Press, 1988), Chapter 15.
5 Franklin Edgerton, 'The Meaning of *sāṃkhya* and *yoga*,' *American Journal of Philology* 45 (1924), pp. 1–47; Gerald James Larson, 'Introduction to the Philosophy of Sāṃkhya,' in Gerald James Larson and Ram Shankar Bhattacharya eds., *Sāṃkhya: A Dualist Tradition in Indian Philosophy*, Encyclopedia of Indian Philosophies, Vol. 4 (Delhi: Motilal Banarsidass, 1987), pp. 3–9, 114–116.
6 Bertrand Russell, *Human Society in Ethics and Politics* (London: Allen and Unwin, 1954), p. viii.
7 *Nyāyabhāṣya* 3, 11–14. All references are to page and line numbers in Thakur's critical edition: *Gautamīyanyāyadarśana with Bhaṣya of Vātsyāyana*, critically edited by Anantalal Thakur (Delhi: Indian Council of Philosophical Research, 1997).
8 *Nyāyabhāṣya* 3, 15–20.
9 *Nyāyabhāṣya* 1, 6–10.
10 *Nyāyabhāṣya* on 4.2.29.
11 Herbert Simon and Allen Newell, *Human Problem Solving* (Englewood Cliffs, N.J.: Prentice-Hall, 1972), pp. 71–105. Robert Nozick, *The Nature of Rationality* (Princeton: Princeton University Press, 1993), pp. 163–174.
12 *Nyāyabhāṣya* 4, 14–18.
13 Uddyotakara. *Nyāyavārttika*, 24, 3.
14 Kalidas Bhattacharya, 'An Idea of Comparative Indian Philosophy,' *All India Oriental Conference* (Santiniketan, 1980), p. 80.
15 *Nyāyavārttika* 28, 19–29, 1.
16 Roderick Chisholm, *Theory of Knowledge* (Englewood Cliffs, N.J.: Prentice-Hall, 1966), pp. 56–69.
17 Bimal Krishna Matilal, *Perception: An Essay on Classical Indian Theories of Knowledge* (Oxford: Clarendon Press, 1986), p. 314.
18 Diṅnāga, *Pramāṇasamuccaya* 1, 17; Uddyotakara, *Nyāyavārttika* 208, 12–237, 5 (under 2.1.33–36).
19 Vātsyāyana's comment under NS 1.1.4, and *Vaiśeṣikasūtra* 3.1.13.
20 *Nyāyavārttika* 36, 1–14 (under 1.1.4).
21 Compare Sartre's criticism of Freud's concept of a 'censor' governing unconscious repression: '. . . the censor in order to apply its activity with discernment must know what it is repressing . . . the censor must choose and in order to choose must be aware of choosing . . .'. J-P. Sartre, *Being and Nothingness: An Essay on Phenomenological Ontology*, translated by H. E. Barnes (London: Methuen & Co., 1966), p. 52.
22 *Nyāyabhāṣya* 19, 2–3 (above 1.1.16).

23 Joerg Tuske, 'Being in Two Minds: The Divided Mind in the *Nyāyasūtra*,' *Asian Philosophy* 9.3 (1999), pp. 229–238. The 'weak' division, in which rationality is attributed only to the whole person and not to any of its subsystems, is that of Davidson: Donald Davidson, 'Paradoxes of Irrationality,' in R. Wollheim and J. Hopkins eds., *Philosophical Essays on Freud* (Cambridge: Cambridge University Press, 1982, pp. 289–305).

24 The classic exposition: Udayana, *Ātmatattvaviveka*, pp. 710–719, p. 752. See also Arindam Chakrabarti, 'I Touch What I Saw,' *Philosophy and Phenomenological Research* 52 (1992), pp. 103–117.

25 For further analysis of the Nyāya anti-reductionist argument: Jonardon Ganeri, 'Cross-modality and the Self,' *Philosophy and Phenomenological Research* (November 2000). There is interesting evidence from developmental psychology that an infant's acquisition of cross-modal capacities, specifically the ability to identify its own tactually perceived facial expressions with the visually perceived facial expressions of an imitating adult, is instrumental in its development of a sense of self; see Andrew Meltzoff, 'Molyneux's Babies: Cross-Modal Perception, Imitation, and the Mind of the Preverbal Infant,' in N. Eilan, R. McCarthy and M. W. Brewer eds, *Spatial Representation: Problems in Philosophy and Psychology* (Oxford: Basil Blackwell, 1993).

26 *Nyāyabhāṣya* 12, 7–16 (below 1.1.5).

27 *Carakasaṃhitā*, sūtrasthāna 11.13–14.

28 *Upāyahṛdaya* or *Prayogasāra*. G. Tucci, *Pre-Diṅnāga Buddhist Texts on Logic from Chinese Sources* (Baroda: Oriental Institute, Gaekwad's Oriental Series 49, 1929), pp. xvii–xviii.

29 G. Tucci, *Pre-Diṅnāga Buddhist Texts on Logic from Chinese Sources*, p. xviii.

30 VS 2.1.8: 'It has horns, a hump, a hairy tail at the extreme and a dewlap – such is the perceived mark of cowness.'

31 *Nyāyabhāṣya* 12, 4 (below 1.1.5).

32 The relations of master to property, matter to its altered condition, cause to effect, efficient cause to caused, matter to form, concurrent occurrence, and hindering to hindered. Further discussion: E. Frauwallner, 'Die Erkenntnislehre des Klassischen Sāṃkhya-Systems,' *Wiener Zeitschrift für die Kunde Süd- und Ost-Asiens* 2 (1958), pp. 84–139, esp. pp. 123, 126–7; Nancy Schuster, 'Inference in the Vaiśeṣikasūtras,' *Journal of Indian Philosophy* 1 (1972), pp. 341–395; M. Nozawa, 'Inferential Marks in the Vaiśeṣikasūtras,' *Saṃbhāṣā: Nagoya Studies in Indian Culture and Buddhism* 12 (1991), pp. 25–38; Claus Oetke, 'Ancient Indian Logic as a Theory of Non-Monotonic Reasoning,' *Journal of Indian Philosophy* 24 (1996), pp. 447–539.

33 *Nyāyabhāṣya* 12, 16–19 (below 1.1.5).

34 Jayarāśi, *Tattvopaplavasiṃha* 74, 8–9.

35 H. N. Randle, *Indian Logic in the Early Schools* (Oxford: Oxford University Press, 1930), p. 148.

36 B. K. Matilal, *The Character of Logic in India* (Albany: State University of New York Press, 1998), p. 32.

37 For an analysis of such reductive attempts in a wider context: Jonardon Ganeri, 'Indian Logic and the Colonisation of Reason,' in Jonardon Ganeri ed., *Indian Logic: A Reader* (London: Curzon Press, 2001).

38 Stanisław Schayer, 'Über die Methode der Nyāya-Forschung,' in O. Stein and W. Gambert eds., *Festschrift für Moritz Winternitz* (Leipzig, 1933), pp. 247–257. Schayer's paper is translated into English by Joerg Tuske in Jonardon Ganeri ed., *Indian Logic: A Reader* (London: Curzon Press, 2001).

39 *Nyāyabhāṣya* 285, 4–8 [below 5.1.3].

40 B. K. Matilal, *The Character of Logic in India* (Albany: State University of New York Press, 1998), p. 63.

41 For detailed analysis: Pradeep P. Gokhale, *Inference and Fallacies Discussed in Ancient Indian Logic* (Delhi: Sri Satguru Publications, 1992).

42 *Nyāyabhāṣya* 14, 4–5.
43 On the status of the *mleccha*: Aloka Parasher, *Mlecchas in Early India: A Study in Attitudes Towards Outsiders upto AD 600* (New Delhi: Munshiram Manoharlal, 1991).
44 *Nyāyabhāṣya* 96, 16–97, 7 (below 2.1.68).
45 Elizabeth Fricker, 'Against Gullibility,' in B. K. Matilal and A. Chakrabarti eds., *Knowing from Words* (Dordrecht: Kluwer, 1994), pp. 125–161.
46 For a fuller development of this defence: Jonardon Ganeri, *Semantic Powers: Meaning and the Means of Knowing in Classical Indian Philosophy* (Oxford: Clarendon Press, 1999), Chapters 1 and 2.
47 *Nyāyabhāṣya* 87, 11–12 (below 2.1.52).

2 Rationality, emptiness and the objective view

1 David Seyfort Ruegg, *The Literature of the Madhyamaka School of Philosophy in India* (Wiesbaden: Otto Harrassowitz, 1981), p. 2.
2 Mark Siderits, 'Nāgārjuna as Antirealist,' *Journal of Indian Philosophy* 16 (1988), pp. 311–326; also his 'Thinking on Empty: Madhyamaka Anti-Realism and Canons of Rationality,' in S. Biderman and B-A Scharfstein eds., *Rationality in Question* (Leiden: E. J. Brill, 1989), pp. 231–250.
3 David Loy, 'The Clôture of Deconstruction: A Mahāyāna Critique of Derrida,' *International Philosophical Quarterly* 27 (1987), pp. 59–80; Harold Coward, *Derrida and Indian Philosophy* (Albany: State University of New York Press, 1990), Chapter 6; Kenneth Liberman, 'The Grammatology of Emptiness,' *International Philosophical Quarterly* 31.4 (1991), pp. 183–195; Bimal K. Matilal, 'Is Prasaṅga a Form of Deconstruction?' *Journal of Indian Philosophy* 20 (1992), pp. 345–362.
4 Thomas Nagel, *The View from Nowhere* (New York: Oxford University Press, 1986), p. 4: 'To acquire a more objective understanding of some aspect of life or the world, we step back from our initial view of it and form a new conception which has that view and its relation to the world as its object. In other words, we place ourselves in the world that is to be understood. The old view then comes to be regarded as an appearance, more subjective than the new view, and correctable or confirmable by reference to it. The process can be repeated, yielding a still more objective conception.'
5 Bernard Williams, *Descartes: The Project of Pure Enquiry* (Harmondsworth: Penguin, 1978), pp. 64–65.
6 E. S. Spelke and G. A. Van De Walle, 'Perceiving and Reasoning about Objects: Insights from Infants,' in Naomi Eilan, Rosaleen McCarthy and Bill Brewer eds., *Spatial Representation* (Oxford: Blackwell, 1993), pp. 132–161.
7 Śāntideva, *Bodhicaryāvatāra* 9.35.
8 On presupposition and truth-value gaps: P. F. Strawson, *Introduction to Logical Theory* (London: Methuen, 1952).
9 Further examples: MK 25.17, 25.18, 27.15–18. Interesting is the suggestion of Richard Robinson that the method of reasoning from the four options has two distinct functions, a positive therapeutic role, as exhibited by the unnegated forms, and a destructive dialectical role, exhibited by the negated forms. Richard H. Robinson, *Early Mādhyamika in India and China* (Madison, Milwaukee and London: University of Winsconsin Press, 1967), pp. 39–58, esp. pp. 55–56.
10 On other patterns in Nāgārjuna's argumentation: Richard H. Robinson, *Early Mādhyamika in India and China*, p. 48.
11 Bimal Krishna Matilal, *The Logical Illumination of Indian Mysticism* (Oxford: Clarendon Press, 1977), p. 7; *cf.* 'Is Prasaṅga a Form of Deconstruction?' *Journal of Indian Philosophy* 20 (1992), p. 353. Richard Hayes, 'Nāgārjuna's Appeal,' *Journal of Indian Philosophy* 22 (1994), pp. 309–410. The translation of MK 15.8–9 below follows Hayes, pp. 368–9.

12 Graham Priest, 'The Structure of the Paradoxes of Self-Reference,' *Mind* 103 (1994), pp. 25–34; *Beyond the Limits of Thought* (Cambridge: Cambridge University Press, 1995).
13 For the comparison: Thomas McEvilley, 'Pyrrhonism and Mādhyamika,' *Philosophy East and West* 32 (1982), pp. 3–35. Against: Mark Siderits, 'Matilal on Nāgārjuna,' in P. Bilimoria and J. N. Mohanty eds., *Relativism, Suffering and Beyond: Essays in Memory of B. K. Matilal* (Delhi: Oxford University Press, 1997), pp. 69–92.
14 Benson Mates, *The Skeptic Way: Sextus Empiricus's Outlines of Pyrrhonism* (New York: Oxford University Press, 1996), p. 176.
15 Richard Robinson, 'Some Logical Aspects of Nāgārjuna's System,' *Philosophy East and West* 6 (1957), pp. 291–308; 'Did Nāgārjuna Really Refute All Philosophical Views?' *Philosophy East and West* 22 (1972), pp. 325–331. Richard Hayes, 'Nāgārjuna's Appeal,' *Journal of Indian Philosophy* 22 (1994), pp. 299–378.
16 Jonardon Ganeri, *Semantic Powers: Meaning and the Means of Knowing in Classical Indian Philosophy* (Oxford: Clarendon Press, 1999), Chapter 5.
17 Ernest Sosa, *Knowledge in Perspective* (Cambridge: Cambridge University Press, 1991), p. 181.
18 My argument in this paragraph follows David Burton, *Emptiness Appraised: A Critical Study of Nāgārjuna's Philosophy* (London: Curzon Press, 1999), pp. 160–172. On the debating trick of 'quibbling' (*chala*): B. K. Matilal, *The Character of Logic in India* (Albany: State University of New York Press, 1998), pp. 47–48.
19 Compare Graham Priest on Sextus Empiricus: *Beyond the Limits of Thought* (Cambridge: Cambridge University Press, 1995), p. 48.
20 Bimal K. Matilal, *Perception: An Essay on Classical Indian Theories of Knowledge* (Oxford: Clarendon Press, 1986).
21 *Pramāṇasamuccaya* II, 1.
22 Kamaleswar Bhattacharya, 'Nāgārjuna's Arguments against Motion: Their Grammatical Basis,' in G. Bhattacharya et al. eds., *A Corpus of Indian Studies: Essays in Honour of Professor Gaurinath Sastri* (Calcutta: Sanskrit Pustak Bhandar, 1980), pp. 85–95; 'The Grammatical Basis of Nāgārjuna's Arguments: Some Further Considerations,' *Indologica Taurinensia*, 8–9 (1980–1), pp. 35–43; 'Nāgārjuna's Arguments Against Motion,' *Journal of the International Association of Buddhist Studies* 8 (1985), pp. 7–16. For criticism: George Cardona, 'A Path Still Taken: Some Early Indian Arguments Concerning Time,' *Journal of the American Oriental Society* 111.3 (1991), pp. 445–464. Reply: Kamaleswar Bhattacharya, 'Back to Nāgārjuna and Grammar,' *The Adyar Library Bulletin* 59 (1995), pp. 178–189.
23 Jonardon Ganeri, *Semantic Powers: Meaning and the Means of Knowing in Classical Indian Philosophy* (Oxford: Clarendon Press, 1999), Chapter 2.1.
24 Bimal K. Matilal, *Epistemology, Logic and Grammar in Indian Philosophical Analysis* (The Hague: Mouton, 1971), pp. 60–2; see also his *The Navya-Nyāya Doctrine of Negation* (Harvard: Harvard University Press, 1968), pp. 72–73.
25 David Lewis, *The Plurality of Worlds* (Oxford: Basil Blackwell, 1986), pp. 202–204; E. J. Lowe, 'Lewis on Persistence versus Endurance,' *Analysis* 47 (1987), pp. 152–154; David Lewis, 'Rearrangement of Particles: Reply to Lowe,' *Analysis* 48 (1988), pp. 65–72. For defences of the adverbial solution: Sally Haslanger, *Change, Persistence and Possibility* (Ph.D. dissertation, University of California, 1985); Mark Johnston, 'Is There a Problem About Persistence?' *Aristotelian Society Supplementary Volume* 61 (1987), pp. 107–135.
26 Mark Siderits and J. Dervin O'Brien, 'Zeno and Nāgārjuna on Motion,' *Philosophy East and West* 26 (1976), pp. 281–299. Brian Galloway, 'Notes on Nāgārjuna and Zeno on Motion,' *The Journal of the International Association of Buddhist Studies* 10 (1987), pp. 80–87.
27 *Physics* 239b11–13; 239b14–16; 239b5–9; 239b30–3; 239b33–40a. Translation: Jonathan Barnes ed., *The Complete Works of Aristotle* (Princeton: Princeton University Press, 1985).

28 Jonathan Lear, 'A Note on Zeno's Arrow,' *Phronesis* 26 (1981), pp. 91–104.

29 Jorge Luis Borges, *Collected Fictions*, translated by Andrew Hurley (London: Penguin Books, 1998), pp. 96–100.

30 David Seyfort Ruegg, 'Does the Mādhyamika have a Thesis and Philosophical Position?' in B. K. Matilal and R. D. G. Evans eds., *Buddhist Logic and Epistemology: Studies in The Buddhist Analysis of Inference and Language* (Dordrecht: Reidel Publishing Company, 1982), pp. 229–238.

31 Some prefer to resolve the tension by dropping the global concept scepticism: David Burton, *Emptiness Appraised: A Critical Study of Nāgārjuna's Philosophy* (London: Curzon Press, 1999), Chapters 1–4.

3 The rational basis of metaphysics

1 Wilhelm Halbfass, *On Being and What There Is: Classical Vaiśeṣika and the History of Indian Ontology* (Albany: State University of New York Press, 1992), esp. p. 54.

2 Gilbert Ryle, *The Concept of Mind* (London: Hutchinson & Co., 1949), Chapter 1.

3 An excellent review of the details of Vaiśeṣika ontology is Karl Potter ed., *Indian Metaphysics and Epistemology – The Tradition of Nyāya-Vaiśeṣika up to Gaṅgeśa*, Encyclopedia of Indian Philosophies, Vol. 2 (Delhi: Motilal Banarsidass, 1977), Introduction.

4 *Kiraṇāvalī*, p. 160.

5 Numbering of the verses in the *Lakṣaṇāvalī* follows Musashi Tachikawa, *The Structure of the World in Udayana's Realism: A Study of the Lakṣaṇāvalī and the Kiraṇāvalī* (Dordrecht: Reidel Publishing Company, 1981).

6 *Vaiśeṣikasūtra* 1.1.14: 'The characteristic of a substance is to possess motions, qualities and to be [their] inherence cause.'

7 In what follows, bold roman letters denote nodes in the graph, and italic letters denote the entities those nodes represent.

8 *Vaiśeṣikasūtra* 1.1.15–6. *Padārthadharmasaṃgraha* 18. Section numbering in the *Padārthadharmasaṃgraha* follows Karl Potter ed., *Indian Metaphysics and Epistemology – The Tradition of Nyāya-Vaiśeṣika up to Gaṅgeśa*, Encyclopedia of Indian Philosophies, Vol. 2 (Delhi: Motilal Banarsidass, 1977), pp. 282–303.

9 *Padārthadharmasaṃgraha* 50–51.

10 *Nyāyabhūṣaṇa*, p. 158.

11 *Vaiśeṣikasūtra* 1.1.16.

12 For later comment on Bhāsarvajña's revision: Karl Potter and Sibajiban Bhattacharyya eds., *Indian Philosophical Analysis – Nyāya-Vaiśeṣika from Gaṅgeśa to Raghunātha Śiromaṇi*, Encyclopedia of Indian Philosophies, Vol. 6 (Delhi: Motilal Banarsidass, 1993), pp. 323, 525–528.

13 *Padārthatattvanirūpaṇa*, p. 43.

14 Musashi Tachikawa, *The Structure of the World in Udayana's Realism: A Study of the Lakṣaṇāvalī and the Kiraṇāvalī* (Dordrecht: Reidel Publishing Company, 1981), p. 41.

15 *Kiraṇāvalī*, p. 161.

16 In favour: Richard Thomason, 'Species, Determinates, and Natural Kinds,' *Noûs* 3 (1969), pp. 95–101; Ian Hacking, 'Working in a New World: The Taxonomic Solution,' in Paul Horwich ed., *World Changes: Thomas Kuhn and the Nature of Science* (Cambridge, Mass., MIT Press, 1993), pp. 275–310; Peter Gärdenfors, 'Induction, Conceptual Spaces, and AI,' in Douglas Stalker ed., *Grue! The New Riddle of Induction* (Chicago: Open Court, 1994), pp. 117–134. Against: Ronald de Sousa, 'The Natural Shiftiness of Natural Kinds,' *Canadian Journal of Philosophy* 14 (1984), pp. 561–580; Muhamad Ali Khalida, 'Natural Kinds and Crosscutting Categories,' *Journal of Philosophy* 95 (1998), pp. 33–50.

17 *Vaiśeṣikasūtra* 1.2.4. Wilhelm Halbfass, *On Being and What There Is: Classical Vaiśeṣika and the History of Indian Ontology* (Albany: State University of New York Press, 1992), Chapter 7.

18 Ian Hacking, 'Working in a New World: The Taxonomic Solution,' in Paul Horwich ed., *World Changes: Thomas Kuhn and the Nature of Science* (Cambridge, Mass., MIT Press, 1993), pp. 286–289.

19 Bimal Krishna Matilal, *Perception: An Essay on Classical Indian Theory of Knowledge* (Oxford: Clarendon Press, 1986), Chapter 12.

20 Aparārkadeva, a follower of Bhāsarvajña. *Nyāyamuktāvalī*, S. S. Sastri and V. S. Sastri ed., (Madras: Madras Government Oriental Series 167, 1961), pp. 120–126; précis by S. S. Sastri in Karl Potter ed., *Indian Epistemology and Metaphysics*, Encyclopedia of Indian Philosophies, Vol. 2 (Princeton: Princeton University Press, 1977), pp. 604–612.

21 Raghunātha. *Kiraṇāvalīprakāśadīdhiti* (Badrinath Sastri ed., Princess of Wales Saraswati Bhavana Texts 38, Benares: Vidya Vilas Press 1932), p. 15. For comment: Karl Potter, *The Padārthatattvanirūpaṇam of Raghunātha Śiromaṇi* (Cambridge, Mass.: Harvard University Press, Harvard Yenching Institute Studies, Vol. 17, 1957), pp. 65–66.

22 Muhamad Ali Khalida, 'Natural Kinds and Crosscutting Categories,' *Journal of Philosophy* 95 (1998), pp. 33–50.

23 Daniel Ingalls, *Materials for the Study of Navya-Nyāya Logic* (Cambridge, Mass.: Harvard University Press, 1951), p. 67.

24 What about the distinction between absential and antinodes? The traditional way of making the distinction is to say that simple absence is the denial of inherence (or some other non-identity relation) and difference is the denial of identity. Graph-theoretically, the distinctive feature of an antinode **x*** is that it absentially qualifies every node other than **x**, while an absential node **x**′ does not. Does this difference fail when *x* is something which inheres in nothing (an atom, an individuator)? No, because such things do not inhere in themselves – so **x**′, unlike **x***, absentially qualifies **x**. Indeed, this second contrast is itself sufficient to discriminate absential nodes and antinodes.

25 Raghunātha, *Padārthatattvanirūpaṇa*, p. 55. Daniel Ingalls, *Materials for the Study of Navya-Nyāya Logic* (Cambridge, Mass.: Harvard University Press, 1951), p. 68. Bimal K. Matilal, *Logic, Language and Reality* (Delhi: Motilal Banarsidass, 1985), p. 149. Roy W. Perrett, 'Is Whatever Exists Knowable and Nameable?' *Philosophy East and West* 49.4 (1999), pp. 410–414, esp. 408–9. I disagree here with the idea of Matilal and Perrett that there is only an intensional difference between an object and the absence of its absence. For me, a type difference in the graph means a type difference in categories of thing.

26 *Padārthatattvanirūpaṇa*, pp. 67–69. Daniel Ingalls, *Materials*, pp. 68–69; Bimal K. Matilal, *Logic, Language and Reality*, pp. 149–150.

27 Daniel Ingalls draws a comparison between Navya-Nyāya and intuitionist logic (*Materials*, p. 68, n. 135), claiming that it is the Elimination rule for double negation that is rejected. However we *are* able, in Navya-Nyāya logic, to infer from the absence of the absence of an entity to the presence of that entity; conversely, we are *not* able to infer from the presence of an entity to the absence of its absence – the non-pervasive node is a counter-example.

28 Daniel Ingalls, *Materials for the Study of Navya-Nyāya Logic* (Cambridge, Mass.: Harvard University Press, 1951), pp. 73–4; Bimal Matilal, *The Navya-Nyāya Doctrine of Negation* (Cambridge, Mass.: Harvard University Press, 1968), pp. 53, 72, 85; *Logic, Language and Reality* (Delhi: Motilal Banarsidass, 1985), pp. 119–122.

29 Frege's notion of 'divisibility' is formally rather analogous. Gottlob Frege, *The Foundations of Arithmetic*, translated by J. L. Austin (Oxford: Basil Blackwell, 1950), p. 66: 'The syllables "letters in the word three" pick out the word as a whole, and as indivisible in the sense that no part of it falls any longer under the same concept. Not

all concepts possess this quality. We can, for example, divide up something falling under the concept "red" into parts in a variety of ways, without the parts thereby ceasing to fall under the same concept "red."'

30 Karl Potter ed., *Indian Metaphysics and Epistemology – The Tradition of Nyāya-Vaiśeṣika up to Gaṅgeśa*, Encyclopedia of Indian Philosophies, Vol. 2 (Delhi: Motilal Banarsidass, 1977), pp. 114–119.

31 Raghunātha, *Padārthatattvanirūpaṇa*, pp. 44–46.

32 Dharmakīrti, *Pramāṇavārttika* II, 85–86; Kamalaśīla, *Pañjikā* under *Tattvasaṃgraha* 592–598.

33 Udayana, *Ātmatattvaviveka*, pp. 586–617. Prabal Kumar Sen, 'The Nyāya-Vaiśeṣika Theory of Variegated Colour (*citrarūpa*): Some Vexed Problems,' *Studies in Humanities and Social Sciences* 3.2 (1996), pp. 151–172.

34 Daniel Ingalls, *Materials*, pp. 73–4; Bimal Matilal, *The Navya-Nyāya Doctrine of Negation* (Cambridge, Mass.: Harvard University Press, 1968), pp. 71–73.

35 Matilal's property-location language, in which properties have both a 'presence range' and an 'absence range' and the two ranges are permitted to overlap, is a different way to capture the same idea; B. K. Matilal, *Logic, Language and Reality*, pp. 112–127.

36 Gaṅgeśa, *Tattvacintāmaṇi*, I, *pramālakṣaṇa*, p. 401.

37 For modern discussions of dialetheism: Graham Priest, *In Contradiction: A Study of the Transconsistent* (Dordrecht: Martin Nijhoff Publishers, 1987), Part Two; Mark Sainsbury, *Paradoxes* (Cambridge: Cambridge University Press, 1995, 2nd edn.), Chapter 6.

38 Gaṅgeśa, *Tattvacintāmaṇi*, II, *vyāptipañcaka*, pp. 27–31.

39 Gaṅgeśa, *Tattvacintāmaṇi*, II, *siddhānta-lakṣaṇa* p. 100.

40 I follow here the explanation of Raghunātha. *Vyāptipañcakadīdhiti* text 3–4 (Ingalls, *Materials*, p. 154).

41 *Vaiśeṣikasūtra* 1.1.9, 7.2.1–8.

42 *Nyāyabhūṣaṇa*, p. 159.

43 For the generalisation to numbers greater than 2: Jonardon Ganeri, 'Objectivity and Proof in a Classical Indian Theory of Number,' *Synthese* (forthcoming).

44 *Śaktivāda* with Kṛṣṇa Bhaṭṭa's *Mañjūṣa*, Mādhava Bhaṭṭācārya's *Vivṛtti* and Sāhitya Darśanācārya's *Vinodini*, G. D. Sastri ed. (Benares: Kashi Sanskrit Series no. 57, 1927), p. 189.

45 *Padārthatattvanirūpaṇa*, pp. 86–87.

46 *Avacchedakatvanirukti with Jagadīśa's Jāgadīśī*, Dharmananda Mahabhaga ed., (Varanasi: Kashi Sanskrit Series 203), p. 38. Translation: Yūkō Miyasaka, *The Concept of Avacchedakatva in Navya-Nyāya (containing the text of Raghunātha Śiromaṇi's Avacchedakatvanirukti and its Commentary Jāgadīśī with an English Translation, Explanatory Notes and a Detailed Introduction)* (Poona: Centre of Advanced Study in Sanskrit, Ph.D. Thesis, 1980).

4 Reduction, exclusion and rational reconstruction

1 For this contrast: Huw Price, 'Metaphysical Pluralism,' *Journal of Philosophy* 89 (1992), pp. 387–410. Price prefers 'additive monism' where I have chosen 'additive realism,' on the reasonable grounds that reductionism and pluralism too are varieties of realism. But 'monism' is a loaded term in Indian philosophical theory, frequently attaching to specific doctrines in the school of Advaita Vedānta, and so I avoid it here.

2 G. F. Stout, 'The Nature of Universals and Propositions,' *Proceedings of the British Academy* 10 (1921), pp. 157–172.

3 D. C. Williams, 'On the Elements of Being,' *Review of Metaphysics* 7 (1953), pp. 171–192.

4 *Pramāṇasamuccaya*. The Sanskrit original is lost. Translations from the Tibetan are taken from (Chapter I) Masaaki Hattori, *Dignāga, On Perception, being the Pratyakṣapariccheda of Dignāga's Pramāṇasamuccaya from the Sanskrit fragments and the Tibetan versions* (Cambridge, Mass.: Harvard University Press, 1968), and (Chapters II and V) Richard Hayes, *Dignāga on the Interpretation of Signs* (Dordrecht: Kluwer Academic Publishers, 1988), revised following Shoryu Katsura, 'Dignāga and Dharmakīrti on *apoha*,' in E. Steinkellner ed., *Studies in the Buddhist Epistemological Tradition* (Vienna: Österreichische Akademie der Wissenschaften, 1991), pp. 129–146. In what follows, these are referred to by chapter number, I, II or V.

5 Theodore Stcherbatsky, *The Central Conception of Buddhism and the Meaning of the Word 'Dharma,'* (London: Royal Asiatic Society, 1922); Fumimaro Watanabe, *Philosophy and its Development in the Nikāyas and Abhidharma* (Delhi: Motilal Banarsidass, 1983); Karl Potter et al. ed., *Abhidharma Buddhism to 150 AD*, Encyclopedia of Indian Philosophies, Vol. 7 (Delhi: Motilal Banarsidass, 1996).

6 Vasubandhu, *Abhidharmakoṣa* VI 14cd.

7 *Dignāga on the Interpretation of Signs* (Dordrecht: Kluwer Academic Publishers, 1988); 'Diṅnāga,' in E. Craig ed., *Routledge Encyclopedia of Philosophy* (1998), Vol. 3, pp. 74–76: 'The first method of securing new knowledge is described as pure sensation (*pratyakṣa*), a form of cognition that is free from all judgment (*kalpanā*). The subject of this type of cognition is particular instances (*svalakṣaṇa*) of colour, sound and other sensible properties' (p. 75).

8 'Diṅnāga's Theory of Perception,' in *Epistemology, Logic and Grammar in Indian Philosophical Analysis* (Mouton: The Hague, 1971), pp. 34–39; 'Imagination, Perception and Language,' in *Perception* (Oxford: Clarendon Press, 1986), pp. 309–356; 'Buddhist Logic and Epistemology,' in B. K. Matilal and R. D. Evans eds., *Buddhist Logic and Epistemology: Studies in the Buddhist Analysis of Inference and Language* (Dordrecht: Reidel Publishing Company, 1982), pp. 1–30; reprinted in his *The Character of Logic in India* (Albany: State University of New York Press, 1998), Chapter 4.

9 Masaaki Hattori, *Dignāga, On Perception, being the Pratyakṣapariccheda of Dignāga's Pramāṇasamuccaya from the Sanskrit fragments and the Tibetan versions* (Cambridge, Mass.: Harvard University Press, 1968); 'Apoha and Pratibhā,' in M. Nagatomi et al. eds. *Sanskrit and Indian Studies: Essays in Honour of Daniel H. H. Ingalls* (Dordrecht: Reidel Publishing Company, 1980), pp. 61–74; 'The Sautrāntika Background of the Apoha Theory,' in Leslie S. Kawamura and Keith Scott eds., *Buddhist Thought and Civilization: Essays in Honour of Herbert V. Guenther on his Sixtieth Birthday* (Emeryville: Dharma Press, 1977), pp. 47–58.

10 Shoryu Katsura, 'Dignāga and Dharmakīrti on *apoha*,' in E. Steinkellner ed., *Studies in the Buddhist Epistemological Tradition* (Vienna: Österreichische Akademie der Wissenschaften, 1991), pp. 129–146.

11 B. K. Matilal, *Epistemology, Logic and Grammar in Indian Philosophical Analysis* (The Hague: Mouton, 1971), pp. 34–36.

12 Jonardon Ganeri, *Semantic Powers* (Oxford: Clarendon Press, 1999), Chapter 6.2.

13 E. Frauwallner, 'Dignāga, sein Werk und seine Entwicklung,' *Wiener Zeitschrift für die Kunde Süd- und Ost-Asiens* 3 (1959), pp. 83–164. Rādhika Herzberger, *Bhartṛhari and the Buddhists* (Dordrecht: Reidel Publishing Company, 1986).

14 Later Buddhist theory makes a clear distinction between 'synchronic' and 'diachronic' modes of grouping; for the Jaina origins of the distinction: Piotr Balcerowicz, 'How Could a Cow be Both Synchronically and Diachronically Homogenous, or On the Jaina Notions of *tiryak-sāmānya* and *ūrdhvatā-sāmānya*,' in N. K. Wagle and Olle Qvarnström eds., *Approaches to Jaina Studies: Philosophy, Logic, Rituals and Symbols* (Toronto: University of Toronto, 1999), pp. 211–235.

15 Nicholas Rescher, 'The Roots of Objectivity,' in *Scientific Realism* (Dordrecht: Reidel Publishing Company, 1987), pp. 111–125. The quotation below is at p. 118.

16 Later Yogācāra philosophers introduce the idea that the meaning of a general term is a mental image (*pratibimba*) which is 'qualified' by an exclusion of others. Śāntarakṣita, *Tattvasaṃgraha* 1005–1010; see also Gopikamohan Bhattacharya, 'Ratnakīrti on Apoha,' in B. K. Matilal and R. D. Evans eds., *Buddhist Logic and Epistemology: Studies in the Buddhist Analysis of Inference and Language* (Dordrecht: Reidel Publishing Company, 1982), pp. 291–298. I do not believe that Diṅnāga himself endorses this view. In any case, the role of the mental image is at best within explanations of the psychology of understanding; it is the exclusion that does the semantic work.

17 Gennaro Chierchia and Sally McConnell-Ginet, *Meaning and Grammar* (Cambridge, Mass.: The MIT Press, 1990). Diṅnāga's semantics analyses terms as generalised quantifiers. Compare D. Westertähl, 'Quantifiers,' in D. Gabbay and F. Guenther eds., *The Handbook of Philosophical Logic*, vol. 4: *Topics in the Philosophy of Language* (Dordrecht: Reidel, 1988).

18 The class-theoretic formula is that, for any classes x and y, $x \subseteq y$ iff $x \cap non\text{-}y = \varnothing$.

19 Shoryu Katsura, 'The apoha Theory of Dignāga,' *Indogaku Bukkyogaku Kenkyū* 28 (1979), pp. (16)–(20). Katsura thinks that Diṅnāga defines exclusion with reference to a presupposed hierarchy. For me, the hierarchy is a consequence of his exclusion theory of meaning.

20 Bimal K. Matilal, *Epistemology, Logic and Grammar in Indian Philosophical Analysis* (The Hague: Mouton, 1971), Chapter 1.6. Jonardon Ganeri, *Semantic Powers* (Oxford: Clarendon Press, 1999), Chapter 4.2.

21 Bimal Krishna Matilal, *The Word and the World* (Delhi: Oxford University Press, 1990), p. 97. Masaaki Hattori, 'Apoha and Pratibhā,' in M. Nagatomi et al. eds., *Sanskrit and Indian Studies: Essays in Honour of Daniel H. H. Ingalls* (Dordrecht: Reidel Publishing Company, 1980), pp. 61–74.

22 *Vākyapadīyam*, II 143.

23 Gottlob Frege, *The Foundations of Arithmetic*, translated by J. L. Austin. (Oxford: Basil Blackwell, 1950), Introduction; see also Michael Dummett, *Frege: Philosophy of Mathematics* (London, Duckworth, 1991), Chapter 16.

24 Masaaki Hattori, 'Apoha and Pratibhā,' in M. Nagatomi et al. eds. *Sanskrit and Indian Studies: Essays in Honour of Daniel H. H. Ingalls* (Dordrecht: Reidel Publishing Company, 1980), p. 66.

25 Brendan S. Gillon and Richard Hayes, 'The Role of the Particle *eva* in (Logical) Quantification in Sanskrit,' *Wiener Zeitschrift für die Kunde Süd- und Ost-Asiens* 26 (1982), pp. 195–203. Jonardon Ganeri, 'Dharmakīrti's Semantics for the Particle *eva*,' in Shoryu Katsura ed., *Dharmakīrti's Thought and Its Impact on Indian and Tibetan Philosophy* (Vienna: Österreichische Akademie der Wissenschaften, 1999), pp. 101–116. Brendan Gillon, 'Another Look at the Sanskrit Particle *eva*,' in Shoryu Katsura ed., *Dharmakīrti's Thought and Its Impact on Indian and Tibetan Philosophy* (Vienna: Österreichische Akademie der Wissenschaften, 1999), pp. 117–130.

26 Shoryu Katsura, 'Dignāga on *trairūpya*,' *Journal of Indian and Buddhist Studies* 32 (1983), pp. (15)–(21).

27 I discuss the behaviour of *only* without this assumption in Jonardon Ganeri, 'Dharmakīrti's Semantics for the Particle *eva (only)*,' pp. 101–116.

28 Jinendrabuddhi; see M. Hattori, 'Apoha and Pratibhā,' in M. Nagatomi et al. eds., *Sanskrit and Indian Studies: Essays in Honour of Daniel H. H. Ingalls* (Dordrecht: Reidel Publishing Company, 1980), pp. 64–65.

29 Tom F. Tillemans, 'On *sapakṣa*,' *Journal of Indian Philosophy* 18 (1990), pp. 53–80.

30 Hans H. Herzberger, 'Three Systems of Buddhist Logic,' in B. K. Matilal and R. D. Evans eds., *Buddhist Logic and Epistemology: Studies in the Buddhist Analysis of Inference and Language* (Dordrecht: Reidel Publishing Company, 1982), pp. 59–76.

31 Bimal Matilal, 'Buddhist Logic and Epistemology,' in B. K. Matilal and R. D. Evans eds., *Buddhist Logic and Epistemology: Studies in the Buddhist Analysis of Inference and Language* (Dordrecht: Reidel Publishing Company, 1982), pp. 1–30; reprinted in his *The Character of Logic in India* (Albany: State University of New York Press, 1998), Chapter 4.

32 *Collection on Knowing* ad II 6. The various possibilities are represented in a different way in Diṅnāga's brief *Chart of Reasons* (HC). There a 3 × 3 grid represents the nine ways for the reason property to be distributed across the likeness and unlikeness classes. Interesting is the proposal of Vijay Bharadwaja to interpret the three conditions as requirements that the reason: (i) be 'relevant' to the thesis; (ii) 'support' the thesis; and (iii) not 'support' the antithesis, with a correlative reading of the chart of reasons and the fallacies of reason. Vijay Bharadwaja, *Form and Validity in Indian Logic* (Shimla: Indian Institute of Advanced Study, 1990), Chapters 1–3.

33 Motoi Ono, 'Dharmakīrti on *asāsāraṇānaikāntika*,' in Shoryu Katsura ed., *Dharmakīrti's Thought and its Impact on Indian and Tibetan Philosophy* (Vienna: Österreichische Akademie der Wissenschaften, 1999), pp. 301–316. Bimal Krishna Matilal, 'Dharmakīrti and the Universally Negative Inference,' in E. Steinkellner ed., *Studies in the Buddhist Epistemological Tradition* (Vienna: Österreichische Akademie der Wissenschaften, 1991), pp. 161–168. Reprinted in *The Character of Logic in India* (Albany: State University of New York Press, 1998), pp. 118–126.

34 Dharmakīrti, *Nyāyabindu* II 11–12.

35 See Mokṣākaragupta's eleventh-century *Tarkabhāṣā or Language of Reason*. Yuichi Kajiyama, *An Introduction to Buddhist Philosophy: An Annotated Translation of the Tarkabhāṣā or Mokṣākaragupta*, Memoirs of the Faculty of Letters (Kyoto) 10 (1966), pp. 74–76.

36 *Pramāṇavārttika* I, 39–42.

37 Douglas Walton, *Arguments from Ignorance* (Penn.: The Pennsylvania State University Press, 1996).

38 Shoryu Katsura, 'Dharmakīrti's Concept of Truth,' *Journal of Indian Philosophy* 12 (1984), pp. 213–235. Georges B. J. Dreyfus, *Recognizing Reality: Dharmakīrti's Philosophy and its Tibetan Interpretations* (Albany: State University of New York Press, 1997), Chapter 17.

39 *Ālambanaparīkṣā* (ĀP).

40 There is an analogy in the Epicurean account of what it is for a perceptual state to have informational content. Richard Sorabji, *Animal Minds and Human Morals* (London: Duckworth, 1993), p. 47. For modern defences of the matching condition: David Lewis, 'Veridical Hallucination and Prosthetic Vision,' in *Philosophical Papers II* (Oxford: Oxford University Press, 1986), pp. 273–290; F. Dretske, *Knowledge and the Flow of Information* (Oxford: Basil Blackwell, 1981).

41 *Pramāṇavārttika*, III, 68–69. Shoryu Katsura, 'On Perceptual Judgement,' in N. K. Wagle and F. Watanabe eds., *Studies in Buddhism in Honour of Professor A. K. Warder* (Toronto: University of Toronto Centre for South Asian Studies, 1993), pp. 66–75; see also his 'Dignāga and Dharmakīrti on *apoha*,' in E. Steinkellner ed., *Studies in the Buddhist Epistemological Tradition* (Vienna: Österreichische Akademie der Wissenschaften, 1991), p. 138, n. 40. Georges B. J. Dreyfus, *Recognizing Reality: Dharmakīrti's Philosophy and its Tibetan Interpretations* (Albany: State University of New York Press, 1997), pp. 359–361.

42 *Collection on Knowing* I 2c–3b.

5 Rationality, harmony and perspective

1 Haribhadra, *Anekāntajayapatākā*, H. R. Kapadia ed. (Baroda: Oriental Institute, 1940), esp. p. ix. B. K. Matilal, *The Central Philosophy of Jainism* (Ahmedabad: L. D. Institute of Indology, 1981), p. 25.

2 Richard Fynes, *Hemacandra: The Lives of the Jaina Elders* (Oxford: Oxford University Press, 1998).
3 Hemacandra, *Pramāṇamīmāṃsā*. Paragraph numbering follows the edition of Mookerjee and Tatia.
4 Y. J. Padmarajiah, *Jaina Theories of Reality and Knowledge* (Bombay: Jain Sahitya Vikas Mandal, 1963), pp. 126–127.
5 *Sanmatitarkaprakaraṇa* 3.49.
6 *Brahmasūtrabhāṣya* 2.2.33.
7 *Tattvasaṃgraha*, verse 1722.
8 *Bhagavatīsūtra* 2.1.90. Bansidhar Bhatt, *The Canonical Nikṣepa: Studies in Jaina Dialectics* (Leiden: E.J. Brill, 1978), pp. xiv and 68.
9 Jonardon Ganeri, *Semantic Powers: Meaning and the Means of Knowing in Classical Indian Philosophy* (Oxford: Clarendon Press, 1999), Chapters 3, 6.
10 P. F. Strawson, 'On Referring,' *Mind* 59 (1950), pp. 320–344. David Kaplan, 'Demonstratives: An Essay on the Semantics, Logic, Metaphysics and Epistemology of Demonstratives and Other Indexicals,' in J. Almog, J. Perry, and H. Wettstein eds., *Themes From Kaplan* (Oxford: Clarendon Press, 1989).
11 Stephen Schiffer, 'Descriptions, Indexicals and Belief Reports: Some Dilemmas,' *Mind* 104 (1995), pp. 107–131.
12 Siddhasena, *Nyāyāvatāra* 29.
13 Vidyānanda, *Tattvārthaślokavārttika* 1.6.21, 1.6.25.
14 Paul Dundas, *The Jains* (London: Routledge, 1992), p. 198.
15 *Jaina Tarkabhāṣā* p. 24; see also Sukhlalji Sanghvi, 'Anekāntavāda: The Principal Jaina Contribution to Logic,' in his *Advanced Studies in Indian Logic and Metaphysics* (Calcutta: Indian Studies Past and Present, 1961), pp. 24–26.
16 Huw Price, 'Metaphysical Pluralism,' *Journal of Philosophy* 89 (1992), pp. 387–410.
17 *Pramāṇanayatattvālokālaṃkāra* 4.13.
18 *Pramāṇasamuccaya* 5.1.
19 R. C. Pandeya, 'The Conception of Syādvāda,' in R. A. Kumar, T. M. Dak and A. D. Mishra eds., *Anekāntavāda and Syādvāda* (Landun: Jain Visva Bharati, 1996), pp. 314–322. Quotation: p. 321.
20 *Syādvādamañjarī* below verse 23.
21 Pradeep P. Gokhale, 'The Logical Structure of *Syādvāda*,' *Journal of Indian Council of Philosophical Research* 8 (1991), pp. 73–81.
22 Graham Priest, Richard Routley and Jean Norman eds., *Paraconsistent Logic: Essays on the Inconsistent* (Munchen: Philosophia Verlag, 1989), pp. 16–17.
23 Stanisław Jaśkowski, 'Propositional Calculus for Contradictory Deductive Systems,' *Studia Logica* 24 (1969), pp. 143–157. Quotation: p. 149.
24 B. K. Matilal, '*Anekānta*: both yes and no?' *Journal of Indian Council of Philosophical Research* 8 (1991), pp. 1–12. Reprinted as 'The Jaina Contribution to Logic,' in *The Character of Logic in India* (Albany: State University of New York Press, 1998), pp. 127–139. Quotation: p. 137.
25 D. H. H. Ingalls, *Materials for the Study of Navya-Nyāya Logic* (Cambridge, Mass.: Harvard University Press, 1951), p. 63.
26 It may accord slightly better with some Jaina formulations to parameterise over properties or states, and treat 'exists' and 'does not exist' as assigning truth-values to points (x, F) in the parameter space.
27 This interpretation of the value 'unassertible' resembles a standard interpretation of the third value in Kleene's three-valued system. Nicholas Rescher, *Many-Valued Logic* (New York: McGraw Hill, 1963), p. 34.
28 *Jaina Tarkabhāṣā*, pp. 19–20.
29 *Syādvādamañjarī* below verse 23.
30 A. L. Basham, *History and Doctrines of the Ājīvikas* (London: Luzac & Co., 1951). Translation, p. 274, slightly revised.

31 *Laghīyastraya*, verse 12.
32 On Akalaṅka on Dharmakīrti: Nagin J. Shah, *Akalaṅka's Criticism of Dharmakīrti's Philosophy* (Ahmedabad: L. D. Institute, 1967), pp. 267–270.
33 *Nyāyakumudacandra*, pp. 421–425.
34 *Pravacanapraveśa*, verse 62 and autocommentary.
35 B. K. Matilal, *The Central Philosophy of Jainism* (Ahmedabad: L. D. Institute of Indology, 1981).
36 *Uttarādhyayanasūtra* 28.24; cited by K. N. Jayatilleke, *Early Buddhist Theory of Knowledge* (London: George Allen and Unwin, 1963), p. 164.

6 Reason in equilibrium

1 Jayarāśi (*c.* AD 800) is a principal source for the sceptical argument: *Tattvopaplasiṃha*, pp. 64–65. Jayarāśi is taken on by at least two Naiyāyikas – Bhāsarvajña and Vyomaśiva – in the centuries immediately subsequent to him; see Eli Franco, *Perception, Knowledge and Disbelief: A Study of Jayarāśi's Scepticism*, 2nd edn. (Delhi: Motilal Banarsidass, 1994), pp. 13–14, 554. A second radical critic, Śrīharṣa (twelfth century AD) presses the sceptical position with great vigour – his critique is at least a part of what drives the so-called New Epistemology (Navya-Nyāya) of Gaṅgeśa and his followers towards a reform of the earlier theory; see Stephen Phillips, *Classical Indian Metaphysics* (La Salle: Open Court, 1995). On both: Esther Solomon, *Indian Dialectics*, 2 volumes (Ahmedabad: B. J. Institute of Learning and Research, 1976), Chapter 13.
2 For a survey of the literature on this theory, see Karl Potter ed., *Indian Epistemology and Metaphysics*, Encyclopedia of Indian Philosophies, Vol. 2 (Princeton: Princeton University Press, 1977), pp. 203–206; Karl Potter and Sibajiban Bhattacharyya eds., *Indian Analytical Philosophy: Gaṅgeśa to Raghunātha*, Encyclopedia of Indian Philosophies, Vol. 6 (Princeton: Princeton University Press, 1993), pp. 187–192.
3 Ernest Sosa, *Knowledge in Perspective* (Cambridge: Cambridge University Press, 1991), pp. 225–244, esp. p. 240.
4 See also Bimal K. Matilal, *Perception: An Essay on Classical Indian Theories of Knowledge* (Clarendon Press, Oxford, 1986), pp. 153–167; Eli Franco, 'Bhāsarvajña and Jayarāśi: The Refutation of Scepticism in the *Nyāyabhūṣaṇa*,' *Berliner Indologische Studien* 3 (1987), pp. 23–49.
5 Nandita Bandyopadhyay, 'The Concept of Contradiction in Indian Logic and Epistemology,' *Journal of Indian Philosophy* 16.3 (1988), pp. 225–246, n. 1.
6 *Nyāyavārttikatātparyaṭīkā*, p. 261 (below 1.1.40).
7 *Tattvacintāmaṇi*, 1892 (Vol. 2), pp. 210–212. The relevant passage is quoted in full in Chapter 6.6.
8 *Ātmatattvaviveka*, p. 863.
9 Douglas Walton, *Arguments from Ignorance* (Penn.: The Pennsylvania State University Press, 1996).
10 On Śrīharṣa: Phyllis Granoff, *Philosophy and Argument in Late Vedānta: Śrīharṣa's Khaṇḍanakhaṇḍakhādya* (Dordrecht: Reidel Publishing Company, 1978); Stephen Phillips, *Classical Indian Metaphysics* (La Salle: Open Court, 1995), Chapter 3.
11 *Khaṇḍanakhaṇḍakhādya* IV, 19 (*aprasaṅgātmakatarkanirūpaṇa*, pp. 777–788, 1979 edition; section numbering follows this edition). Śrīharṣa the negative dialectician wants to criticise even the varieties of suppositional reasoning, although his own method depends upon it. So he says: 'By us indeed were suppositional reasonings installed in place, and so we do not reject them with [such] counter-arguments. As it is said – "it is wrong to cut down even a poisonous tree, having cultivated it oneself" (p. 787).
12 *Ātmatattvaviveka*, p. 533.

13 *Khaṇḍanakhaṇḍakhādya* II, 2 (*pratibandīlakṣaṇakhaṇḍana*, pp. 571–572). The full quotation is given by Śaṃkara Miśra in his commentary.
14 Stanisław Schayer, 'Studies on Indian Logic, Part II: Ancient Indian Anticipations of Propositional Logic' [1933], translated into English by Joerg Tuske in Jonardon Ganeri ed., *Indian Logic: A Reader* (London: Curzon Press, 2000).
15 Morris R. Cohen and Ernest Nagel, *An Introduction to Logic and Scientific Method* (London: Routledge & Kegan Paul, 1934), p. 384.
16 Bhimacarya Jhalakikar, *Nyāyakośa or Dictionary of Technical Terms of Indian Philosophy* (Poona: Bhandarkar Oriental Research Institute, 1928), under *laghutvam*.
17 A useful chart is in S. Bagchi, *Inductive Reasoning*, interleaved between p. 182 and p. 183.
18 Udayana, *Pariśuddhi*, p. 304 (under NS 1.1.40).
19 *Nyāyakośa*, under *āhāryam*.
20 Viśveśvara Paṇḍit. *Alaṅkārakaustubham*, M. P. Sivadatta and K. P. Parab eds. (Bombay: Nirnaya-sagara Press, 1898; Kavyamala no. 66), pp. 207–208.
21 Mukund Lath, 'The Concept of Āhārya-jñāna: Some Queries,' *Journal of the Indian Council of Philosophical Research* 13.1 (1995), pp. 175–181.
22 N. S. Dravid, 'Āhārya Cognition in Navya-Nyāya,' *Journal of the Indian Council of Philosophical Research* 14.2 (1996), pp. 164–168.
23 Vijay Bharadwaja, *Form and Validity in Indian Logic* (Shimla: Indian Institute of Advanced Study, 1990), Chapter 5.
24 S. Bagchi, *Inductive Reasoning*, p. 59.
25 Bimal K. Matilal, *Perception: An Essay on Classical Indian Theories of Knowledge* (Clarendon Press, Oxford, 1986), Chapter 6, esp. 6.6; Jonardon Ganeri, *Semantic Powers: Meaning and the Means of Knowing in Classical Indian Philosophy* (Oxford: Clarendon Press, 1999), pp. 138–154.
26 Especially Thomas Nagel's reflections on the possibility of what he calls a 'general concept of truth' in *The View from Nowhere* (Oxford: Oxford University Press, 1987), pp. 93–99. Also: David Lewis, 'Elusive Knowledge,' *Australasian Journal of Philosophy* 74 (1996), pp. 549–567.
27 *Nyāyakusumāñjali* 3.7.
28 *Khaṇḍanakhaṇḍakhādya* I, 29 (*vyāptilakṣaṇatadgrahopāyakhaṇḍana*; pp. 395–396). Translation: Stephen Phillips, *Classical Indian Metaphysics* (La Salle: Open Court, 1995), pp. 154–156, and for the wider context Mrinalkanti Gangopadhyay, *Indian Logic in its Sources* (Delhi: Munshiram, 1987), pp. 67–118.
29 *Tattvacintāmaṇi*, II, *tarkaprakaraṇa* (1892, pp. 232–233); translation Stephen Phillips, *Classical Indian Metaphysics*, pp. 162–4, and for the wider context Mrinalkanti Gangopadhyay, 'Gaṅgeśa on *vyāptigraha*: The Means for the Ascertainment of Invariable Concomitance,' *Journal of Indian Philosophy* 3 (1975), pp. 167–208.
30 *Tattvacintāmaṇi*, II, *vyāptilakṣaṇatadgrahopāyasiddhānta* (1892, pp. 210–212).
31 Nelson Goodman, *Fact, Fiction and Forecast* (Indianapolis: Bobbs-Merrill, 1965), pp. 66–67.
32 The phrase is due to John Rawls, *A Theory of Justice* (Oxford: Clarendon Press, 1972), pp. 20–1, 48–51.
33 Norman Daniels, 'On Some Methods of Ethics and Linguistics,' *Philosophical Studies* 37 (1980), pp. 21–36.
34 Stephen Stich and R. Nisbett, 'Justification and the Psychology of Human Reasoning,' *Philosophy of Science* 47 (1980), pp. 188–202; Stephen Stich, 'Reflective Equilibrium, Analytic Epistemology and the Problem of Cognitive Diversity,' *Synthese* 74 (1988), pp. 391–413.
35 On the distinction: John Rawls, 'The Independence of Moral Theory,' *Proceedings and Addresses of the American Philosophical Society* 48 (1974), pp. 4–22; Norman Daniels, 'Wide Reflective Equilibrium and Theory Acceptance in Ethics,' *Journal of Philosophy* 76 (1979), pp. 256–282; Ernest Sosa, 'Equilibrium in Coherence?' in his *Knowledge in Perspective* (Cambridge: Cambridge University Press, 1991), Chapter 15.

36 The domain of principles meets an 'independence constraint' analogous to the one Norman Daniels finds in the domain of particular judgments.

37 J. N. Mohanty, *Reason and Tradition in Indian Thought* (Oxford: Clarendon Press, 1992). The quotation is at p. 271.

38 Roderick Chisholm, *Theory of Knowledge* (Englewood Cliffs, N.J.: Prentice-Hall, 1966), pp. 56–69; see also his 'The Problem of the Criterion,' *The 1973 Aquinas Lecture* (Milwaukee: Marquette University Press, 1973).

39 Rohinton Mistry, *A Fine Balance* (London: Faber & Faber, 1995). Gaṅgeśa's epistemology is related in important ways to the bi-level virtue epistemology of Ernest Sosa. Ernest Sosa, 'Reflective Knowledge in the Best Circles,' *The Journal of Philosophy* 94 (1997), pp. 410–430. See also: Richard Foley, 'Skepticism and Rationality,' in M. D. Roth and G. Ross (eds.), *Doubting* (Dordrecht: Kluwer Academic Publishers, 1990), pp. 69–81.

Texts

For the newest editions and translations of the texts, consult Karl Potter's excellent and regularly updated online bibliography on the philosophical literature of India – http://faculty.washington.edu/kpotter/

AJP *Anekāntajayapatākā*, by Haribhadra; ed. with *Vṛtti* and Municandra Sūri's *Vivaraṇa*, H. R. Kapadia (Baroda: Gaewkwad Oriental Series 88, 1940), 2 volumes.

ĀM *Āptamīmāṃsā*, by Samantabhadra; ed. Gajadharalal Jain (Benares: Sanantana Jaina Granthamala, 1914).

ĀP *Ālambanaparīkṣā* (*Examination of Supports*), by Diṅnāga; 'restored' N. Aiyaswami Shastri, *Ālambanaparīkṣā and vṛtti by Diṅnāga with the Commentary of Dharmapāla, restored into Sanskrit from the Tibetan and Chinese Versions and Edited with an English Translation and Notes* (Madras: The Adyar Library, 1942).

—— ed. with Vinītadeva's and Dharmapāla's commentaries, N. Aiyaswami Shastri, *Bulletin of Tibetology* (1980), pp. 1–170.

TRANSLATIONS Fernando Tola and Carmen Dragonetti, 'Dignāga's Ālambanaparīkṣāvṛtti,' *Journal of Indian Philosophy* 10 (1982), pp. 105–134. See also Shastri, 1942, 1980.

AŚ *Arthaśāstra*, by Kauṭilya; critical ed. R. P. Kangle, *The Kauṭilya Arthaśāstra* (2nd edn., Bombay: Bombay University Press, 1972), Part I.

TRANSLATION R. P. Kangle, *The Kauṭilya Arthaśāstra* (2nd edn., Bombay: Bombay University Press, 1972), Part II.

ĀTV *Ātmatattvaviveka*, by Udayana; ed. V. P. Dvivedin and L. S. Dravida (Calcutta: Asiatic Society, 1986).

TRANSLATIONS Kisor Kumar Chakrabarti, *Classical Indian Philosophy of Mind: The Nyāya Dualist Tradition* (Albany: State University of New York Press, 1999), pp. 219–276.

—— N. S. Dravid, *Ātmatattvaviveka of Udayanācārya* (Shimla: Indian Institute of Advanced Study, 1995).

AYVD *Anyayogavyavacchedadvātriṃśikā*, by Hemacandra. See SM.

HC *Hetucakraḍamaru* (*Chart of Reasons*), by Diṅnāga; 'reconstructed' from Tibetan by Durgacharan Chatterji, '*Hetucakranirṇaya* – A Translation,' *Indian Historical Quarterly* 9 (1933), pp. 266–272, 511–514.

—— Richard S. Y. Chi, *Buddhist Formal Logic: A Study of Dignāga's Hetucakra and K'uei-chi's Great Commentary on the Nyāyapraveśa* (London: Royal Asiatic Society, 1969).

TRANSLATIONS D. Chatterji, R. S. Y. Chi.

JTB *Jaina Tarkabhāṣā*, by Yaśovijaya; ed. D. Bhargava (Delhi: Motilal Banarsidass, 1973).

TRANSLATION D. Bhargava.

KĀ *Kiraṇāvalī*, by Udayana; ed. with Vardhamāna's *Prakāśa*, Siva Candra Sarvvabhouma (fasc. 1–3, 1911) and Narendra Chandra Vedantatirtha (fasc. 4, 1956) (Calcutta: The Asiatic Society, Bibliotheca Indica No. 200).

TRANSLATIONS B. K. Matilal (précis), in Karl Potter ed., *Indian Metaphysics and Epistemology – The Tradition of Nyāya-Vaiśeṣika up to Gaṅgeśa*, Encyclopedia of Indian Philosophies, Vol. 2 (Delhi: Motilal Banarsidass, 1977), pp. 589–603.

—— Musashi Tachikawa [sections on earth, fire, water], *The Structure of the World in Udayana's Realism: A Study of the Lakṣaṇāvalī and the Kiraṇāvalī* (Dordrecht: Reidel Publishing Company, 1981), pp. 109–147.

KhKh *Khaṇḍanakhaṇḍakhādya*, by Śrīharṣa; ed. Swami Yogindrananda Nyayacarya (Varanasi: Udasina Sanskrit Press, 1979).

—— ed. with selections from the commentaries by Śaṃkara Miśra and Raghunātha Śiromaṇi, S. N. Śukla (Varanasi: Chowkhamba Oriental Series 82, 1904–1914).

TRANSLATIONS Ganganath Jha, *The Khaṇḍanakhaṇḍakhādya of Śrī Harṣa* (Delhi: Sri Satguru, 1986), 2 volumes.

—— Phyllis Granoff [Book I, Introduction], *Philosophy and Argument in Late Vedānta: Śrīharṣa's Khaṇḍanakhaṇḍakhādya* (Dordrecht: Reidel Publishing Company, 1978), pp. 71–208.

—— Mrinalkanti Gangopadhyay [Book I, Inference], *Indian Logic in its Sources* (Delhi: Munshiram Manoharlal, 1984), pp. 67–118.

LĀ *Lakṣaṇāvalī*, by Udayana; ed. Musashi Tachikawa, *The Structure of the World in Udayana's Realism: A Study of the Lakṣaṇāvalī and the Kiraṇāvalī* (Dordrecht: Reidel Publishing Company, 1981).

TRANSLATION Musachi Tachikawa.

LT *Laghīyastraya*, by Akalaṅka; ed. with Akalaṅka's *Nyāyaviniścaya* and *Pramāṇasaṃgraha* in *Akalaṅka Granthatrayam*, Mahendra Kumar Sastri (Calcutta: Sanchalaka Singhi Jaina Granthamala, 1939).

MK *Mūlamadhyamakakārikā (The Middle Stanzas)*, by Nāgārjuna; ed. with Candrakīrti's *Prasannapadā*, Dwarikadas Shastri (Varanasi: Bauddha Bharati, 1989, 2nd edn.).

TRANSLATIONS Jay L. Garfield, *The Fundamental Wisdom of the Middle Way* (New York: Oxford University Press, 1995).

—— David Kalupahana, *Nāgārjuna: The Philosophy of the Middle Way* (Albany: SUNY Press 1986).

—— Kenneth Inada, *Nāgārjuna: A Translation of his Mūlamadhyamakakārikā* (Tokyo: Hokuseido Press, 1970).

—— Frederick Streng, *Emptiness: A Study in Religious Meaning* (Nashville: Abingdon Press, 1967), pp. 183–220.

NA *Nyāyāvatāra*, by Siddhasena Divākara; ed. A. N. Upadhye (Bombay: Jaina Sahitya Vikasa Mandala, 1971).

TRANSLATIONS Piotr Balcerowicz, *Epistemology in Historical and Comparative Perspective. Critical Edition and English Translation of Logical-Epistemological Treatises: Nyāyāvatāra, Nyāyāvatāra-virti and Nyāyāvatāra-ṭippana with Introduction and Notes* (Hamburg: Franz Steiner Verlag, 2000).

—— Satkari Mookerjee, 'A Critical and Comparative Study of Jaina Logic and Epistemology on the Basis of the *Nyāyāvatāra* of Siddhasena Divākara,' *Vaishali Institute Research Bulletin* 1 (1971), pp. 1–144.

NB *Nyāyabindu*, by Dharmakīrti; ed. with Dharmottara's *Ṭīkā* and an anonymous *Ṭippaṇī,* Dwarikadas Sastri (Varanasi: Baudhha Bharati, 1985).

TRANSLATIONS Mrinalkanti Gangopadhyaya, *Vinītadeva's Nyāyabinduṭīkā* (Calcutta: Indian Studies Past and Present, 1971).

—— Theodore Stcherbatsky, 'A Short Treatise of Logic by Dharmakīrti with its Commentary by Dharmottara,' in his *Buddhist Logic*, Vol. 2 (New York: Dover Publications, 1962), pp. 1–253.

—— G. C. Pande, *Nyāyabindu* (Sarnath, 1996).

NBh *Nyayabhāṣya,* by Vātsyāyana Pakṣilasvāmin, see NS.

TRANSLATION See NS.

NBhū *Nyāyabhūṣaṇa*, by Bhāsarvajña; ed. S. Yogindrananda (Varanasi: Saddarsan Prakasan Pratisthanam, 1968).

TRANSLATION B. K. Matilal (précis), in Karl Potter ed., *Indian Metaphysics and Epistemology – The Tradition of Nyāya-Vaiśeṣika up to Gaṅgeśa*, Encyclopedia of Indian Philosophies, Vol. 2 (Delhi: Motilal Banarsidass, 1977), pp. 410–424.

NK *Nyāyakandalī*, by Śrīdhara; ed. Durgadhara Jha (Varanasi: Sampurnanand Sanskrit Vishvavidyalaya, Ganganatha Jha Granthamala, Vol. 1, 1977).

TRANSLATION See PDS.

NKA *Nyāyakusumāñjali*, by Udayana; ed. Padmaprasada Upadhyaya and Dhundhiraja Sastri (Benares: Chowkhamba Sanskrit Series Office, Kash Sanskrit Series 30, 1957).

TRANSLATION N. S. Dravid, *Nyāyakusumāñjali of Udayanācārya* (Delhi: Indian Council of Philosophical Research, 1996).

NKC *Nyāyakumudacandra*, by Prabhācandra (a commentary on Akaṅkara's *Laghīyastraya*); ed. Mahendra Kumar Nyayacharya (Bombay: Manik Chandra Dgambara Jain Series, 1938; reprinted in 2 volumes, Sri Satguru, 1991).

NM Jayanta. *Nyāyamañjarī*; ed. S. N. Shukla (Benares: Chowkhamba Sanskrit Series 106, 1936).

TRANSLATION J. V. Bhattacharyya, *Nyāyamañjarī: The Compendium of Indian Speculative Logic* (Delhi: Motilal Banarsidass, 1978).

NS *Nyāyasūtra*, by Gautama Akṣapāda; *Gautamīyanyāyadarśana with Bhaṣya of Vātsyāyana*, critical ed. Anantalal Thakur (Delhi: Indian Council of Philosophical Research, 1997).

TRANSLATION *Gautama's Nyāyasūtra with Vātsyāyana's Commentary*, translated by Mrinalkanti Gangopadhyaya, with an introduction by Debiprasad Chattopadhyaya (Calcutta: Indian Studies Past and Present, 1982).

NV *Nyāyavārttika* by Bhāradvāja Uddyotakara; critical ed. Anantalal Thakur (Delhi: Indian Council of Philosophical Research, 1997).

TRANSLATION Ganganatha Jha, *The Nyāyasūtras of Gautama with the Bhāṣya of Vātsyāyana and the Vārttika of Uddyotakara* (Delhi: Motilal Banarsidass, 1984), Vols. 1–4.

NVTP *Nyāyavārttikatātparyapariśuddhi*, by Udayana, critical ed. Anantalal Thakur (Delhi: Indian Council of Philosophical Research, 1996).

NVTṬ *Nyāyavārttikatātparyaṭīkā*, by Vācaspati; critical ed. Anantalal Thakur (Delhi: Indian Council of Philosophical Research, 1996).

TRANSLATIONS B. K. Matilal (précis), in Karl Potter ed., *Indian Metaphysics and Epistemology – The Tradition of Nyāya-Vaiśeṣika up to Gaṅgeśa*, Encyclopedia of Indian Philosophies, Vol. 2 (Delhi: Motilal Banarsidass, 1977), pp. 455–483.

—— Theodore Stcherbatsky, sections translated in his *Buddhist Logic*, Vol. 2 (New York: Dover Publications, 1962), pp. 287–298, 303–308, 405–432.

P *Prasannapadā*, by Candrakīrti; see MK.

TRANSLATION Mervyn Sprung, *Lucid Exposition of the Middle Way: The Essential Chapters from the Prasannapadā of Candrakīrti* (Boulder, Colorado: Prajña Press, 1979).

PDS *Padārthadarmasaṃgraha* aka *Praśastapādabhāṣya*, by Praśastapāda; ed. with Śaṅkara Miśra's *Upaskāra*, Dundhiraja Sastri (Varanasi: Chaukhamba Sanskrit Series Office, Kashi Sanskrit Series 3, 1923).

TRANSLATION Ganganatha Jha, *Padārthadharmasaṃgraha with Śrīdhara's Nyāyakandalī*, *The Pandit*, n.s. Vols. 25–37 (1903–15).

PKM *Prameyakamalamārtaṇḍa*, by Prabhācandra; ed. Mahendra Kumar Shastri (Bombay: Nirnayasagar Press, 1941; reprinted Sri Satguru 1990).

PM *Pramāṇamīmāṃsā*, by Hemacandra; ed. Sukhlalji Sanghvi (Calcutta: Shri Bahadur Singh Singhi Jaina Series 9, 1939).

TRANSLATION Satkari Mookerjee and N. Tatia, *Hemacandra's Pramāṇamīmāṃsā, Text and Translation with Critical Notes* (Varanasi: Tara Publications, 1970).

PNTĀ *Pramāṇanayatattvālokālaṃkāra*, by Vādideva Sūri, ed. Hari Satya Bhattacharya (Bombay: Jaina Sahitya Vikas Mandala, 1967).

TRANSLATION H. S. Bhattacharya.

PS *Pramāṇasamuccaya* (*Collection on Knowing*), by Diṅnāga; for editions of the Tibetan translations, see Richard Hayes, *Dignāga on the Interpretation of Signs* (Dordrecht: Kluwer Academic Publishers, 1988), p. 338.

—— partly 'reconstructed' into Sanskrit by Muni Sri Jambuvijaya in *Vaiśeṣikasūtra of Kaṇāda, with the Commentary of Candrānanda*, Appendix 7 (Baroda: Oriental Institute, Gaekwad's Oriental Series 136, 1961).

—— H. N. Randle, *Fragments from Dignāga* (London, 1926).

—— Shoryu Katsura, 'New Sanskrit Fragments of the *Pramāṇasamuccaya*,' *Journal of Indian Philosophy* 3 (1975), pp. 67–78.

TRANSLATIONS Chapter I. Masaaki Hattori, *Dignāga, On Perception, being the Pratyakṣapariccheda of Dignāga's Pramāṇasamuccaya from the Sanskrit fragments and the Tibetan versions* (Cambridge, Mass.: Harvard University Press, 1968), pp. 21–70.

—— Chapters II, V. Richard P. Hayes, *Dignāga on the Interpretation of Signs* (Dordrecht: Kluwer Academic Publishers, 1988), pp. 231–248, 252–299.

PTN *Padārthatattvanirūpaṇa*, by Raghunātha; ed. Karl H. Potter, *The Padārthatattvanirūpaṇam of Raghunātha Śiromaṇi* (Cambridge, Mass.: Harvard University Press, Harvard Yenching Institute Studies, Vol. 17, 1957).

TRANSLATION K. H. Potter.

PV *Pramāṇavārttika* (*Commentary on Knowing*), by Dharmakīrti; ed. with Manorathanandin's *Vṛtti*, Dwarikadas Shastri (Varanasi: Baudhha Bharati, 1968).

—— ed. Raniero Gnoli, *The Pramāṇavārttikam of Dharmakīrti: The First Chapter with the Autocommentary* (Rome: Istituto Italiano per Il Medio ed Estremo Oriente, 1960).

TRANSLATIONS (ongoing)

—— Chapter I (*svārthānumāna*, 'inference for oneself'). [1–10] Richard P. Hayes and Brendan S. Gillon, 'Introduction to Dharmakīrti's Theory of Inference as Presented in Pramāṇavārttika Svopajñavṛtti 1–10,' *Journal of Indian Philosophy* 19 (1991), pp. 1–74.

—— Chapter II (*pramāṇasiddhi*, 'establishment of knowing'). [1–6] Shoryu Katsura, 'Dharmakīrti's Theory of Truth,' *Journal of*

Indian Philosophy 12 (1984), pp. 215–235. [34–72] Eli Franco, *Dharmakīrti on Compassion and Rebirth* (Vienna: Arbeitskreis für Tibetische und Buddhistische Studien Universität Wien, 1997).

—— Chapter III (*pratyakṣa*, 'perception'). [1–51] Satkari Mookerjee and Hojun Nagasaki, *The Pramāṇavārttika of Dharmakīrti – An English Translation of the First Chapter with the Autocommentary* (Nalanda: Nava-Nalanda Mahavira Research Publication, 1964).

—— Chapter IV (*parārthānumāna*, 'inference for others'). [1–148] Tom J. F. Tillemans, *Dharmakīrtis Pramāṇavārttika – An Annotated Translation of the Fourth Chapter (parārthānumāna)* Vol. 1 (Vienna: Österreichische Akademie der Wissenschaften, 2000). [202–206] Shoryu Katsura, 'Pramāṇavārttika IV 202–206 – Towards the Correct Understanding of *svabhāvapratibandha*,' *Journal of Indian and Buddhist Studies* 40 (1992), pp. 35–40.

SM *Syādvādamañjarī*, by Malliṣeṇa; ed. with Hemacandra's *Anyayogavyavacchedadvātriṃśikā*, A. B. Dhruva (Bombay: Bombay Sanskrit and Prakrit Series 83, 1933).

TRANSLATIONS S. K. Saksena and C. A. Moore, in S. Radhakrishnan and C. A. Moore eds., *A Sourcebook in Indian Philosophy* (Princeton: Princeton University Press, 1957), pp. 260–268.

—— F. W. Thomas, *The Flower-Spray of the Quodammodo Doctrine* (Berlin: Akademia Verlag, 1960).

ST *Saptabhaṅgītaraṅginī*, by Vimaladāsa; ed. T. P. Sharma (Bombay: Rayacandra Jaina Sastra Mala, 1905, 1916, 1977).

STP *Sanmatitarkaprakarana*, by Siddhasena Divākara; ed. with Abhayadevasūri's *Tattvabodhavidhāyanī* by S. Sanghvi and B. Doshi (Ahmedabad: Gujarat Puratattva Mandira Granthavali, 1924–31).

TĀ *Tattvārthasūtra*, by Umāsvāti; ed. J. L. Jain (Arah: Bibliotheca Jainica, 1920).

TRANSLATION K. K. Dixit, Sukhlalji Sanghvi's *Commentary on Tattvārthasūtra of Vācaka Umāsvāti* (Ahmedabad: L. D. Institute of Indology, 1974).

TC *Tattvacintāmaṇi*, by Gaṅgeśa; ed. with Mathuranātha's *Rahasya* and Jayadeva Miśra's *Āloka*, Kamakhyanatha Tarkavagisa, 6 volumes (Calcutta: Asiatic Society, 1884–1901).

TRANSLATIONS Thorough précis in Karl Potter and Sibajiban Bhattacharyya eds., *Indian Philosophical Analysis – Nyāya-Vaiśeṣika from Gaṅgeśa to Raghunātha Śiromaṇi* Encyclopedia of Indian Philosophies, Vol. 6 (Delhi: Motilal Banarsidass, 1993), pp. 85–311.

—— Chapter I (*pratyakṣa*, 'perception'). Stephen Phillips, *Gaṅgeśa's 'Jewel of Reflection on Reality,' the Perception Chapter* (New York: Oxford University Press, 2000). Also:

(2 *prāmāṇyavāda*) J. N. Mohanty, *Gaṅgeśa's Theory of Truth* (Santiniketan, 1966), pp. 73–210. (8 *abhāvavāda*) Bimal K. Matilal, *The Navya-Nyāya Doctrine of Negation* (Harvard: Harvard University Press, 1968), pp. 173–188. (14 *nirvikalpakavāda*) Sibajiban Bhattacharyya, *Gaṅgeśa's Theory of Indeterminate Perception* (Delhi: Indian Council of Philosophical Research, 1993), Part Two.

—— Chapter II (*anumāna*, 'inference'). (1 *anumitinirūpaṇa* and 2–8 *vyāptipañcaka* to *viśeṣavyāpti*) Cornelius Goekoop, *The Logic of Invariable Concomitance in the Tattvacintāmaṇi* (Dordrecht: Reidel Publishing Co., 1967), pp. 55–154. (2 *vyāptipañcaka*) Daniel H. H. Ingalls, *Materials for the Study of Navya-Nyāya Logic* (Harvard: Harvard University Press, 1951), p. 86. (9 *vyāptigrahopāyaprakaraṇa*) Mrinalkanti Gangopadhyay, 'Gaṅgeśa on *vyāptigraha*: The Means for the Ascertainment of Invariable Concomitance,' *Journal of Indian Philosophy* 3 (1975), pp. 167–208. (10 *tarkaprakaraṇa*) Stephen Phillips, *Classical Indian Metaphysics* (La Salle: Open Court, 1995), pp. 158–164. (14 *pakṣatā*) A. K. Rai, 'Pakṣatā in Navya-Nyāya,' *Journal of Indian Philosophy* 23 (1995), pp. 3–4. (21 *īśvarānumāna*) John Vattanky, *Gaṅgeśa's Philosophy of God* (Madras, 1984).

—— Chapter IV (*śabda*, 'language'). (1 *śabdaprāmāṇyavāda*) Pradyot Kumar Mukhopadhyay, *The Nyāya Theory of Linguistic Performance: A New Interpretation of Tattvacintāmaṇi* (Calcutta: K.P. Bagchee & Co., 1992). (8 *vidhivāda*) V. N. Jha, *The Philosophy of Injunctions* (Delhi: Sri Satguru Publications, 1988). (11 *apūrvavāda*) V. N. Jha, *The Philosophy of the Intermediate Causal Link* (Delhi: Sri Satguru Publications, 1986).

TS *Tarkasaṃgraha,* Annambhaṭṭa; ed. with author's *Dīpikā*, Satkari Sarma Vangiya (Varanasi, 1969).

TRANSLATION Gopinath Bhattacharya, *Tarkasaṃgrahadīpikā on Tarkasaṃgraha by Annambhaṭṭa* (Calcutta: Progressive Publishers, 1983; reprinted 1994).

TUS *Tattvopaplasiṃha*, by Jayarāśi; ed. Sukhlalji Sanghavi and Rasiklal C. Parikh (Varanasi: Bauddha Bharati, 1987).

TRANSLATIONS Chapter 1 (Perception). Eli Franco, *Perception, Knowledge and Disbelief: A Study of Jayarāśi's Scepticism* (2nd Edition, Delhi: Motilal Banarsidass, 1994).

—— Chapter 2 (Inference). S. N. Shastri and S. N. Saksena, in Sarvepalli Radhakrishnan and Charles Moore eds., *A Sourcebook in Indian Philosophy* (Princeton: Princeton University Press, 1957), pp. 236–246.

U *Upaskāra*, by Śaṅkara Miśra; see PDS.

TRANSLATION See: VS.

V *Vigrahavyāvartanī (Reply to Critics)*, by Nāgārjuna; critical ed.

E. H. Johnston and A. Kunst in *The Dialectical Method of Nāgārjuna: Vigrahavyāvartanī* (Delhi: Motilal Banarsidass, 1986).
TRANSLATION Kamaleswar Bhattacharya, in critical ed.

VN *Vādanyāya*, by Dharmakīrti; ed. Pradeep P. Gokhale, *Vādanyāya of Dharmakīrti: The Logic of Debate* (Delhi: Sri Satguru Publications, 1993).
TRANSLATION P. P. Gokhale.

VS *Vaiśeṣikasūtra*, by Kaṇāda; critical ed. with Candrānanda's *Vṛtti*, Muni Sri Jambuvijayaji (Baroda: Oriental Institute, Gaekwad's Oriental Series 136, 1961).
TRANSLATION Nandalal Sinha, *The Vaiśeṣikasūtras of Kaṇāda, with the commentary of Śaṅkara Miśra* (Allahabad: The Panini Office, Bhuvaneswari Asrama, 1911).

Bibliography

Alsdorf, Luwig, 'Nikṣepa – A Jaina Contribution to Scholastic Methodology,' *Journal of The Oriental Institute, Baroda* 22 (1973), pp. 455–463.

Bagchi, Sitansusekhar, *Inductive Reasoning: A Study of Tarka and its Role in Indian Logic* (Calcutta: Munishchandra Sinha, 1953).

Balcerowicz, Piotr, 'How Could a Cow be Both Synchronically and Diachronically Homogenous, or On the Jaina Notions of *tiryak-sāmānya* and *ūrdhvatā-sāmānya*,' in N. K. Wagle and Olle Qvarnström eds., *Approaches to Jaina Studies: Philosophy, Logic, Rituals and Symbols* (Toronto: University of Toronto, 1999), pp. 211–235.

Bandyopadhyay, Nandita, 'The Concept of Contradiction in Indian Logic and Epistemology,' *Journal of Indian Philosophy* 16.3 (1988), pp. 225–246.

Barnes, Jonathan ed., *The Complete Works of Aristotle* (Princeton: Princeton University Press, 1985).

Basham, A. L., *History and Doctrines of the Ājīvikas* (London: Luzac & Co., 1951).

Bhaduri, S., *Studies in Nyāya-Vaiśeṣika Metaphysics* (Poona: Bhandarkar Oriental Research Institute, 1947).

Bharadwaja, Vijay, 'Rationality, Argumentation and Philosophical Embarrassment: A Study of Four Logical Alternatives (*catuṣkoṭi*) in Buddhist Logic,' *Philosophy East and West* 34 (1984), pp. 303–319; reprinted in his *Form and Validity in Indian Logic*, Chapter 4.

—— *Form and Validity in Indian Logic* (Shimla: Indian Institute of Advanced Study, 1990).

Bhatt, Bansidhar, *The Canonical Nikṣepa: Studies in Jaina Dialectics* (Leiden: E. J. Brill, 1978).

Bhattacharya, Gopikamohan, 'Ratnakīrti on Apoha,' in B. K. Matilal and R. D. Evans eds., *Buddhist Logic and Epistemology: Studies in the Buddhist Analysis of Inference and Language* (Dordrecht: Reidel Publishing Company, 1982), pp. 291–298.

Bhattacharya, Kalidas, 'An Idea of Comparative Indian Philosophy,' *All India Oriental Conference* (Santiniketan, 1980).

Bhattacharya, Kamaleswar, 'On the Relationship Between Nāgārjuna's *Vigrahavyāvartanī* and the *Nyāyasūtras*,' *Journal of Indo-European Studies (USA)* 5 (1977), pp. 265–273.

—— 'Nāgārjuna's Arguments against Motion: Their Grammatical Basis,' in G. Bhattacharya et al. eds., *A Corpus of Indian Studies: Essays in Honour of Professor Gaurinath Sastri* (Calcutta: Sanskrit Pustak Bhandar, 1980), pp. 85–95.

—— 'The Grammatical Basis of Nāgārjuna's Arguments: Some Further Considerations,' *Indologica Taurinensia* 8–9 (1980–1), pp. 35–43.

—— 'Nāgārjuna's Arguments Against Motion,' *Journal of the International Association of Buddhist Studies* 8 (1985), pp. 7–16.

—— 'Back to Nāgārjuna and Grammar,' *The Adyar Library Bulletin* 59 (1995), pp. 178–189.
Bhattacharyya, Sibajiban, 'The Navya-Nyāya Theory of Universals,' in his *Gadādhara's Theory of Objectivity*, Part 1: General Introduction to Navya-Nyāya Concepts (New Delhi: Indian Council of Philosophical Research, 1990), Chapter 3.
Bronkhorst, J., 'Nāgārjuna and The Naiyāyikas,' *Journal of Indian Philosophy* 13 (1985), pp. 107–132.
Burton, David, *Emptiness Appraised: A Critical Study of Nāgārjuna's Philosophy* (London: Curzon Press, 1999).
Cardona, George, 'Anvaya and Vyatireka in Indian Grammar,' *Adyar Library Bulletin* 31 (1967–8), pp. 313–352.
—— 'On Reasoning from Anvaya and Vyatireka in Early Advaita,' in his *Studies in Indian Philosophy* (Ahmedabad: L.D. Series, 1981), pp. 79–104.
—— 'A Path Still Taken: Some Early Indian Arguments Concerning Time,' *Journal of the American Oriental Society* 111.3 (1991), pp. 445–464.
Chakrabarti, Arindam, 'I Touch What I Saw,' *Philosophy and Phenomenological Research* 52 (1992), pp. 103–117.
—— 'Rationality in Indian Philosophy,' in Eliot Deutsch and Ron Bontekoe eds., *A Companion to World Philosophies* (Oxford: Blackwell Publishers, 1997), pp. 259–278.
—— *Denying Existence* (Dordrecht: Kluwer Academic Publishers, 1997).
Chakrabarti, Kishor, *Indian Philosophy of Mind: The Nyāya Dualist Tradition* (Albany: State University of New York Press, 1999).
Chakrabarti, Kishor and Chandana Chakrabarti, 'Towards Dualism: The Nyāya-VaiśeṣIka Way,' *Philosophy East and West* 41 (1991), pp. 477–491.
Chierchia, Gennaro and Sally McConnell-Ginet, *Meaning and Grammar* (Cambridge, Mass.: MIT Press, 1990).
Chisholm, Roderick, *Theory of Knowledge* (Englewood Cliffs, N.J.: Prentice-Hall, 1966).
—— 'The Problem of the Criterion,' *The 1973 Aquinas Lecture* (Milwaukee: Marquette University Press, 1973).
Cohen, Morris R. and Ernest Nagel, *An Introduction to Logic and Scientific Method* (London: Routledge & Kegan Paul, 1934).
Coward, Harold, *Derrida and Indian Philosophy* (Albany: State University of New York Press, 1990).
Daniels, Norman, 'Wide Reflective Equilibrium and Theory Acceptance in Ethics,' *Journal of Philosophy* 76 (1979), pp. 256–282.
—— 'Reflective Equilibrium and Archimedean Points,' *Canadian Journal of Philosophy* 10 (1980), pp. 83–103.
—— 'On Some Methods of Ethics and Linguistics,' *Philosophical Studies* 37 (1980), pp. 21–36.
Davidson, Donald, 'Paradoxes of Irrationality,' in R. Wollheim and J. Hopkins eds., *Philosophical Essays on Freud* (Cambridge, Cambridge University Press, 1982), pp. 289–305.
Dravid, N. S., 'Āhārya Cognition in Navya-Nyāya,' *Journal of the Indian Council of Philosophical Research* 14.2 (1996), pp. 164–168.
Dretske, Fred, *Knowledge and the Flow of Information* (Oxford: Basil Blackwell, 1981).
Dreyfus, Georges B. J., *Recognizing Reality: Dharmakīrti's Philosophy and its Tibetan Interpretations* (Albany: State University of New York Press, 1997).
Dummett, Michael, *Frege: Philosophy of Mathematics* (London, Duckworth, 1991).
Dundas, Paul, *The Jains* (London: Routledge, 1992).

Edgerton, Franklin, 'The Meaning of *sāṃkhya* and *yoga*,' *American Journal of Philology* 45 (1924), pp. 1–47.

Franco, Eli, 'Bhāsarvajña and Jayarāśi: The Refutation of Scepticism in the Nyāyabhūṣaṇa,' *Berliner Indologische Studien* 3 (1987), pp. 23–49; reprinted as an Appendix in his *Perception, Knowledge and Disbelief.*

—— *Perception, Knowledge and Disbelief: A Study of Jayarāśi's Scepticism*, 2nd edition (Delhi: Motilal Banarsidass, 1994).

Frauwallner, E., 'Die Erkenntnislehre des Klassischen Sāṃkhya-Systems,' *Wiener Zeitschrift für die Kunde Süd- und Ost-Asiens* 2 (1958), pp. 84–139.

—— 'Dignāga, sein Werk und seine Entwicklung,' *Wiener Zeitschrift für die Kunde Süd- und Ostasiens* 3 (1959), pp. 83–164.

Frege, Gottlob, *The Foundations of Arithmetic*, translated by J. L. Austin (Oxford: Basil Blackwell, 1950).

Fricker, Elizabeth, 'Against Gullibility' in B. K. Matilal and A. Chakrabarti eds., *Knowing from Words* (Dordrecht: Kluwer, 1994), pp. 125–161.

Fynes, Richard, *Hemacandra: The Lives of the Jaina Elders* (Oxford: Oxford University Press, 1998).

Galloway, Brian, 'Notes on Nāgārjuna and Zeno on Motion,' *The Journal of the International Association of Buddhist Studies* 10 (1987), pp. 80–87.

—— 'Some Logical Issues in Madhyamaka Thought,' *Journal of Indian Philosophy* 17 (1989), pp. 1–35.

Ganeri, Jonardon, 'Numbers as Properties of Objects: Frege and the Nyāya,' *Studies in Humanities and Social Sciences* (3) – *Epistemology, Logic and Ontology After Matilal* (Shimla: Indian Institute of Advanced Studies, 1996), pp. 111–121.

—— *Semantic Powers: Meaning and the Means of Knowing in Classical Indian Philosophy* (Oxford: Clarendon Press, 1999).

—— 'Dharmakīrti's Semantics for the Particle *eva (only)*' in Shoryu Katsura ed., *Dharmakīrti's Thought and Its Impact on Indian and Tibetan Philosophy* (Vienna: Österreichische Akademie der Wissenschaften, 1999), pp. 101–116.

—— 'Objectivity and Proof in an Indian Theory of Number,' in *Synthese* (forthcoming).

—— 'Cross-modality and the Self,' *Philosophy and Phenomenological Research* 61 (2000).

—— 'Indian Logic and the Colonization of Reason,' in Jonardon Ganeri ed., *Indian Logic: A Reader* (London: Curzon Press, 2001).

Gangopadhyay, Mrinalkanti, 'Gaṅgeśa on Vyāptigraha: The Means for the Ascertainment of Invariable Concomitance,' *Journal of Indian Philosophy* 3 (1975), pp. 167–208.

—— *Indian Logic in its Sources* (Delhi: Munshiram Manoharlal, 1984).

Gärdenfors, Peter, 'Induction, Conceptual Spaces, and AI,' in Douglas Stalker ed., *Grue! The New Riddle of Induction* (Chicago: Open Court, 1994), pp. 117–134.

Gillon Brendan S. and Richard Hayes, 'The Role of the Particle *eva* in (Logical) Quantification in Sanskrit,' *Wiener Zeitschrift für die Kunde Süd- und Ost-Asiens* 26 (1982), pp. 195–203.

Gillon Brendan, 'Another Look at the Sanskrit Particle *eva*,' in Shoryu Katsura ed., *Dharmakīrti's Thought and Its Impact on Indian and Tibetan Philosophy* (Vienna: Österreichische Akademie der Wissenschaften, 1999), pp. 117–130.

Gokhale, Pradeep P., 'The Logical Structure of *Syādvāda*,' *Journal of Indian Council of Philosophical Research* 8 (1991), pp. 73–81.

—— *Inference and Fallacies Discussed in Ancient Indian Logic* (Delhi: Sri Satguru Publications, 1992).

Goodman, Nelson, *Fact, Fiction and Forecast* (Indianapolis: Bobbs-Merrill, 1965).

Goody, Jack, 'East and West: Rationality in Review,' *Ethnos* (1992), pp. 6–36.

Granoff, Phyllis, *Philosophy and Argument in Late Vedānta: Śrīharṣa's Khaṇḍanakhaṇḍakhādya* (Dordrecht: Reidel Publishing Company, 1978).

Gutting, Gary, *Michel Foucault's Archaeology of Scientific Reason* (Cambridge: Cambridge University Press, 1989).

Hacker, Paul, 'Ānvīkṣikī,' *Wiener Zeitschrift für die Kunde Süd-und Ostasiens* 2 (1958), pp. 54–83.

Hacking, Ian, 'Working in a New World: The Taxonomic Solution,' in Paul Horwich ed., *World Changes: Thomas Kuhn and the Nature of Science* (Cambridge, Mass., MIT Press, 1993), pp. 275–310.

Halbfass, Wilhelm, 'Darśana, Ānvīkṣikī, Philosophy,' in his *India and Europe: an Essay in Understanding* (Albany: State University of New York Press, 1988), pp. 263–286.

—— *On Being and What There Is: Classical Vaiśeṣika and the History of Indian Ontology* (Albany: State University of New York Press, 1992).

Haslanger, Sally, *Change, Persistence and Possibility* (Ph.D. dissertation, University of California, 1985).

Hattori Masaaki, *Dignāga, On Perception, being the Pratyakṣapariccheda of Dignāga's Pramāṇasamuccaya from the Sanskrit fragments and the Tibetan Versions* (Cambridge, Mass.: Harvard University Press, 1968).

—— 'The Sautrāntika Background of the *apoha* Theory,' in Leslie S. Kawamura and Keith Scott eds., *Buddhist Thought and Civilization: Essays in Honour of Herbert V. Guenther on his Sixtieth Birthday* (Emeryville: Dharma Press, 1977), pp. 47–58.

—— 'Apoha and Pratibhā,' in M. Nagatomi et al. eds. *Sanskrit and Indian Studies: Essays in Honour of Daniel H. H. Ingalls* (Dordrecht: Reidel Publishing Company, 1980), pp. 61–74.

Hayes, Richard P., 'On the Reinterpretation of Dharmakīrti's *svabhāvahetu*,' *Journal of Indian Philosophy* 15 (1987), pp. 319–332.

—— *Dignāga on the Interpretation of Signs* (Dordrecht: Kluwer Academic Publishers, 1988).

—— 'Nāgārjuna's Appeal,' *Journal of Indian Philosophy* 22 (1994), pp. 309–410.

Herzberger, Hans H., 'Three Systems of Buddhist Logic,' in B. K. Matilal and R. D. Evans eds., *Buddhist Logic and Epistemology: Studies in the Buddhist Analysis of Inference and Language* (Dordrecht: Reidel Publishing Company, 1982), pp. 59–76.

Herzberger, Rādhika, *Bhartṛhari and the Buddhists* (Dordrecht: Reidel Publishing Company, 1986).

Hiriyanna, M., *Outlines of Indian Philosophy* (London: G. Allen & Unwin, 1932).

Hoffman, Frank J., 'Rationality in Early Buddhist Four-Fold Logic,' *Journal of Indian Philosophy* 10 (1982), pp. 309–337.

—— *Rationality and Mind in Early Buddhism* (Delhi: Motilal Banarsidass, 1992; first published 1987).

Hume, David, *Dialogues Concerning Natural Religion* (London: Routledge, 1991).

Huntington, C. W., *The Emptiness of Emptiness: An Introduction to Early Indian Madhyamaka* (Honolulu: University of Hawaii Press, 1989).

Ingalls, Daniel H. H., *Materials for the Study of Navya-Nyāya Logic* (Cambridge, Mass.: Harvard University Press, 1951).

Jacobi, Hermann J., 'A Contribution Towards the Early History of Indian Philosophy,' translated by V. A. Sukthankar, *The Indian Antiquary* XLVII (1918), pp. 101–109.

Jaśkowski, Stanisław, 'Propositional Calculus for Contradictory Deductive Systems,' *Studia Logica* 24 (1969), pp. 143–157.

Jayatilleke, K. N., *Early Buddhist Theory of Knowledge* (London: George Allen and Unwin, 1963).

Jhalakikar, Bhimacarya, *Nyāyakośa, or Dictionary of Technical Terms of Indian Philosophy* (Poona: Bhandarkar Oriental Research Institute, 1928).

Jinpa, Thupten, 'Delineating Reason's Scope for Negation,' *Journal of Indian Philosophy* 26 (1998), pp. 275–308.

Johnston, Mark, 'Is There a Problem About Persistence?' *Aristotelian Society Supplementary Volume* 61 (1987), pp. 107–135.

Kajiyama Yuichi, *An Introduction to Buddhist Philosophy: An Annotated Translation of the Tarkabhāṣā or Mokṣākaragupta*, Memoirs of the Faculty of Letters (Kyoto) 10 (1966).

Kaplan, David, 'Demonstratives: An Essay on the Semantics, Logic, Metaphysics and Epistemology of Demonstratives and Other Indexicals,' in J. Almog, J. Perry, and H. Wettstein eds., *Themes from Kaplan* (Oxford: Clarendon Press, 1989).

Katsura Shōryū, 'The *apoha* Theory of Dignāga,' *Indogaku Bukkyogaku Kenkyū* 28 (1979), pp. (16)–(20).

—— 'Dignāga on *trairūpya*,' *Journal of Indian and Buddhist Studies* 32 (1983), pp. (15)–(21).

—— 'Dharmakīrti's Concept of Truth,' *Journal of Indian Philosophy* 12 (1984), pp. 213–235.

—— 'On *trairūpya* Formulae,' in *Buddhism and Its Relation to Other Religions: Essays in Honour of Dr. Shozen Kumoi on His Seventieth Birthday* (1986), pp. 161–172.

—— 'Dignāga and Dharmakīrti on *apoha*,' in E. Steinkellner ed., *Studies in the Buddhist Epistemological Tradition* (Vienna: Österreichische Akademie der Wissenschaften, 1991), pp. 129–146.

—— 'On Perceptual Judgement,' in N. K. Wagle and F. Watanabe eds., *Studies in Buddhism in Honour of Professor A. K. Warder* (Toronto: University of Toronto Centre for South Asian Studies, 1993), pp. 66–75.

Kellner, Birgit, 'Levels of (Im)Perceptibility: Dharmottara's Views on The *Dṛśya* and *Dṛśānupalabdhi*,' in Shoryu Katsura ed., *Dharmakīrti's Thought and Its Impact on Indian and Tibetan Philosophy* (Vienna: Österreichische Akademie der Wissenschaften, 1999), pp. 193–208.

Khalida, Muhamad Ali, 'Natural Kinds and Crosscutting Categories,' *Journal of Philosophy* 95 (1998), pp. 33–50.

King, Richard, *Indian Philosophy: An Introduction to Hindu and Buddhist Thought* (Edinburgh: Edinburgh University Press, 1999).

Kumar, R. A., Dak, T. M. and Mishra A. D. eds., *Anekāntavāda and Syādvāda* (Landun: Jain Visva Bharati, 1996).

Larson, Gerald James and Ram Shankar Bhattacharya eds., 'Sāmkhya: A Dualist Tradition in Indian Philosophy,' *Encyclopedia of Indian Philosophies*, Vol. IV (Delhi: Motilal Banarsidass, 1987).

Lath, Mukund, 'The Concept of Āhārya-jñāna: Some Queries,' *Journal of the Indian Council of Philosophical Research* 13.1 (1995), pp. 175–181.

Lear, Jonathan, 'A Note on Zeno's Arrow,' *Phronesis* 26 (1981), pp. 91–104.

Lewis, David, 'Veridical Hallucination and Prosthetic Vision,' in *Philosophical Papers II* (Oxford: Oxford University Press, 1986), pp. 273–290.

—— *The Plurality of Worlds* (Oxford: Basil Blackwell, 1986).

—— 'Rearrangement of Particles: Reply to Lowe,' *Analysis* 48 (1988), pp. 65–72.

Loy, David, 'The Clôture of Deconstruction: A Mahāyāna Critique of Derrida,' *International Philosophical Quarterly* 27 (1987), pp. 59–80.

Lowe, E. J., 'Lewis on Persistence versus Endurance,' *Analysis* 47 (1987), pp. 152–154.

Liberman, Kenneth, 'The Grammatology of Emptiness,' *International Philosophical Quarterly* 31.4 (1991), pp. 435–448.

McEvilley, Thomas, 'Pyrrhonism and Mādhyamika,' *Philosophy East and West* 32 (1982), pp. 3–35.

Mates, Benson, *The Skeptic Way: Sextus Empiricus's Outlines of Pyrrhonism* (New York: Oxford University Press, 1996).

Matilal, Bimal Krishna, *The Navya-Nyāya Doctrine of Negation* (Harvard: Harvard University Press, 1968).

—— 'Gaṅgeśa on the Concept of Universal Property (*Kevalānvayin*),' *Philosophy East and West* 18 (1968), pp. 151–161. Reprinted in *Logic, Language and Reality*, pp. 128–139.

—— *Epistemology, Logic and Grammar in Indian Philosophical Analysis* (The Hague: Mouton, 1971).

—— *The Logical Illumination of Indian Mysticism* (Oxford: Clarendon Press, 1977).

—— 'Double Negation in Navya-Nyāya,' in M. Nagatomi et al. eds., *Sanskrit and Indian Studies: Essays in Honour of Daniel H. H. Ingalls* (Dordrecht: Kluwer, 1980), pp. 1–10. Reprinted in *Logic, Language and Reality*, pp. 145–154.

—— 'A Note on the Difference of Difference,' in G. Bhattacharya et al. eds., *A Corpus of Indian Studies: Essays in Honour of Gaurinath Sastri* (Calcutta, Sanskrit Pustak Bhandar, 1980), pp. 69–78. Reprinted in *Logic, Language and Reality*, pp. 155–163.

—— *The Central Philosophy of Jainism* (Ahmedabad: L. D. Institute of Indology, 1981).

—— *Logic, Language and Reality: An Introduction to Indian Philosophical Studies* (Delhi: Motilal Banarsidass, 1985).

—— *Perception: An Essay on Classical Indian Theories of Knowledge* (Clarendon Press, Oxford, 1986).

—— *The Word and the World* (Delhi: Oxford University Press, 1990).

—— '*Anekānta*: both yes and no?' *Journal of Indian Council of Philosophical Research* 8 (1991), pp. 1–12. Reprinted as 'The Jaina Contribution to Logic,' in *The Character of Logic in India*, pp. 127–139.

—— 'Dharmakīrti and the Universally Negative Inference,' in E. Steinkellner ed., *Studies in the Buddhist Epistemological Tradition* (Vienna: Österreichische Akademie der Wissenschaften, 1991), pp. 161–168. Reprinted in *The Character of Logic in India*, pp. 118–126.

—— 'Is Prasaṅga a Form of Deconstruction?' *Journal of Indian Philosophy* 20 (1992), pp. 345–362.

—— 'A Realist View of Perception,' in P. K. Sen and R. R. Verma eds., *The Philosophy of P.F. Strawson* (New Delhi: Indian Council of Philosophical Research, 1995), pp. 305–326. Reprinted in his *Philosophy, Religion, Culture: Collected Essays* (Delhi: Oxford University Press, 2001).

—— *The Character of Logic in India*, Jonardon Ganeri and Heeraman Tiwari eds., (Albany: State University of New York Press, 1998).

—— 'On the Concept of Philosophy in India,' in *Philosophy, Religion, Culture: Collected Essays* (Delhi: Oxford University Press, 2001).

—— *Philosophy, Religion and Culture: Collected Essays*, Jonardon Ganeri ed., (Delhi: Oxford University Press, 2001); Vol. 1: *Mind, Language and World*, Vol. 2: *Ethics and Epics*.

Matilal, Bimal Krishna and R. D. G. Evans eds., *Buddhist Logic and Epistemology: Studies in the Buddhist Analysis of Inference and Language* (Dordrecht: Reidel Publishing Company, 1982).

Matilal, Bimal Krishna and Arindam Chakrabarti eds., *Knowing from Words* (Dordrecht: Kluwer, 1994).

Meltzoff, Andrew, 'Molyneux's Babies: Cross-Modal Perception, Imitation, and the Mind of the Preverbal Infant,' in N. Eilan, R. McCarthy and M. W. Brewer eds., *Spatial Representation: Problems in Philosophy and Psychology* (Oxford: Basil Blackwell, 1993).

Miyasaka Yūkō, *The Concept of Avacchedakatva in Navya-Nyāya (containing the text of Raghunātha Śiromaṇi's Avacchedakatvanirukti and its Commentary Jāgadīśī with an English Translation, Explanatory Notes and a Detailed Introduction)* (Poona: Centre of Advanced Study in Sanskrit, PhD. Thesis, 1980).

Mohanty, J. N., *Gaṅgeśa's Theory of Truth* (Santiniketan, 1966).

—— *Reason and Tradition in Indian Thought* (Oxford: Clarendon Press, 1992).

—— *Essays on Indian Philosophy*, edited by Purushottama Bilimoria (Delhi: Oxford University Press, 1993).

Mondal, Pradyot, 'Some Aspects of Perception in Old Nyāya,' *Journal of Indian Philosophy* 10 (1982), pp. 357–376.

Müller, Max, *The Six Systems of Indian Philosophy* (Oxford, 1899).

Nagel, Thomas, *The View From Nowhere* (New York: Oxford University Press, 1986).

Nenninger, Claudius, 'Analogical Reasoning in Early Nyāya-Vaiśeṣika,' *Asiatische Studien* 48 (1994), pp. 819–832.

Nozawa, M., 'Inferential Marks in the Vaiśeṣikasūtras,' *Saṃbhāṣā: Nagoya Studies in Indian Culture and Buddhism* 12 (1991), pp. 25–38.

Nozick, Robert, *The Nature of Rationality* (Princeton: Princeton University Press, 1993), pp. 163–174.

Oberhammer, Gerhard R. F., 'Pakṣilasvāmin's Introduction to his Nyāyabhāṣyam,' *Asian Studies* (Philippines) 2 (1964), pp. 302–322.

Oetke, Claus, *'Ich' und das Ich* (Stuttgart: Franz Steiner Verlag Wiesbaden Gmbh, 1988).

—— *Studies on the Doctrine of Trairūpya* (Vienna: Wiener Studien für Tibetologie und Buddhismuskunde, 1993).

—— 'Ancient Indian Logic as a Theory of Non-Monotonic Reasoning,' *Journal of Indian Philosophy* 24 (1996), pp. 447–539.

Oliver, Curtis, 'Perception in Early Nyāya,' *Journal of Indian Philosophy* 6 (1978), pp. 243–266.

Ono Motoi, 'Dharmakīrti on *asāsāraṇānaikāntika*,' in Shoryu Katsura ed., *Dharmakīrti's Thought and its Impact on Indian and Tibetan Philosophy* (Vienna: Österreichische Akademie der Wissenschaften, 1999), pp. 301–316.

Padmarajiah, Y. J., *Jaina Theories of Reality and Knowledge* (Bombay: Jain Sahitya Vikas Mandal, 1963).

Pandeya, R. C., 'The Conception of Syādvāda,' in R. A. Kumar, T. M. Dak and A. D. Mishra eds., *Anekāntavāda and Syādvāda* (Landun: Jain Visva Bharati, 1996), pp. 314–322.

Parasher, Aloka, *Mlecchas in Early India: A Study in Attitudes Towards Outsiders up to* AD *600* (New Delhi: Munshiram Manoharlal, 1991).

Perrett, Roy W. 'A Note on the Navya-Nyāya Account of Number,' *Journal of Indian Philosophy* 13 (1985), pp. 227–234.

—— 'Is Whatever Exists Knowable and Nameable?' *Philosophy East and West* 49.4 (1999), pp. 410–414.

Phillips, Stephen H., *Classical Indian Metaphysics: Refutations of Realism and the Emergence of 'New Logic'* (La Salle: Open Court, 1995).

Potter, Karl, 'Astitva Jñeyatva Abhidheyatva,' *Wiener Zeitschrift für die Kunde Süd- und Ost-Asiens und Archiv für Indische Philosophie* 12–13 (1968), pp. 275–280.

Potter, Karl ed., *Indian Metaphysics and Epistemology – The Tradition of Nyāya-Vaiśeṣika up to Gaṅgeśa*, Encyclopedia of Indian Philosophies, Vol. 2 (Delhi: Motilal Banarsidass, 1977).

Potter, Karl and Sibajiban Bhattacharyya eds., *Indian Philosophical Analysis – Nyāya-Vaiśeṣika from Gaṅgeśa to Raghunātha Śiromaṇi*, Encyclopedia of Indian Philosophies, Vol. 6 (Delhi: Motilal Banarsidass, 1993).

Potter, Karl, with Robert Buswell, Padmanabh Jaini and Noble Ross Keat eds., *Abhidharma Buddhism to 150 AD*, Encyclopedia of Indian Philosophies, Vol. 7 (Delhi: Motilal Banarsidass, 1996).

Preisendanz, Karin, *Studien zu Nyāyasūtra III.1 Mit dem Nyāyatattvāloka Vācaspati Miśras II*, Tiel 1 und 2 (Stuttgart: Franz Steiner Verlag, 1994).

Price, Huw, 'Metaphysical Pluralism,' *Journal of Philosophy* 89 (1992), pp. 387–410.

Priest, Graham, 'Can Contradictions Be True?' *Supplementary Proceedings of the Aristotelian Society* 67 (1993), pp. 35–54.

—— 'The Structure of the Paradoxes of Self-Reference,' *Mind* 103 (1994), pp. 25–34.

—— *Beyond the Limits of Thought* (Cambridge: Cambridge University Press, 1995).

Priest, Graham, Richard Routley and Jean Norman eds., *Paraconsistent Logic: Essays on the Inconsistent* (Munchen: Philosophia Verlag, 1989).

Radhakrishnan, Sarvepalli, *Indian Philosophy* (London: George Allen and Unwin, 1923).

Radhakrishnan, Sarvepalli and Charles Moore eds., *A Sourcebook in Indian Philosophy* (Princeton: Princeton University Press, 1967).

Raja, K. K., 'Apoha and Pre-Diṅnāga Views on Sentence Meaning,' in B. K. Matilal and R. D. Evans eds., *Buddhist Logic and Epistemology: Studies in the Buddhist Analysis of Inference and Language* (Dordrecht: Reidel Publishing Company, 1982), pp. 185–192.

Ramakrishnan, Lakshmi, 'On Talk of Modes of Thought,' *Journal of the Indian Council of Philosophical Research* 13.2 (1996), pp. 1–17.

Ramanujan, A. K., 'Is There an Indian Way of Thinking?' *Contributions to Indian Sociology* 23 (1989), pp. 41–58.

Ram-Prasad, C., 'Immediacy and the Direct Theory of Perception: Problems from Śrīharṣa,' *Studies in Humanities and Social Sciences* 3.2 (1996) – *Epistemology, Logic and Ontology After Matilal* (Shimla: Indian Institute of Advanced Studies), pp. 33–56.

—— *Knowledge and the Highest Good: Liberation and Philosophical Inquiry in Classical Indian Thought* (Basingstoke: Macmillan, 2000).

Randle, H. N., *Indian Logic in the Early Schools* (Oxford: Oxford University Press, 1930).

Rawls, John, *A Theory of Justice* (Oxford: Clarendon Press, 1972).

—— 'The Independence of Moral Theory,' *Proceedings and Addresses of the American Philosophical Society* 48 (1974), pp. 4–22.

Rescher, Nicholas, *Many-Valued Logic* (New York: McGraw Hill, 1963).

—— 'The Roots of Objectivity,' in *Scientific Realism* (Dordrecht: Reidel Publishing Company, 1987), pp. 111–125.

Robinson, Richard H., 'Some Logical Aspects of Nāgārjuna's System,' *Philosophy East and West* 6 (1957), pp. 291–308.

—— *Early Mādhyamika in India and China* (Madison, Milwaukee and London: University of Winsconsin Press, 1967).

—— 'Did Nāgārjuna Really Refute All Philosophical Views?' *Philosophy East and West* 22 (1972), pp. 325–331.

Ruegg, David Seyfort, 'The Uses of the Four Positions of the Catuṣkoṭi and the Problem of the Description of Reality in Mahāyāna Buddhism,' *Journal of Indian Philosophy* 5 (1977), pp. 1–71.

—— *The Literature of the Madhyamaka School of Philosophy in India* (Wiesbaden: Otto Harrassowitz, 1981).

—— 'Does the Mādhyamika Have a Thesis and Philosophical Position?' in B. K. Matilal and R. D. G. Evans eds., *Buddhist Logic and Epistemology: Studies in the Buddhist Analysis of Inference and Language* (Dordrecht: Reidel Publishing Company, 1982), pp. 229–238.

Russell, Bertrand, *Human Society in Ethics and Politics* (London: Allen and Unwin, 1954).

Ryle, Gilbert, *The Concept of Mind* (London: Hutchinson & Co., 1949).

Sagal, Paul, 'Nāgārjuna's Paradox,' *American Philosophical Quarterly* 29.1 (1992), pp. 79–85.

Sainsbury, Mark, *Paradoxes*, 2nd edn (Cambridge:Cambridge University Press, 1995).

Sanghvi, Sukhlalji, *Advanced Studies in Indian Logic and Metaphysics* (Calcutta: Indian Studies Past and Present, 1961).

Sartre, J-P., *Being and Nothingness: An Essay on Phenomenological Ontology*, translated by H. E. Barnes (London: Methuen & Co., 1966).

Schayer, Stanisław, 'Studies on Indian Logic, Part II: Ancient Indian Anticipations of Propositional Logic' (1933), translated by Joerg Tuske in Jonardon Ganeri ed., *Indian Logic: A Reader* (London: Curzon Press, 2001).

—— 'Über die Methode der Nyāya-Forschung,' in O. Stein and W. Gambert eds., *Festschrift für Moritz Winternitz* (Leipzig, 1933, pp. 247–257), translated by Joerg Tuske in Jonardon Ganeri ed., *Indian Logic: A Reader* (London: Curzon Press, 2001).

Schiffer, Stephen, 'Descriptions, Indexicals and Belief Reports: Some Dilemmas,' *Mind* 104 (1995), pp. 107–131.

Schuster, Nancy, 'Inference in the Vaiśeṣikasūtras,' *Journal of Indian Philosophy* 1 (1972), pp. 341–395.

Sen, Prabal Kumar, 'The Nyāya-Vaiśeṣika Theory of Variegated Colour (*citrarūpa*): Some Vexed Problems,' *Studies in Humanities and Social Sciences* 3.2 (1996) – *Epistemology, Logic and Ontology After Matilal* (Shimla: Indian Institute of Advanced Studies), pp. 151–172.

Shah, Nagin J., *Akalaṅka's Criticism of Dharmakīrti's Philosophy* (Ahmedabad: L. D. Institute, 1967).

Shaw, J. L., 'The Nyāya on Existence, Knowability and Nameability,' *Journal of Indian Philosophy* 5 (1978), pp. 255–266.

—— 'Number: From the Nyāya to Frege-Russell,' *Studia Logica* 41 (1982), pp. 283–291.

Siderits, Mark, 'Nāgārjuna as Anti-Realist,' *Journal of Indian Philosophy* 16 (1988), pp. 311–326.

—— 'Thinking on Empty: Madhyamaka Anti-Realism and Canons of Rationality,' in S. Biderman and B-A. Scharfstein eds., *Rationality in Question* (Leiden: E. J. Brill, 1989), pp. 231–250.

—— *Indian Philosophy of Language* (Dordrecht: Kluwer Academic Publishers, 1991).

—— 'Matilal on Nāgārjuna,' in P. Bilimoria and J. N. Mohanty eds., *Relativism, Suffering and Beyond: Essays in Memory of B. K. Matilal* (Delhi: Oxford University Press, 1997), pp. 69–92.

Siderits, Mark and J. Dervin O'Brien, 'Zeno and Nāgārjuna on Motion,' *Philosophy East and West* 26 (1976), pp. 281–299.

Simon, Herbert and Allen Newell, *Human Problem Solving* (Englewood Cliffs, N.J.: Prentice-Hall, 1972).

Solomon, Esther, 'Scepticism or Faith and Mysticism – A Comparative Study of the *Tattvopaplasiṃha* and the *Khaṇḍanakhaṇḍakhādya*,' *Journal of the Oriental Institute* (Baroda) 8 (1959), pp. 219–233, 349–368.

—— *Indian Dialectics*, 2 volumes (Ahmedabad: B. J. Institute of Learning and Research, 1976).

Solomon, Robert, 'Existentialism, Emotions, and the Cultural Limits of Rationality,' *Philosophy East and West* 42 (1992), pp. 597–621.

Soni, Jayandra, 'Dravya, Guṇa and Paryāya in Jaina Thought,' *Journal of Indian Philosophy* 19.1 (1991), pp. 75–88.

Sorabji, Richard, *Animal Minds and Human Morals* (London: Duckworth, 1993).

Sosa, Ernest, *Knowledge in Perspective* (Cambridge: Cambridge University Press, 1991).

Sousa, Ronald de, 'The Natural Shiftiness of Natural Kinds,' *Canadian Journal of Philosophy* 14 (1984), pp. 561–580.

Spelke, E. S. and G. A. Van De Walle, 'Perceiving and Reasoning about Objects: Insights from Infants,' in Naomi Eilan, Rosaleen McCarthy and Bill Brewer eds., *Spatial Representation* (Oxford: Blackwell, 1993).

Stcherbatsky, Theodore, *The Central Conception of Buddhism and the Meaning of the Word 'Dharma'* (London: Royal Asiatic Society, 1922).

Steinkellner, Eric Von, 'On the Interpretation of the *svabhāvahetuḥ*,' *Wiener Zeitschrift für die Kunde Süd- und Ost-Asiens* 18 (1973), pp. 117–129.

Stich, Stephen, 'Reflective Equilibrium, Analytic Epistemology and the Problem of Cognitive Diversity,' *Synthese* 74 (1988), pp. 391–413.

Stich, Stephen and R. Nisbett, 'Justification and the Psychology of Human Reasoning,' *Philosophy of Science* 47 (1980), pp. 188–202.

Stout, G. F., 'The Nature of Universals and Propositions,' *Proceedings of the British Academy* 10 (1921), pp. 157–172.

Strawson, P. F., 'On Referring,' *Mind* 59 (1950), pp. 320–344.

—— *Introduction to Logical Theory* (London: Methuen, 1952).

Tachikawa Musashi, *The Structure of the World in Udayana's Realism: A Study of the Lakṣaṇāvalī and the Kiraṇāvalī* (Dordrecht: Reidel Publishing Company, 1981).

Taylor, Charles, 'Rationality,' in his *Philosophy and the Human Sciences: Philosophical Papers 2* (Cambridge: Cambridge University Press, 1985), pp. 134–151.

Thomason, Richard, 'Species, Determinates, and Natural Kinds,' *Noûs* 3 (1969), pp. 95–101.

Tillemans, Tom F., 'On *sapakṣa*,' *Journal of Indian Philosophy* 18 (1990), pp. 53–80.

Tucci, G., *Pre-Diṅnāga Buddhist Texts on Logic from Chinese Sources* (Baroda: Oriental Institute, Gaekwad's Oriental Series 49, 1929).

Tuske, Joerg, 'Being in Two Minds: The Divided Mind in the *Nyāyasūtra*,' *Asian Philosophy* 9.3 (1999), pp. 229–238.

Uno Atishi, 'Vyāpti in Jainism,' in N. K. Wagle and F. Watanabe eds., *Studies on Buddhism in Honour of Professor A. K. Warder* (Toronto: University of Toronto, 1993), pp. 160–167.

Van Den Bossche, Frank, 'Jain Relativism: an Attempt at Understanding,' in R. Smet and K. Watanabe eds. *Jain Studies in Honour of Jozef Deleu* (Tokyo: Hon-No-Tomosha, 1993), pp. 457–474.

—— 'Existence and Non-Existence in Haribhadra Sūri's *Anekāntajayapatakā*,' *Journal of Indian Philosophy* 23 (1995), pp. 429–468.

Wada, Toshihiro, *Invariable Concomitance in Navya-Nyāya* (Delhi: Sri Satguru, 1990).

Walton, Douglas, *Arguments from Ignorance* (Penn.: Pennsylvania State University Press, 1996).

Watanabe Fumimaro, *Philosophy and its Development in the Nikāyas and Abhidharma* (Delhi: Motilal Banarsidass, 1983).

Westertähl, D., 'Quantifiers,' in D. Gabbay and F. Guenther eds., *The Handbook of Philosophical Logic*, Vol. 4: *Topics in the Philosophy of Language* (Dordrecht: Reidel, 1988).

Williams, Bernard, *Descartes: The Project of Pure Enquiry* (Harmondsworth: Penguin, 1978).

Williams, D. C., 'On the Elements of Being,' *Review of Metaphysics* 7 (1953), pp. 171–192.

Zong-qi, Cai, 'Derrida and Mādhyamika Buddhism,' *International Philosophical Quarterly* 33.2 (1993), pp. 183–195.

Index

Abhidharma 100–3, 124–5, 171, 177
absence (*abhāva*) 12, 21, 72, 74, 82–91, 95, 98, 175–6; versus non-existence 82, 144–7
absolute conception *see* objective conception
Advaita Vedānta *see* Vedānta
Ājīvikas, the 143–4, 180
Akalaṅka 144, 147–8, 181, 185
Annambhaṭṭa 86, 190
Aparārkadeva 175
Aristotle 65, 97; Aristotelian syllogism 31
Arthaśāstra (*Treatise on Gains*) 8–10, 184
associate condition (*upādhi*) 79, 145, 152, 154, 162
association and dissociation, method of (*anvaya-vyatireka*) 109–10, 118
ataraxia or equipoise 39, 55
atoms 10, 34, 72–5, 77–8, 124–5, 175
attention, faculty of 22–5
authority 2, 10–11, 37, 166; *see also* testimony

Bagchi, Sitansusekhar 167, 182
Balcerowicz, Piotr 5, 177
Bandyopadhyay, Nandita 181
Basham, A. L. 180
Bhaduri, S. 95
Bharadwaja, Vijay 69, 167, 179, 182
Bhartṛhari 58, 109, 111–12
Bhāsarvajña 71, 76–8, 91–2, 95, 174–5, 181, 186, 194
Bhatt, Bansidhar 180
Bhattacharya, Gopikamohan 178
Bhattacharya, Kalidas 17, 170
Bhattacharya, Kamaleswar 63, 69, 173
Bhattacharya, Ram Shankar
Bhattacharyya, Sibajiban 95, 174, 181
Bhāvaviveka 49
Bilimoria, Purushottama 169, 173
bogus reason (*hetvābhāsa*) 32–3, 37–9, 119; the 'unproven' (*sādhyasama*) 33, 39, 59
Borges, Jorges Luis 66, 174
Buddha, the 42, 48, 51, 67, 132
Buddhapālita 49
Buddhism *see* Abhidharma, Madhyamaka, Yogācāra
burden of proof 59, 151, 153–7, 160, 163
Burton, David 69, 173–4

Candrakīrti 49, 68, 185, 187
Canguilhem, G. 4
Caraka 26, 171
Cardona, George 69, 173
Cārvāka 135, 160
catuṣkoṭi 'four-limbed' refutation 48–51, 52–6
causation 44, 46, 50–8, 62, 77
Chakrabarti, Arindam 5, 40–1, 171–2
Chakrabarti, Kisor 41, 95, 184
change 53–4, 72–3, 125–6, 128–30
Chisholm, Roderick 21, 166, 170, 183
Cohen, M. R. 157, 182
Colebrooke, Henry 29
collecting relation (*paryāpti*) 92
colour, problem of mixed 81, 88, 131–2
common-sense 27–8, 40, 131–2; scheme 43–7, 50, 57, 67–8, 97–8, 100
concepts, Diṅnāga's theory of 99–100, 106, 137
conceptual construction (*kalpanā*) 100–6, 177
connectedness of the world 81–2; *see also* unity
consciousness 23–5, 166
contact (*saṃyoga*) 26, 47, 76–7, 82, 88; sensory 17–22, 125

content, Nyāya theory of 19, 158–9
contradiction 37, 129–34, 138, 141, 146, 153, 155–6, 159–61, 163, 165, 181; *see also* paraconsistency.
counterfactuals 36, 122, 153, 158–61, 163
Coward, Harold 172
critical inquiry (*ānvīkṣikī*) 7–17; and problem-solving 14
culture 2–3, 5

Daniels, Norman 182–3
Davidson, Donald 171
debate 2, 10, 13, 15, 17, 26, 28–35 *passim*, 37–9, 119, 128
deep case (*kāraka*) 63
definition, nature of 17–8, 33, 63–5, 75–7, 130
demonstration (*avayava*) 13–15, 17, 28–9, 32, 37, 49, 62; *see also* extrapolation, inference
Descartes, René 37–8, 72, 156
dharma, as basic ingredient 48, 101–3, 177
dharma, as proper conduct 3, 7–8, 169
Dharmakīrti 21, 118, 121–4, 126–7, 145, 176–9, 181, 186, 188–9, 191
Diṅnāga 2, 33–4, 40, 50, 58, 62, 68, 97–127 *passim*, 129, 137, 144, 146–7, 152, 170–2, 177–9, 184–5, 188
dialetheic logic *see* paraconsistency
doubt (*saṃśaya*) 13–4, 20, 24, 131, 151–168 *passim*
doxastic ascent 58–9, 159–62
Dravid, N. S. 182, 184, 186
Dretske, Fred 179
Dreyfus, Georges B. J. 179
duḥkha 15–16, 22–4, 36, 44, 48, 50–2
Dummett, Michael 178
Dundas, Paul 135, 180

Edgerton, Franklin 170
emptiness (*śūnyatā*) 1, 42–70 *passim*, 97, 123, 172–4
epistemic closure, principles of 110
error 23, 28, 44; 58, 128, 157; Nyāya theory of 158–9
ethics 3–4, 10, 15–17, 23, 36, 44, 98, 172
Eubulides 94
example (*udāharaṇa*) 14, 28–35, 50, 62, 81, 114–22, 144–7, 152, 154–5, 162
exclusion (*apoha*) 100, 106–15, 137, 148, 178
extraction (*apoddhāra*), method of 111
extrapolation 22, 25–35 *passim*, 38–40, 62, 99, 114–23 *passim*, 144–7 *passim*, 152–4, 158, 162–4, 167; *see also* inference

five-limbed inference schema *see* demonstration
Franco, Eli 181, 189–90
Frauwallner, E. 171, 177
Frege, Gottlob 4, 96, 175, 178
Freud, Sigmund 170
Fricker, Elizabeth 172
Fynes, Richard 180

Gadādhara 91–2
Galloway, Brian 69, 173
gambler's fallacy 164–5
Ganeri, Jonardon 41, 96, 127, 169, 171–3, 176–8, 180, 182
Gaṅgeśa 89–91, 95, 154–5, 158–67, 176, 181, 189–90
Gangopadhyay, Mrinalkanti 41, 168, 182, 185–7, 190
Gautama Akṣapāda 10, 13, 21, 27–8, 40, 60, 187
Gillon, Brendan 5, 178, 188
Goekoop, Cornelius 96, 190
Gokhale, Pradeep 150, 171, 180, 191
Goodman, Nelson 163, 182
Goody, Jack 169
Gośāla 143
Granoff, Phyllis 167, 181, 185
Gutting, Gary 175

Hacker, Paul 9, 170
Hacking, Ian 80, 174–5
Halbfass, Wilhelm 40, 71, 95, 170, 174–5
Haribhadra 129, 150, 169, 179, 184
Hattori, Masaaki 102–3, 112, 126–7, 177–8, 188
Hayes, Richard 69, 102, 126–7, 172–3, 177–8, 188
Hemacandra 129–32, 140–1, 149, 180, 184, 188–9
Herzberger, Hans H. 178
highest goal, the (*niḥśreyasa*) *see* liberation
Hoffman, Frank 69
Hume, David 5, 36, 160, 170
Huntington, C. W. 69

imagination (*vikalpa*) 21; *see also* conceptual construction
individuator (*viśeṣa*) 72–80, 93, 175

induction, problem of 116, 118, 122, 151–2, 160, 164
inference 10–11, 14, 21–2, 24, 26–38, 49, 61–2, 89–91, 100–2, 103, 106, 110, 114–23, 125, 134, 144–7, 151–4, 159–60, 163–5, 171, 174, 177–9; from sampling 26, 30, 33, 35, 121, 154; of the 'residual' 27; from non-observation (*anupalabdhi*) 21, 110, 121, 122; and the universal rule (*vyāpti*) 31, 33, 37, 118, 122, 145–7, 151, 160
Ingalls, Daniel 81, 95, 142, 175–6, 180, 190
inherence (*samavāya*) 26, 72–6, 79, 82, 84–7, 92, 97–9, 111, 174–5

Jacobi, Hermann 9, 70
Jagadīśa 92, 151, 176
Jainism 2–3, 30, 40, 98, 126, 128–50 *passim*, 177, 179–81
Jaśkowski, S. 140, 180
Jayarāśi 27–8, 167, 171, 181, 190
Jayatilleke, K. N. 181
Jhalakikar, Bhimacarya 182
justification 162–3, 165–7; virtuous circle of 163–4

Kamalaśīla 176
Kaṇāda 130, 188, 191
Kaplan, David 180
kāraka see deep case
karma theory of moral retribution 16, 23, 44
Katsura, Shoryu 102–3, 126–7, 177–9, 188–9
Kauṭilya 2, 8–12, 16, 28, 184
Khalida, Muhamad Ali 174–5
knowing, method of (*pramāṇa*) 10, 12–14, 27, 32, 35, 58–62, 77, 100, 106, 125, 129, 134, 148–9, 152–3, 157, 162, 166
Kumārila 156

language 2, 4, 58, 98, 102–5, 128, 133, 135–7, 141, 143; limits to 1, 42; propositional 89–90
Larson, Gerald James 170
Lear, Jonathan 65, 174
Lewis, David 173, 179
liberation 9, 15–17
Liberman, Kenneth 172
likeness *see* similarity
Lokāyata 7–9, 27

Loy, David 172

Madhyamaka Buddhism 1, 39–40, 42–70, 98, 124, 172–4, 185
Magritte, René 83
Mahābhārata, the 7
Mahāvīra 132, 149
Malliṣeṇa 139–40, 143, 189
Manu 1, 8
many-sidedness, theory of (*anekāntavāda*) 128–30, 134, 148, 150
Masaaki, Hattori 102–3, 112, 126–7, 177–8, 188
mathematics 72–3, 94; *see also* number
Matilal, Bimal Krishna 3, 5, 19, 21, 28, 33, 40–1, 69–70, 81, 95–6, 102, 126–7, 147, 149–50, 167–82, 185–7, 190
maximal property *see* universally present property
McEvilley, Thomas 173
meaning 4, 9, 58, 60, 104–6, 133, 135–7; as basis for application (*pravṛtti-nimitta*) 106–7; exclusion theory of 106–14, 178; Jaina theory of 137–43, 148; of names 91, 104–5; of sentences 111–14
Meltzoff, Andrew 171
memory 24–5, 101
metaphysical pluralism 98, 137, 176
mind, the (*manas*) 1, 10, 22–5, 171
Mistry, Rohinton 183
Mohanty, J. N. 3, 41, 96, 166, 169, 173, 183, 190
Mokṣākaragupta 151, 179
moral theory *see* ethics
motion (*karma*) 44, 46, 51, 58, 63–6, 69, 72–8, 93, 98, 107, 126, 173
Müller, Max 2, 169

Nāgārjuna 1, 26, 39, 42–70, 94, 97–8, 123, 156–7, 172–4, 185–6, 191
Nagel, Ernest 157, 182
Nagel, Thomas 172, 182
natural kinds: cross-cutting systems of 80–1; *jāti* as 81
Navya-Nyāya 71, 81–95, 141, 151–68, 174–6, 181–3, 189–90
negation 53, 67, 82–91, 94, 107, 113, 132, 140–1, 159, ; rules of Double Negation Elimination and Introduction 87, 89, 175
Nenninger, Claudius 41
nikṣepa 133, 180
nirvāṇa 42

Nisbett, R. 164, 182
nominalism 2, 43, 97, 104–5
non-monotonicity 41, 62
non-observation, inference from *see* inference, from non-observation
norms of reason 2–3, 15, 29, 31, 35, 119, 169
number 52, 91–4, 176
Nyāya 10–41, 46, 65, 88, 94, 99, 114, 125, 132, 137, 152, 157, 170–2; *see also* Navya-Nyāya
nyāya 11, 15, 37
Nyāyasūtra, the 10–41, 60, 154, 171, 187

O'Brien, J. Dervin 173
objective conception 1, 43–7, 66–8, 172
objective support (*ālambana*) *see* support, objective
objectivity 22, 50, 129, 176
Oetke, Claus 41, 127, 171
'only' (*eva*), as a quantifier 112–14, 127, 139–41, 178
Ono, Motoi 127, 179

Padmarajiah, Y. J. 130, 150, 180
pain *see duḥkha*
Pandeya, R. C. 138, 180
Pāṇini 113, 142
paraconsistency 141, 143, 165–6; and non-adjunctive logics of discourse 141–2; *see also* contradiction
paradox 54, 94, 141, 173; of origin 50–9; of motion 51, 58, 63–6; of change 53–4
Parasher, Aloka 172
perception 10, 15, 17–25, 37–9, 45–7, 51, 61–2, 100–4, 106, 115, 122–6, 134, 148, 154, 158, 170, 176–7
Perrett, Roy W. 96, 175
persistence *see* change
perspective *see* standpoint
Phillips, Stephen 5, 168, 181–2, 189–90
Plato 10
pleasure 16, 22–4, 136
pluralism *see* metaphysical pluralism
Potter, Karl 95, 174–7, 181, 184–9
pramāṇa epistemology, *see* knowing, method of
Pramāṇasamuccaya (*Collection on Knowing*) 97–121, 126, 170, 173, 177, 180, 188
prasaṅga 47–54, 155–7, 172
Praśastapāda 22, 58, 76, 187
pretence (*āhārya*) 158–9
Price, Huw 176, 180
Priest, Graham 54, 140, 173, 176, 180
problem of the criterion 166–7

quality (*guṇa*) 27, 72–8, 88, 91–4, 98, 100, 104, 107, 111–12, 126, 148
quibbling (*cchala*) 11, 60, 173

Radhakrishnan, Sarvepalli 2, 169, 189–90
Raghunātha 71, 77–8, 85–6, 91–2, 95, 175–6, 185, 188
Ramakrishnan, Lakshmi 169
Ramanujan, A. K. 3, 169
Rāmāyaṇa, the 7
Ram-Prasad, C. 40, 168
Randle, H. N. 28, 171, 188
Rawls, John 182
realism 17, 58, 88, 98, 125, 176
reason property (*hetu*) 12, 14, 26–35, 57, 89–91, 114–23, 144–7, 151–3, 162–7
reductionism 2, 97–8, 107, 125, 171, 176
reflective equilibrium 153, 164–7
Rescher, Nicholas 105, 177, 180
resemblance *see* similarity
Robinson, Richard H. 70, 172–3
Ruegg, David Seyfort 4, 42, 69–70, 170, 172, 174
Russell, Bertrand 10, 91, 170
Ryle, Gilbert 72, 174

Sāṃkhya 8–9, 26, 170–1
sādhyasama see bogus reason
Sagal, Paul 70
Śaṃkara 130, 180
Sanghvi, Sukhlalji 148, 150, 180, 188–9
Sañjaya 94
Sāntarakṣita 130, 180
Śāntideva 49, 172
Sartre, Jean Paul 170
scepticism 2, 7–8, 11, 27–8, 38–40, 42–3, 67, 148, 152–4, 156–7, 159–61, 163, 174, 181; Pyrrhonic 55–7
Schayer, Stanisław 31, 157, 171, 182
Schiffer, Stephen 180
scientific explanation 26, 57–8, 68, 77, 80–1
self *see* soul
self-marked (*svalakṣaṇa*) 100–4, 106
self-refutation 66–8
self-standing nature (*svabhāva*) 44–5, 47, 66–8
semantic model 89
Sen, Prabal Kumar 95, 176
sense–reference distinction 3–4, 136

senses, the 18–9, 22–5, 38, 58, 61, 101, 105, 124–5; inner sense 22, 101
seven-fold division (*saptabhaṅgī*) 137–40, 149, 189
Sextus Empiricus 55–7, 173
Shah, Nagin J. 150, 181
Shaw, J. L. 96
Siddhasena 130, 134, 144–5, 149, 180, 186, 189
Siderits, Mark 69, 172–3
similarity 27, 29–38 *passim*, 75, 99–127 *passim*, 144, 147, 153, 179
simplicity (*laghutva*) 2, 97, 157
Solomon, Esther 41, 167, 169,181
'somehow' (*syāt*), as a modal operator 138–41, 147–9
Soni, Jayandra 150
sophistical resemblance-based rejoinder (*jāti*) 13, 31–3
Sorabji, Richard 5, 179
Sosa, Ernest 58, 152, 173, 181–2
soul, the (*ātman*) 8–9, 11, 13, 22–5, 34, 44, 128, 143, 171; soul-mind division 22–5
Sousa, Ronald de 174
Stout, G. F. 99, 176
Śrīharṣa 2, 94, 156–68 *passim*, 181, 185
standpoint (*naya*) 133–7, 143, 150
Stcherbatsky, Theodore 177, 186–7
Steinkellner, E. 126, 177, 179
Stich, Stephen 164, 182
Strawson, P. F. 40, 172, 180
substance (*dravya*) 27, 64, 72–9, 87–8, 91, 101, 104, 111–2, 129–33, 135–6, 138–9, 143, 148–9, 174
substitution, property-, model of inference 29
support, objective (*ālambana*) 45, 48, 123–6
suppositional reasoning (*tarka*) 13–4, 24, 144–4, 151, 153–68, 181
syādvāda see 'somehow'

Tachikawa, Masashi 79, 174, 185
Taylor, Charles 169
testimony 10, 14, 24, 35–40, 61, 134
Thakur, Anantalal 170, 187
theory revision 3, 46, 71, 76–8, 89, 94, 132, 164–7, 174
Thomason, Richard 174
Tillemans, Tom F. 127, 178, 189
time 8, 23–6, 44, 52, 132–3; the three times 56–7; and the *now* 64–6, 136
Trairāśikas, the 143–3
trope 72, 99–111, 122, 125–6
truth 42, 57, 89–91, 120, 123, 128, 134, 137–41, 149, 152–3, 162, 179, 182; 'conventional' vs. 'ultimate' 45, 101
truth-aptness 50, 158
truth-value 48, 89, 114, 149, 172, 180; links 66
Tucci, G. 171
Tuske, Joerg 171, 182

Udayana 71, 73–81, 95, 154–62, 171, 176, 182, 184–7
Uddyotakara 18, 21, 23, 38, 62, 170, 187
unity 2, 17, 81, 97, 101–2, 107, 111
universal (*sāmānya*) 10, 22, 33, 52, 72–81, 86, 91, 98–100, 104, 107, 109, 111, 119, 135, 176
universally present property (*kevalānvayin*) 90
unpervaded occurrence (*avyāpya-vṛttitva*) 82, 88–90
Upaniṣads, the 1, 11, 97, 169

Vācaka Umāsvāti 130, 189
Vācaspati 153–4, 187
Vādideva Sūri 137–8, 140, 145, 149, 188
Vaiśeṣika 2, 47, 58, 68, 71–96 *passim*, 98–9, 104, 111, 119, 125, 130–2, 137, 174–6
Vaiśeṣikasūtra 26, 41, 170–1, 176, 188, 191
validity 89–91
Van Den Bossche, Frank 150
Vātsyāyana Pakṣilasvāmin 10–20, 23–4, 26–7, 32, 34–5, 37–40, 170, 186–7
Vedānta 2, 8, 135, 162, 176
Vedas, the 2, 7–8, 35
Vidhyabhusana, S. C. 29
Vigrahavyāvartanī (*Reply to Critics*) 43–4, 59–62, 66–8, 191
Vyāḍi 113
Vyomaśiva 181

Wada, Toshihiro 96
Walton, Douglas 122, 179, 181
wholes 10, 13, 18, 21–3, 26, 72, 88, 97–9, 101, 147–9, 171, 175
William of Occam 97
Williams, Bernard 172
Williams, D. C. 99, 176

Yaśovijaya 136, 141–4, 185
Yoga 8–9, 170
Yogācāra Buddhism 2, 40, 178

Zeno 65, 94, 173–4